Reformers to Radicals

Reformers to Radicals

The Appalachian Volunteers and the War on Poverty

Thomas Kiffmeyer

The University Press of Kentucky

Scholarly publisher for the Commonwealth,
serving Bellarmine University, Berea College, Centre
College of Kentucky, Eastern Kentucky University,
The Filson Historical Society, Georgetown College,
Kentucky Historical Society, Kentucky State University,
Morehead State University, Murray State University,
Northern Kentucky University, Transylvania University,
University of Kentucky, University of Louisville,
and Western Kentucky University.
All rights reserved.

Editorial and Sales Offices: The University Press of Kentucky
663 South Limestone Street, Lexington, Kentucky 40508-4008
www.kentuckypress.com

12 11 10 09 08   5 4 3 2 1

Library of Congress Cataloging-in-Publication Data

Kiffmeyer, Thomas, 1963-
  Reformers to radicals : the Appalachian Volunteers and the war on poverty /
Thomas Kiffmeyer.
     p. cm.
  Includes bibliographical references and index.
  ISBN 978-0-8131-2509-1 (hardcover : alk. paper)
  1. Appalachian Region—Social conditions. 2. Appalachian Region—
Economic conditions. 3. Social reformers—Appalachian Region. I. Title.
  HN79.A127K45 2008
  306.0975—dc22   2008028014

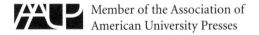

To Laura and Theresa
angels always

Contents

Acknowledgments

During the "long strange trip" that led to this book, I accumulated many, many debts. Though this brief statement will not come close to repaying those intellectual, financial, and emotional obligations, it brings me great pleasure to acknowledge those generous individuals who were instrumental in bringing this project to completion.

Quite a few years ago, Nancy Forderhase of Eastern Kentucky University related to me, a young graduate student, that Berea College housed a virtually untouched collection of papers generated by a certain organization—the Appalachian Volunteers—that operated out of Berea in the 1960s. This collection, she rightly contended, would make the basis for a wonderful study. Thus it was Nancy who started me on this strange trip. Despite our frequent debates on the merits, or lack thereof, of the Volunteers, her guidance was, without a doubt, critical to my development as a historian. I do hope that I have lived up to the faith in me that she demonstrated. Others at EKU, especially Bill Ellis, David Sefton, Gene Forderhase, and Walter Odum, also contributed as both advisers and friends.

The second stop along the road was Berea College. Though I do not remember the exact day I first walked into the special collections department in Berea's Hutchins Library, which was then crammed into a tiny space on the second floor, I do remember the two men, Gerald Roberts and Shannon Wilson, that I met. Shannon, the college archivist at Berea, has been a part of this project since the beginning (Gerald retired some years ago). I have known Shannon for more than twenty years now, and it is impossible to overstate how important and how special he is to me as a colleague and friend. I know he realizes that, given the complexity of the War on Poverty, the Appalachian Volunteers, the Council of the Southern Mountains, and the Appalachian region itself, I will be in "my chair" in the reading room for years and years to come. I also want to thank Steve Gowler, who took over as head of the Hutchins Library's special collections after Gerald's retirement. Also a special thanks to the staff, especially Jim Pritchard, at the Kentucky Department of Libraries and Archives.

As the journey continued, I incurred more debts at the University of Kentucky. Ron Eller, Theda Perdue (now at the University of North Carolina–Chapel Hill), and David Hamilton all went beyond the call of duty, pushing me not merely to graduate but to produce the best work possible. While Ron offered probing insights into Appalachian history, David never let me forget that the War on Poverty was also a 1960s story. Professor Hamilton still gives me thorough, *written* comments whenever I ask him to review a piece I am working on. Theda is in a class by herself. She did everything, from overpaying me to clean her gutters to boosting my confidence when I needed it. She is a very special, unique person. In addition, I want to thank Mike Green of UNC, who could teach a student a lot in the time it took to drink a twelve-ounce beer, and George Herring of UK. George is both an inspiration and a great friend. I also owe a special debt of gratitude to Robert Hodges and Andy McIntire, great friends and great historians.

The next stop along the road, Morehead State University in Kentucky, also blessed me with a talented group of colleagues. John Ernst, John Hennen, Steve Parkansky, Yvonne Baldwin, Alana Scott, Adrian Mandzy, Kris Durocher, and Jason Holcomb are the core of the best department at MSU. I wish to extend a special thanks to Jason (he knows why) and to Gregory Goldey. The tragic loss of "Big Daddy" Goldey to cancer in late 2007 left a void that will never be filled.

The last stop on the journey was, of course, the University Press of Kentucky. Without the guidance, help, and faith of individuals such as press director Steve Wrinn, acquisitions editor Anne Dean Watkins, and editing supervisor David Cobb, this study would never have come to fruition. Thanks also to copyeditor Joseph Brown, who gave me more than a few grammar lessons.

Still, the road is not all of the journey, so, before I slip my bicycle into its rack, I need to remember the people who assisted me in unexpected ways and made the trip worth taking. Paul D. Newman of the University of Pittsburgh–Johnstown is a brilliant historian, great friend, and relentless task master (I mean that positively). Thanks, Paul, for keeping the fire. Also at UPJ is Dan Santoro, who, along with Paul, gave me the opportunity to present my ideas to his classes. My students at Morehead State University, especially Jessica Pugh, Holly Beach, Tony Curtis, Phil Howard, and Valerie Edgeworth, provided the inspiration to keeping plugging away even while we discussed the Jacksonian era. Chad Berry, director of Berea College's

Appalachian Center, provided fantastic insights, as did the former Appalachian Volunteers and Council of the Southern Mountains members whom I interviewed all those years ago.

A special thanks goes to the cats at the Drum Center of Lexington, especially the late Kevin Toole, another dear friend lost to cancer in 2007, and the folks at the Cave Run Bicycle and Outdoor Center, especially John and April Haight. These people provided the outlets needed—the escape—to refresh the brain.

Finally, I would like to thank my family. Bill and Mary Jo Kiffmeyer and Bob and Audry Dwyer helped me financially and, more important, emotionally. Their support was crucial this last, most difficult year. Kathleen, Laura, and Theresa gave me the strength, courage, and drive required to finish this project. Without their love and support, on every level imaginable, I would not have completed it. This project is as much a part of their lives as it is of mine. Kathleen has sacrificed more than any one person should, and, while acknowledging this in no way comes close to paying the debt—really a debt that can never be paid—I hope that it is a start. Laura and Theresa have never known me to be doing much of anything else except writing this book (Laura actually sat through two days of War on Poverty discussions at the University of Virginia in November 2007—probably not a fifteen-year-old's idea of a good time). I owe them time and attention, and I cannot wait to start repaying them—they deserve it. While I hope that I can learn from the past and make this world a better place, I pray that Laura and Theresa learn from my mistakes and make their world even better still.

Introduction

A Time for Change

Looking back on the 1960s, one activist recalled that he was "motivated by a desire to do . . . good works and to be involved in change that was going on all over the country." "It was a time for doing things; was a time of social activism," he declared, "and that was sanctioned and supported and our President had told us to do that—President Kennedy." Inspired by the new president's 1961 inauguration speech, "where he challenged the American youth to do something for the country," this individual eventually did take action and, toward the middle of the decade, joined an antipoverty organization known as the Appalachian Volunteers (AVs).[1]

About six years after Kennedy's inauguration, this same activist and the whole of the Appalachian Volunteers made national headlines as they faced accusations that they were "seditious" and "un-American." Initially leveled by local officials in Pike County, Kentucky, these accusations reflected the growing frustrations that many people felt with the reform efforts that emerged from Kennedy's 1960 campaign rhetoric, his promise of another "New Deal" for Appalachia. While traveling through the West Virginia coalfields during that state's Democratic primary campaign, the senator from Massachusetts promised, if elected, to end the human devastation he witnessed in one of the poorest regions in the country. Though Kennedy did not live to fulfill his promise, the Appalachian Volunteers became, in 1964, one of the first programs funded by the War on Poverty. Created that year by Kennedy's successor, Lyndon Johnson, the War on Poverty sought to make good on the late president's pledge, end the plight of want in the country, and help create what the new president called a "Great Society."[2]

The period during which the Appalachian Volunteers existed certainly was a time of change. Young Americans in particular, overcome with self-confidence precipitated by the victory in World War II and the subsequent economic boom of the 1950s, truly believed that they could solve the nation's social problems. Blessed with university educations, a material culture that featured products and technologies unimaginable just a few years earlier, and rising levels of personal affluence, baby boomers—nearly 20 percent of the U.S. population in 1960—maintained that they and their government had, according to the historian James Patterson, "the knowledge and the resources to create a progressive, advanced society like none before in human history." Calling the twenty-five years following the end of the war a period of "grand expectations," Patterson observed that optimism "lay at the heart of American liberalism in the sixties."[3]

While Americans' confidence came from success in the war and the growing economy, their conscience came from a small but growing cadre of critics. Perhaps most influential was Michael Harrington. His *The Other America,* published in 1962, exposed what he called the nation's "invisible" problem—poverty. Buried in inner-city ghettos under mountainous skyscrapers of glass and steel, and hidden in the country's "forgotten" regions, including Appalachia, as many as 50 million citizens, Harrington argued, felt the grip of poverty. His was not the only voice raised. While individuals such as Rosa Parks and Martin Luther King Jr. contributed significantly to the beginning of the modern struggle for civil rights and brought racial discrimination to the nation's attention, it was the spontaneous actions of four African American college students from North Carolina A&T in Greensboro that, on February 1, 1960, precipitated the national "movement." After purchasing a few items at the local Woolworth's, the four sat down at the lunch counter and ordered coffee. The store's refusal to serve them highlighted the pervasiveness of discrimination in the country. How, young Americans, black and white, asked, could these problems exist in their country? The United States had, after all, just defeated fascism and stood as the protector and guarantor of freedom and democracy in the face of a growing Communist threat. Its economy, moreover, generated more wealth than did that of any other nation on the planet. These two issues—poverty and discrimination—because they directly countered those sources of confidence, became the new enemies, threats to the real America that needed the same degree of attention that the country had given its wartime enemies in the 1940s. Nothing short of the heart and soul of the United States was at stake.[4]

Young America entered the fray through a variety of organizations. In the South, many blacks, but also some whites such as the Alabama native Bob Zellner, joined the Student Nonviolent Coordinating Committee (SNCC), commonly referred to as "Snick." Founded in 1960 as a direct result of the Greensboro sit-in, SNCC "became a community for a small but growing number of idealist activists, whites as well as blacks." A predominately African American organization, it welcomed, in the early years of its existence, any and all support in its "grassroots efforts to overcome racial oppression." Northern white students created their own vehicle for change: Students for a Democratic Society (SDS). Rising Phoenix-like from the student wing of the languid League for Industrial Democracy, SDS offered a biting critique of the United States in its 1962 declaration called the "Port Huron Statement." Issued following a meeting of some sixty SDS participants at Port Huron, Michigan, the "Statement" expressed concern over nuclear weapons proliferation and the denial of civil rights to Southern blacks. Nevertheless, it also echoed a fundamental belief in democracy, the principle that differentiated the United States from all other nations. In the early years of the decade, then, both organizations, SNCC and SDS, sought the same basic goal, the integration of African Americans into American society so that the blessing of the nation could be extended to each and every citizen.[5]

Relative latecomers to the "movement" were the poverty warriors. Though charitable institutions, such as the American Friends Service Committee and other religious organizations, had always maintained a presence in the country's impoverished areas, a concerted, national effort to deal with this problem did not begin until President Johnson launched his antipoverty crusade in 1964. Equipped with the same confidence and conscience as their civil rights counterparts, young Americans joined organizations such as Volunteers in Service to America (VISTA) and the Appalachian Volunteers and relocated to economically depressed areas for periods as short as a weekend or as long as a year, hoping to improve the lives of their beneficiaries. Through remedial academic instruction, health education, job training, and home and school refurbishing, the poverty warriors thought that they could bring that affluence from which they came to the nation's poor. Like the civil rights activists, they had as their goal "integration." They believed that if they overcame the obstacles to integration—which to the initial reformers in rural Appalachia, for example, included a dysfunctional culture, an inadequate education system, and geographic isolation—then poverty would disappear from the land. As the battle against want in the nation progressed, however, this notion of integration took a different form. Rather than simply immersing the poor in a "mainstream" culture and environment, the poverty warriors undertook to integrate them more fully in the nation's political and social dialogue, explore and then explain to them the root causes of poverty, and suggest alternative paths—often different than those proffered by the local, state, and national administrators of the War on Poverty. This new version of integration, then, also offered a critique of the country's prevailing social, political, and economic structures, and this assessment located the cause of poverty in inequities in the nation's political economy, as opposed to "cultural deficiencies."[6]

When the antipoverty activists began to question the fundamental causes of poverty and to move away from conventional explanations that focused on the shortcoming of individuals, their thoughts and actions resembled those of their counterparts in the civil rights struggle. In his study of SNCC, Clayborne Carson traces the evolution of an organization that, through such efforts as "Freedom Summer," attempted to integrate Southern blacks into the American political mainstream. Though SNCC took the lead by moving to areas, such as rural Mississippi, where few civil rights workers ventured, the goal still was political integration. Following Lyndon Johnson's rejection of the Mississippi Freedom Democratic Party, a freely elected delegation from that state to the Democratic National Convention in 1964, however, SNCC workers began to question the efficacy of working with mainstream American liberals. "They also questioned," Carson observed, "whether their remaining goals could be best achieved through continued confrontation with existing institutions or through the building of alternative institutions controlled by the poor and powerless." Unfortunately, these alternative organizations often led to internecine conflicts over leadership, direction, and issues. The Appalachian Volunteers, for example—under attack by antireform forces, and weakened by internal strife— like their SNCC brethren, "withered in the face of the same tactics of subtle cooptation and ruthless repression that stifled the entire black struggle."[7]

Young America, nevertheless, was not the only agent for change in the years following World War II. Beginning immediately after Japan's surrender in August 1945, the Cold War caused many older Americans—those who had lived through the trauma of global conflict—to fear for their continued safety. In the "dual world" of the 1950s, in which one was in either the Soviet or the American camp, the "fall" of China to communism and the detonation of a nuclear device by the Soviet Union, both in 1949, heightened these fears. Just as the existence of poverty was an affront to some Americans' sensibilities, Communist "successes" particularly frustrated the World War II generation. How could these nations, devastated by the recent war and technologically inferior, equal American successes in the scientific arena? Equally frightening was the extension of communism in Asia. Convinced of its monolithic nature, these Americans interpreted any and all "Red" advances as a loss for the free world. By the dawn of the 1950s, America believed that it faced a serious new threat to its freedom, a threat that would require it to match the vigilance, determination, and unity of its enemies.[8]

America's view of the world as dominated by the two irreconcilable forces of freedom and communism was perhaps best expressed in the National Security Act and National Security Council Report 68 (NSC-68). Passed in 1947, the National Security Act expanded the powers of the president through the creation of the White House–controlled National Security Council and the Central Intelligence Agency. Set up to gather information and "perform other such functions and duties related to intelligence affecting the national security as the National Security Council may from time to time direct," the CIA was yet another addition to the "centralized power of the State." Written by the State Department official George Kennan in 1950, NSC-68 argued that "a defeat of free institutions anywhere is a defeat everywhere." It also reflected the belief that the superior productive capacity of the United States (along with higher taxes but *not* true economic sacrifice) would enable the country to easily increase defense spending to the point where it could protect the entire free world. The United States thus embarked on a global strategy of "containing" communism wherever it existed.[9]

More important than the finances involved, policy makers argued, a successful counter to the Soviet challenge "would require the mobilization of American society and the creation of a 'consensus' that 'sacrifice' and 'unity' were necessary." This sacrifice was, of course, personal and political, not just economic. Subjected to loyalty boards, the McCarran Act of 1950, the Communist Control Act of 1954, and "attorney general lists" that enumerated suspected political subversives, Americans saw their political freedoms severely restricted in the name of national security. While under presidents Harry S. Truman and Dwight D. Eisenhower the loyalty boards fired twenty-seven hundred federal employees for being associated with "totalitarian" ideologies and through fear and intimidation caused another twelve thousand to resign, the McCarran Act required Communist Party members to register with the national government. When President Eisenhower signed the Communist Control Act, the government terminated "all rights, privileges, and immunities" of the Party. The country, moreover, "denied Communists their passports, terminated their social security and military disability payments, and deported those who were not citizens."[10]

It did not stop at the federal level. As "McCarthyism" took hold of the nation, Ohio State University restricted speakers, and the University of California fired those employees who refused to sign loyalty oaths. Institutions of higher learning, both large and small, across the country followed suit, and, in the early years of the Cold War, America's centers of learning were anything but a marketplace of ideas. In her study of the academy and anticommunism, Ellen Schrecker claims that over six hundred teachers and professors lost their jobs because they refused to sign loyalty oaths or bow to state laws or institutional pressure. Finally, many states, including Pennsylvania and Kentucky, enacted their own versions of these laws. Most important were state antisedition laws patterned after the federal Smith Act of 1940. With many linking any type of deviance with communism, fitting in rendered one immune from charges of disloyalty. Of course, those who advocated change—even the relatively modest changes of the first half of the 1960s—failed to fit the criteria for loyal citizens. Even more sinister were the activists of the later 1960s, those who openly questioned the country's economic and social institutions.[11]

At the dawn of the 1960s, these two opposing forces, one stressing increased state controls over dissidence and the other focusing on the nation's problems, dramatically clashed. Though their battlefields seem obvious to many, the nature and causes of the conflicts run deeper and are much more complex. Beyond the immediate issues of national security and the Communist threat, civil rights, and the war in Southeast Asia exist questions concerning the nature of American liberalism, the identification of the country's radicals, the role of local people in reform (or antireform) issues, the political uses of anticommunism, the methods of community development employed, and, especially in the case of Appalachia, Americans' image of themselves. These questions—essentially the same issues that civil rights scholars confront—place the Appalachian Volunteers and the War on Poverty squarely within the context of the decade of the 1960s. Though the AVs operated in the southern mountain region, their experience reveals much about the nation's history. Essentially, they were American, not just Appalachian, activists.

Appalachia, nevertheless, was a natural battleground for the War on Poverty. Harboring some of the poorest counties in the United States, the Southern mountains long held the interest of reformers. In the 1890s, the local color movement—a literary movement that highlighted the deplorable living conditions of the people in the more remote sections of the mountains—brought national attention to the region, and women such as Katherine Pettit and May Stone founded settlement schools there. Modeled after their urban counterparts, including Hull House in Chicago, these turn-of-the-century mountain schools instructed students in proper living as well as academic subjects. Like their 1960s descendants, reformers designed these efforts to lift Appalachians out of their depressed conditions. Critical to the settlement school program, however, was the maintenance of those aspects of mountain culture that set it apart from the new immigrants, mostly Southern and Eastern Europeans, who were flooding into the United States at that time.[12]

Using labels such as *contemporary ancestors* and *a strange land and peculiar people*, reformers, from William Goodell Frost, the president of Berea College at the turn into the twentieth century, to the settlement schools' teachers, described a "culture of poverty" that existed in the mountains.[13] By perpetuating outmoded customs, values, and traditions, this culture explained the impoverishment of the rural mountaineer. Because at the dawn of the twentieth century the people of the mountains still lived in log cabins, spoke the language of Chaucer, dressed in "sorry clothing," and exhibited an "awkward demeanor," as Frost wrote in 1899, Appalachia became not just a land of primitive people but a place "in" but not "of" America, especially when viewed in light of the achievements of the late nineteenth century and the early twentieth. Briefly, Appalachia's "otherness" equaled poverty. According to this explanation, mountaineer lifestyles more closely resembled those of generations past, typified as they were by sparsely settled communities, subsistence farming, a Calvinistic sense of fatalism, and, most important, a value system that was incongruent with modern, urban standards. In response, proponents of the modern model advocated a system of education, economic stimulation, and a cultural reorientation that would align the region and its people with the rest of America. Underlying this argument was the unquestioned assumption that the values and lifestyles of the dominant culture were inherently superior to those of the mountaineer. Naturally, to those who visited the region and reported what they found, this impoverished, "other" area cried out for aid. Reformers of many types—settlement school teachers, benevolent organizations, and churches—then entered the mountains with the hope of uplifting the impoverished mountaineers out of their deplorable conditions. Thus began the first efforts to reconstruct the Southern mountains. Though rooted in the progressive movement of the late nineteenth and early twentieth centuries, this model resonated through the later reform efforts of the New Deal and the Great Society. Jack Weller's *Yesterday's People*—perhaps the best example of this model—actually served as a training manual for those reformers, including the Appalachian Volunteers, who entered Appalachia during the first few years of the War on Poverty.[14]

Interestingly, a contemporary of Weller's, the Whitesburg, Kentucky, lawyer Harry Caudill, highlighted how industrialists monopolized coal and timber, exploited the labor force, and turned local politics in their favor. The result, Caudill declared, was a "depressed area." Though he recognized the arbitrary destructiveness of extractive industries such as coal and timber, Caudill saw Appalachia in the 1960s as a region inhabited by people with a culture as depressed as the economy. It was this interpretation—one that was nearly a century old—that dominated the earliest of the antipoverty efforts of the Appalachian Volunteers. Ultimately, however, Caudill's interpretation, coupled with the experiences of the Volunteers, precipitated different interpretations that, by the 1980s, included modernization theory, labor issues, and sociology.[15]

Scholars, including John Gaventa, Ron Eller, David Corbin, and John Hevener, have identified the virtual dictatorial control of the coal industry, not the region's culture, as the cause of poverty. Asking (in *Power and Powerlessness*) the fundamental question of why people stoically accepted the power of the coal industry in the region, Gaventa makes the argument—reminiscent of John Steinbeck's depiction in *The Grapes of Wrath* (1939) of the eviction of farmers from their homes during the Great Depression—that the nature of power and its physical location outside the region prevented local people from ever confronting the source of poverty in the coalfields.

Using modernization as his theoretical model in *Miners, Millhands, and Mountaineers,* Eller argued that the process of industrialization, coupled with factors including absentee ownership, resulted in the destruction of traditional Appalachian economic structures, the depletion of the region's resources, and the impoverishment of the rural population. More than just wages and working conditions, Eller states, the "elimination of mine guards, overpricing at the company store, assembly and visitation restrictions, and other issues of civil liberties were almost always major areas of concern" to mountaineers.[16]

Specifically focusing on the repressive policies of the coal industry, Corbin's *Life, Work, and Rebellion in the Coal Fields* and Hevener's *Which Side Are You On?* convincingly document the arbitrary power of the coal operators. According to Hevener and Corbin, labor troubles in the coal-fields in the first half of the twentieth century resulted from the nearly complete subservience of the miner in a quasi-feudal society, dominated by coal operators and their local allies. The union struggles in the mountain coal industry were, Hevener contends, "both an attempt to remedy unsatisfactory working conditions and a miners' revolt against the Harlan mine owners' arbitrary economic, political, and social power."[17]

Within the past decade, historians have recognized that simply blaming outside corporate interests for Appalachian poverty ignores the role of residents of the region. What role, if any, scholars began to ask, did Appalachians themselves play in the industrial development of the region. Building, in her *Feud,* on Eller's work, which recognized that "insiders" such as John C. C. Mayo contributed to industrial domination, Altina Waller reinterprets the conflict between these two infamous families. While outside corporate interests played a major role in both the causes and longevity of the feud, Waller argues that the Hatfields and McCoys themselves were torn between traditional local economic relationships and participation in a broader national market economy. Waller's contribution charted a new course in Appalachian studies. Historians began to reexamine the paths that coal operators traveled to ensure their domination of the labor force.

Crandall Shifflett answers Gaventa's query by illustrating, in *Coal Towns,* how mountain residents sought the "stable ideal," which included mobility and fecundity rather than stasis. Owing to declining fortunes on the family farm prior to the coming of industry, mountaineers accepted and adapted to the coal industry in the hope of perpetuating preindustrial cultural patterns. "In other words," according to Shifflett, "mountain culture has not caused mobility, but cultural ideals have given context and shape to the movement." This did not mean, however, that coal operators faced a passive, reticent labor force. On the contrary, operators, through what Shifflet labels "contentment sociology," provided company town residents with health care, amusements, and schools with the goal "that a satisfied laboring population would be stable and productive" and should, moreover, "[prevent] unions and lockouts."[18]

As illuminating as these more recent accounts are, they too often see easy dichotomies: they pit modernizers against traditionalists or coal operators against an uncertain, volatile workforce. While their general interpretations are accurate, they minimize the diversity of experience in the region. Included in this group is David Whisnant. Published in 1980, Whisnant's *Modernizing the Mountaineer* places the Appalachian Volunteers first in a conservative "Appalachia as culture of poverty" camp, after which they travel to a much more "radical activist" camp. In reality, as the trajectory of the Appalachian Volunteers illustrated, the organization was much more complex. Further, the Volunteers themselves underwent a number of transformations. In their initial phase, the AVs were exactly that: volunteers from Appalachia. By 1965, however, the Volunteers had entered a second phase; while they were still volunteers, they increasingly hailed from outside Appalachia. In their third phase, when the organization focused on issue organizing (Whisnant's "radical" phase), the AVs were, for the most part, neither Appalachian nor volunteers, most being paid "fieldmen" from outside the region. Eventually, in their final phase, as the War on Poverty ground to a halt at the start of the 1970s, they found themselves Appalachians again, if still not volunteers. Instead, the organization employed the services of local people to carry on the organizing agenda.[19]

As the Appalachian Volunteers story shows, the history of the Southern mountains is more than a struggle between the haves and the have-nots. On the contrary, the War on Poverty in Appalachia illuminates the multiplicity of problems that the various poverty warriors faced no matter where they operated. Though the exploitation of the region by both native and outside industrialists was at the root of many problems, others were the result of the clash of values and cultures. More than just a conflict between different socioeconomic classes within the area, what emerged as the reform effort progressed was a clash between Appalachians and non-Appalachians. In short, the War on Poverty magnified the social, political, economic, and cultural problems precipitated by the collision of class, culture, urban and rural values, and corporate domination—and not just in Appalachia, but nationwide.

Because the Community Action Program—the centerpiece of the Economic Opportunity Act of 1964, by means of which Johnson launched the War on Poverty—required the input of virtually every segment of society, this multiplicity of problems led to a plethora of proposed solutions that would result in a confused concept of "community development." Given that, at the start, the poverty warriors viewed their target communities as characterized by both economic and cultural impoverishment and considered the two states to be equivalently evil, they conceptualized development in these terms. Other participants, however, including public and private interests as well as the poor themselves, had their own sets of values, harboring their own versions of what *community development* meant and how to achieve it. As a result, communities, and those who sought to help them, experienced extreme difficulty defining the term and forging solutions that addressed the problems they encountered. As the War on Poverty progressed, battles arose more over whose definitions and solutions would prevail than over poverty itself. Unfortunately, for those who lost these struggles, the results were devastating.[20]

This concern with how different individuals or groups understood the designs and functions of the War on Poverty sheds light on the philosophical underpinning of the reform effort and on the history of American liberal reform movements generally. As Alice O'Connor argues in *Poverty Knowledge,* the history of American reform, especially since the advent of "professional social researchers" in the early twentieth century, has focused on the *poor,* not on *poverty.* As a result, she claims, reformers tried to change the impoverished rather than those factors, including racial inequities and gender biases, that placed people in a disadvantaged position in the first place. Focused in this manner, "poverty knowledge has been perhaps most effective as a form of cultural affirmation: a powerful reassurance that poverty occurs outside or in spite of core American values and practices." Though her primary concern is poverty within a decaying urban core, in her discussion of poverty research in the 1960s, "when this theme became virtually institutionalized," O'Connor echoed the attitude held by most poverty planners and warriors *throughout the twentieth century*—and especially those in Appalachia. "Poverty," she concluded, "to use the terminology of the day, occurs in some 'other' separate America; as an aberration, an exception, a 'paradox' of plenty rather than as an integral or necessary condition of the affluent society." From the Progressive era through the 1960s, American reformers entered battle armed with the unquestioning belief that they, not the targets of their efforts, held the proper attitudes concerning social, economic, and political structures. What held the poor back was not the prevailing political economy but an inability to accept and embrace those proper attitudes.[21]

O'Connor's evaluation of the Office of Economic Opportunity's performance in America's urban sectors reveals that the same range of problems and proposed solutions existed there as in rural America. To policy makers at the national level, antipoverty measures involved integrating the poor, whether blacks in urban slums or mountaineers in rural Appalachia, into U.S. society. To their counterparts at the local level, they involved overhauling the existing service delivery systems. To the poor, however—whether living in Syracuse, New York, or Pike County, Kentucky—they involved greater personal autonomy. It was this desire on the part of the poor to exert their own agenda that caused the worst of the conflicts for which the Great Society is, unfortunately, known.

As the battle for control of the reform agenda became increasingly heated, one of the contending groups came into its own. As recent scholarship on the civil rights movement demonstrates, that group that John Dittmer calls "local people" was instrumental in the struggle for racial equality. While not overlooking the contributions of such individuals as Martin Luther King and Ralph Abernathy to the movement, Dittmer argues that it was the efforts of the many unnamed, unsung local people who made the difference. Without the willingness of these local people to persevere in the face of violent repression—much of which was in reaction to the speeches King made and the demonstrations he led—the movement, Dittmer believes, never would have succeeded. Dittmer's analysis, moreover, questions the identity of the movement's leaders. It reverses the relationship between those traditionally seen as leaders and the rank and file activists and places the latter in the forefront of social change.[22]

Among the Appalachian Volunteers working in the Southern mountains, the power of local people became most apparent when some of the broader issues of the decade, for example, the Vietnam War, intruded into their discussions about the nature of their work. Already engaged by 1966 in a serious battle with local elected officials in eastern Kentucky for control of the reform agenda, the Volunteers lost the support of the local people—those very people who, they claimed, determined AV action—when a number of them took a stand in opposition to the war. This, coupled with the forces already aligned against them, spelled disaster for the reformers.[23]

Beyond the significance of the role of the impoverished mountaineers, the manner in which the Volunteers' antagonists mobilized against them bears scrutiny and points toward a new understanding of American radicalism. Defined by Daniel Pope as a relative term that is bound by the context in which it occurs, *radicalism* is about change. In the postwar period, however, when change was the goal of policy makers and activists at both the national and the local levels, this simple definition is of little help. Fortunately, Pope provides further clarification. "Equality," he claims, "[is] a central objective and core value of American radical movements and ideas." Radicals are those who use "illegitimate means" to achieve their objectives.[24]

While both civil rights and antipoverty advocates, especially toward the end of the decade, sought political, economic, and social equality, the question of "illegitimacy" obscures the issue. On an immediate level, how can a group that professes the desirability of equality gain the label of *radical* in a nation whose very ideology claims a like goal? More fundamental concerns involve Pope's all-important "context" and "illegitimate means." As both civil rights activists and antipoverty warriors increased their efforts, their opposition countered with police dogs, fire hoses, nightsticks, charges of sedition, the manipulation of the judicial system, and their own brand of violence. Given the context and the means employed, those opposed to the Great Society and civil rights used illegitimate means and are as deserving of the label *radicals* as are the activists.[25]

In the face of an all-out attack by their opponents, the War on Poverty activists, in and beyond the Southern mountains, crumbled. Questions remain, however, regarding the success of their antipoverty programs. Certainly, poverty still exists, and it would be foolhardy to expect its eradication within the span of one presidential administration. Nevertheless, the effort did suffer from the "political demand" for "quick and visible results." Beyond this, the activists themselves had trouble reconciling their hierarchical organization with their notions of equality. They struggled to replace older institutions that they interpreted as oppressive with more equitable ones, and they were decidedly less than successful working within the established system. More important, however, the trouble with evaluating the accomplishments of the War on Poverty and its participants lies within that war itself. How can community development and community action be evaluated when those notions lacked clear definitions and were understood differently by the various people involved? To local officials and program planners, they essentially meant solidifying their control over any new federally sponsored programs, while, to local people, they involved "political organizing and genuinely local autonomy."[26] In the end, to determine whether the War on Poverty met the criteria for failure—or success—the perspective from which the criteria were drawn must be identified.

Ultimately, the War on Poverty produced neither victors nor heroes. In the case of the Volunteers, though their analysis of the sources of Appalachian poverty was headed in the right direction and they compelled the enforcement of existing laws, they lost when they abandoned their focus on local people, asserted their own agenda, and attempted a frontal assault on their more powerful adversaries. Likewise, while the "radicals" on the right halted the War on Poverty, watched the activist organizations disband, and maintained their control of the social, political, and economic hierarchy, they faced a reinvigorated local population that continued to seek greater autonomy. Unfortunately, the results of the "war" for the local people were also mixed. While many gained at least economically from the federal largesse that the poverty programs brought to the mountains, they were caught between two external forces, a reform movement (the AVs) that thought it knew better and those industrial interests (particularly coal) that had dominated the region since the dawn of the twentieth century.

Finally, the nation too won and lost as a result of 1960s activism. On the positive side of the ledger, with the passage of such measures as the Civil Rights Act of 1964 and the Voting Rights Act of the following year, along with the social programs of the era, the United States did come closer to achieving its democratic ideal. Nevertheless, on the negative side, the trajectory of the activism of the decade—the self-serving nature of many of the participants and their attitudes toward those they came to help—reveals the shortcomings of America's reform tradition. By focusing on vague notions of community development and education (something seen as necessarily accompanying community development), War on Poverty planners and participants adopted, as did many of their civil rights counterparts, a reform philosophy that saw victims as the source of poverty and ignored their attempts to better their own condition.[27]

1

On the Brink of War

The Council of the Southern Mountains and the Origins of the War on Poverty in Appalachia

I can believe anything after seeing this area. I cannot describe it. . . . I wish I could do something for this string of coal camp communities. Wish I could talk to you and wish some responsible, able agency could turn some wheels favorably in this place. . . . It is under my skin, and deeper.

—Alvin Boggs, Pine Mountain Settlement School,
to the Council of the Southern Mountains,
describing the area around Black Mountain, Kentucky, 1961

The Oak Ridge, Tennessee, native George Brosi was probably atypical even for a college student, and in particular for a Southerner, in the early 1960s. In the summer of 1961, following his first year at Carlton College in Minnesota, Brosi "for the first time in [his] life . . . was exposed to Yankees that were appalled by the whole notion of anybody being from the [segregated] South or being from the hills." "A lot of them . . . guilt-tripped" him about being from the "wrong part of the country." "And it was true," Brosi recalled. "I had been raised in segregation . . . with the colored and white restrooms and drinking fountains and restaurants and everything." When he got back to Oak Ridge that summer, the "guilt-tripping" apparently had affected him. He became involved in the civil rights movement that was then "happening" and picketed a segregated laundromat in his hometown.[1]

In the winter of 1962, the "whole cultural contrast" between the elite at his Northern private school and the situation in the South precipitated Brosi's decision to leave college and return to Tennessee, where he gained employment at a hotel in Gatlinburg. It was the same hotel that the Council of the Southern Mountains (CSM)—then the leading Appalachian benevolent organization—held its annual conference. Led by Perley Ayer, the CSM, housed at Berea College in Berea, Kentucky, attempted to incorporate every possible interest, from corporations and churches to state and county governments, into its reform efforts. By the summer of 1963, Brosi, who increasingly became involved in the emerging youth movement in the early part of the decade, made the connection that poor whites needed their own movement and joined the CSM. Interestingly, Brosi claimed that he was one of only two CSM employees who, in late 1963, supported the Democrat Lyndon Johnson over the Republican Barry Goldwater.[2]

While at the Council, Brosi worked closely with Milton Ogle, the CSM's community development specialist and the eventual leader of the Appalachian Volunteers (AVs), a college student–based reform project started by the Council. In fact, Brosi asserts that he was on the very first AV project. Though he had returned to Carlton by then, Brosi "happened" during the Christmas break of 1963–1964 "to stop by [the CSM office] . . . to shoot the shit with Ogle, . . . [who] said 'hey we're going out to this schoolhouse, why don't you come along?' and I said what the hell. . . . This is the very first time we've ever gone out on this new program." Thus, Brosi accompanied CSM staff and a number of college volunteers on a school-repainting effort in Harlan County, Kentucky. "At this point," Brosi contends, "[Ogle] was . . . very, very conservative politically and at that point his vision of the AVs was a 'Perley Ayer, power company, chamber of commerce kind of vision: that it's too bad this schoolhouse needs paint . . . if we paint it the situation will be better.'" This initial AV project reflected the growing national attention paid to impoverished areas, such as Appalachia, in the post–World War II era and the cooperative, New Deal, top-down approach that influenced reformers on virtually every level at that time.[3]

Though Brosi claimed that he attempted to debate Ogle concerning the merits—or the lack thereof—of a simple school-painting project, he also contended that Ogle remained wedded to his conservative ideology, and the discussion did not go far. Nevertheless, many Americans other than Brosi wanted to talk about Appalachia during the postwar years. Always part of the national conversation, especially since the coal industry entered the region at the dawn of the twentieth century, Appalachia—or, more precisely, Appalachians—took on added importance in the 1950s and 1960s. Responding to a number of developments, including the mechanization of the coal industry and the labor demands precipitated by global conflict, Appalachians now inhabited urban industrial centers, particularly those in the Upper Midwest, in unprecedented numbers. This "great migration," as James S. Brown of the National Institute of Mental Health and the University of Kentucky demographer George A. Hillery Jr. called it in 1962, created a host of social, economic, and political problems for those cities and for Appalachia. While the region suffered the drain of its most productive citizens, urban centers such as Cleveland, Cincinnati, and Chicago witnessed a massive influx of Southerners who were, many established residents determined, ill suited for city life.[4]

Focusing on these Southern migrants, the Cleveland resident Adelbert Bodnar informed the Council of the Southern Mountains that his city had "trouble . . . with 'Sam' [an acronym for 'southern Appalachian migrant'] . . . in the area of behavior." While the adults were responsible for drunken brawls, robbery, burglary, vandalism, and gang fights, their children used the foulest language. No wonder, Bodnar wrote, that decent people call them "poor white trash." These new migrants also threatened the economic security of established residents. Since the 1930s, industry increasingly relocated to the South, lured by right-to-work laws and tax breaks, and Cleveland now faced "hordes of hillbillies [who came] up here to take away what jobs [it had] left for [its] own citizenry." "Keep them back in the hills," Bodnar admonished the CSM, "where they belong." He also implored that the "hillbillies" be taught to have respect for order and property.[5]

Bodnar's admonition reflected the dual nature of the problem faced by the Council. On the one hand, the CSM needed to help this "poor white trash" adjust to city life, and, on the other, it hoped to stem the "brain and talent" drain that plagued the region. This latter goal in particular fit the CSM's long-standing mission in Appalachia. Founded in 1913 in Atlanta by John C. Campbell, the Council of Southern Mountain Workers—later renamed the Council of the Southern Mountains—brought together "mountain workers" to discuss the difficulties of their labors. Composed mostly of rural doctors, ministers, and social workers, the Council became the permanent organization for those who sought to improve living conditions in the hills. Membership was open to all persons, institutions, or foundations working toward the betterment of the mountaineers.[6]

In 1925, the CSM established a permanent headquarters at and a close working relationship with Berea College, in Berea, Kentucky. The association between the two remained until 1949, when dwindling funds forced the Berea office to close. With money and influence rapidly fading, the Council hired Perley Ayer, a rural sociologist from New Hampshire then working in Tennessee, to oversee the organization's supposed final days. Though the CSM was all but bankrupt when he took control in 1951, after he reopened the Berea office Ayer revived an association that, by the mid-1960s, would become the largest, most significant social service agency operating in the Appalachian coalfields and in those Northern cities to which Appalachians had migrated in search of employment.[7]

Though the CSM was the Appalachian region's leading advocacy organization, its members certainly were not the only people concerned about Appalachia, America's cities, and the relationship between the two. Critics as diverse as the economist John Kenneth Galbraith, the journalist Michael Harrington, and the psychiatrist Robert Coles reflected the growing concern and contributed to the emerging ideas about poverty's causes and solutions. Galbraith contrasted a "new" poor, a minority of the population that had failed to tap into the economic, political, and social gains accruing to most Americans since the advent of the New Deal, with an older general, societywide poverty of the late nineteenth century. Because this new poverty encompassed a numeric minority, he concluded, the larger *affluent society* could effectively ignore it. It was the hidden poor that Harrington recognized in his influential 1963 *The Other America*. Adding a cultural element to Galbraith's demographic characterization, Harrington claimed: "To be impoverished is to be an internal alien, to grow up in a culture that is radically different from the one that dominates the society." Not just ignored, Harrington's poor were invisible, hidden by urban skyscrapers and Appalachia's hills. Focusing on children, Coles directly linked urban and rural poverty. "Many of the children I observed in Southern cities," he reported, "have cousins whose parents are migrant farmers, or sharecroppers, or 'mountain folk' from the Appalachia hills." Coles looked further into the lives of those "cousins" who remained on farms or in the mountains "and eventually the children of Northern cities who must also face social isolation, segregation, desegregation—in brief, the dislocated, hard living that is still America's gift to some of its young."[8]

Coupled with the ideas of an "alien" culture, this identification of an invisible poor about which public officials need not concern themselves suggested certain reform strategies. Most obvious was the integration of mountain people into the fabric of American society. "[If] the problem of Appalachia is to be met," noted the sociologist Rupert Vance in 1962, "it must be interpreted in the context of national development." Of greatest concern to Vance was the "extent to which the Region has lagged behind in the processes of population redistribution, of economic and cultural development, and in the equalization of opportunity." While this analysis rejected the notion of Appalachian isolation, it recognized the existence of "chronic pockets of poverty" that hindered the "development of a single, national community in which regional urban-rural and social class differences [would] become less important."[9] In short, the region could address, and possibly end, its chronic poverty if it could develop in the context of, and in relation to, the nation.

While isolation characterized the relationship—or the lack thereof—between Appalachia and the rest of the United States, urbanization was both the way in which this isolation could be overcome and the ultimate end of any reform process. Central to this reform was "pluralism," a political theory that was at once the problem and the solution to Appalachian poverty. Popular in the postwar United States, pluralism was the process by which interest groups influenced the distribution of goods and services in a given society and "achieve[d] their various rights." Because the theory maintained that the give-and-take between these various groups resulted in the equitable distribution of a given society's wealth, it essentially equated pluralism with democracy. Implicit in this analysis was the notion that urban space, with its ready access to markets, government services, and educational and cultural facilities—those very resources for which interest groups vied—was conducive to the formation of these interest groups. Appalachians were invisible, as Harrington suggested, because they were isolated both from the urban stage on which groups acted and from each other.[10]

Interestingly, the Council's first attempt to reform Appalachia happened not in the Southern mountains but in a Northern metropolis. Responding to concerns such as those outlined by Bodnar, the CSM, at the behest of the Mayor's Friendly Relations Committee of Cincinnati,[11] conducted its first "urban workshop" in 1959. Designed to acquaint city officials, social service workers, and the police with their new Appalachian neighbors, the urban workshops introduced urban professionals to a dysfunctional culture ill suited to city life. According to the historian Bruce Tucker, urban workshop speakers "described a society weak in institutional structures, lacking in political and social cohesion, deprived of material resources, and burdened by archaic family and religious customs." Of the many criticisms offered by workshop speakers, two of the more significant were Appalachians' "environmental circumstances," which city workers needed to understand in order to "help . . . the mountain migrant," and the notion that their highly individualistic, family-oriented culture prevented them, as one workshop speaker claimed, from realizing that "voluntary cooperation [was] required for urban living." In short, Appalachians had no real sense of community. Overcoming these archaic burdens to community involvement, both in the city and in the mountains, became the goal of later-twentieth-century Appalachian reform. Because the source of the trouble was Appalachia, reformers looked to the mountains, hoping to change mountaineers before their inevitable arrival in the nation's cities.[12]

Complementing the urban workshops, which stressed the "weak institutional structures" of mountaineers and reinforced the notion of an isolated Appalachia, were other sources, including major national newspapers and the Council itself, that reflected the belief in an urban-pluralist solution to mountain poverty. Writing in October 1963, the New York Times reporter Homer Bigart, in an article that reputedly motivated President Kennedy to lay the foundation of what would become the War on Poverty, exposed the poor housing, inadequate educational facilities, and, perhaps most important, the "native clannishness" that made mountaineers' "adjustment to urban life painfully difficult." Though he recognized corruption in local government, inadequate services, and chronic unemployment, Bigart concluded that the people, more than the social, political, and economic structures, needed a transformation.[13]

Commonly called Ayer's "call to partnership," the Council's strategy closely resembled the pluralist theory that dominated the thinking of so many postwar Americans. Ayer argued that, in the mountains, every action had a "social consequence." It was the Council's job, he continued, to "bring together and relat[e] in effective cooperation all the positive interests and efforts in the area." In that sense, Ayer considered the Council to be a coordinating body, not an action program, ensuring that all mountain citizens—individual and corporate—operated "in such a way that the quality of living [would be] improved in the area." Far from naive concerning the devastating effects of the extractive industries, Ayer nonetheless sought to enlist them in his reform efforts. By representing a unified front of Appalachian interests, the Council of the Southern Mountains could increase the level of knowledge about mountain issues at all levels of society and influence potential government legislation and the resultant action.[14]

Ayer's ideas about community development closely resembled the Council's original "Program for the Mountains" outlined in 1925 in the very first issue of the organization's official publication, *Mountain Life and Work.* Focusing on a "cooperative community development" idea, Ayer's program too called for improved educational, recreational, and health facilities as well as enhanced economic opportunity for mountaineers.[15] His conception of the Council and his conviction of what form welfare should take demonstrated how the organization sought to aid needy mountaineers. At the same time, he hoped to alter, or at least limit the adverse effects of, industrialization in the coalfields. Rooted in notions of traditional communal relationships, the "call to partnership" implored those with the time and resources to act selflessly for the benefit of the entire Appalachian South. Defined in terms of economic self-sufficiency, an egalitarian social structure, and the people's "rel[iance] upon themselves and their neighbors for both the necessities and pleasures of life," this traditional community ideal guided Ayer's Council of the Southern Mountains.[16]

Religious principles, moreover, were fundamental to the CSM's desire to effect positive change. These principles were, however, tempered by a strong sense of humanism and communal responsibility. The Council of the Southern Mountains, Ayer wrote to George Bidstrup, the director of the John C. Campbell Folk School, "serves the Appalachian South in a religiously motivated fellowship which has united leaders and efforts of almost every conceivable interest and diversity in one common cause." It was essential "that the basic principles of religion and humanitarianism be kept alive and dominant in both policy and practice." To Council members, these basic religious tenets and motivations did not imply the missionary zeal commonly attributed to them. Rather, the Council called on people—the wealthy, business interests, local and national governments, and even ordinary mountain residents—to work for Appalachian improvement. "Education and better living," the Council member W. Ross Baley told the *West Virginia Hillbilly*, "are not the sole province of the church."[17]

This religiously influenced, communal view placed the Council of the Southern Mountains squarely in line with other reform agents of the early 1960s, including the Student Nonviolent Coordinating Committee (SNCC). Speaking for that organization, James Lawson, a civil rights leader from Nashville, declared that the SNCC "affirm[ed] the philosophy or religious ideal of nonviolence as the foundation of our purpose, the presupposition of our faith, and the manner of our action." Part of the Judeo-Christian heritage, nonviolence sought "a social order of justice permeated by love. . . . *Integration of human endeavor represents the crucial first step towards such a society. . . . Mutual regard cancels enmity. Justice for all overthrows injustice. The redemptive community supersedes systems of gross social immorality. . . . By appealing to conscience and standing on the moral nature of human existence, nonviolence nurtures the atmosphere in which reconciliation and justice become actual possibilities.*"[18] Substitute cooperation or partnership for nonviolence, and the philosophies of SNCC and the CSM are strikingly similar.

At its annual conference, the CSM promoted its own conception of a "redemptive community" in the Southern mountains. It recruited new members, educated those already active, and presented a united front in the battle against Appalachian poverty. Topics discussed at these yearly gatherings centered on educational concerns, health issues, and the recreational needs of mountain children. Interestingly, the broad base of participation envisioned by the Council provided the foundation for the organization's reform efforts in the middle of the decade. Participation in the conferences was not limited to dues-paying members of the CSM; anyone believed able to contribute to the knowledge and understanding of the region received an invitation. Included in this group were governors, congressmen, and local college students, the latter because the Council had begun to attract the interest of an increasing number of young people. One young 1960 conference participant discovered: "I was not the only one interested in medicine and the nursing needs of mountain people. [The conference] helped me to really see where my people need my help the most."[19]

Perhaps more significant, the conferences created a dialogue between the CSM and the federal government. Following John F. Kennedy's promise of another "New Deal" for the depressed areas of Appalachia during the West Virginia primary of 1960 and the creation of the Area Redevelopment Administration (ARA) in May 1961, the Council actively sought federal participation in its programs. Calling on Kennedy to attend the fiftieth annual conference in 1962, the governor of Kentucky, Bert T. Combs, on behalf of the CSM, urged the president to openly support an organization that lived up to the challenge in his inaugural address: "Ask not what your country can do for you, ask what you can do for your country." In its efforts to gain a presidential visit, the Council of the Southern Mountains won the support of many influential legislators, such as Congressman Carl Perkins of Kentucky's eastern mountain district and Senator John Sherman Cooper, as well as of William Batt, the chief executive of the ARA. Perhaps most significant, the Council established a link with the politician most responsible for the reform efforts of the 1960s—Lyndon Baines Johnson, Kennedy's vice president.[20]

Beyond the personal connections, finances remained a priority for the Council of the Southern Mountains, and the federal government's seemingly growing financial commitment, as illustrated by the nascent ARA, to aid depressed areas, especially Appalachia, made a relationship with Washington extremely attractive. Despite the Council's disadvantageous position, however, the mountain reformers refused to allow the national government to assume control over its efforts or to establish a simple charity approach to aid depressed areas. "I cannot bear the impression," Ayer wrote to Assistant Secretary of State Brooks Hays, "that we are idle and helpless until saved by others." Just because the people needed help, it did not follow that they should be seen as mere pawns by any group, including the CSM. Not the states, and not the Council, declared the CSM staff member Milton Ogle, but the people themselves "will have to assume the final responsibility of executing any program for regional betterment." Part of that burden, again, was the coordination of all attempts to improve the lot of impoverished Appalachians. "We operate on the theory," the executive director asserted, "that neither welfare nor education nor health interests nor economic development nor federal assumption of responsibility can . . . adequately meet the needs of this area . . . without adequate knowledge of and voluntary coordination with all other efforts at work in the same cause."[21] In Council members' eyes, the CSM was the best-equipped vehicle to coordinate the activities of governments, churches, schools, and other mountain interests.

This open orientation, coupled with the desire to avoid a program of charity, significantly influenced Council membership, the activities of the organization, and its conception of welfare. It permitted the Council to actively solicit the support of those entities, such as extractive industries, that some believed were responsible for many of the region's problems and required the membership to push the bounds of Southern mores. Recognizing that the coal industry was the backbone of the economy in most central Appalachian counties, and in adherence to its inclusive philosophy, the Council of the Southern Mountains hoped to minimize the destructive tendencies of mining by bringing operators to the discussion table under the banner of "humanitarian concerns." Because membership in the Council meant acceptance of its philosophy—that of acting for the good of all in the region—coal companies who joined essentially promised to aid mountain reform. It was on the basis of this conception that Ayer solicited memberships from Island Creek Coal, the Turner-Elkhorn Mining Company, the Chesapeake and Ohio Railroad, and the American Electric Power Company of New York. At the same time, the CSM advocated measures to make mining a feasible means of making a living. His stance on strip mining, for example, highlighted the delicate balance that Ayer hoped to strike between the concerns of coal operators and the need for jobs in central Appalachia. Though he favored stronger anti-strip-mining legislation in the state, Ayer feared that, if only Kentucky, or only any one state, for that matter, passed such a law, the result would penalize that particular state and further encourage the "continu[ed] destruction of the countryside" in the others. Thus, he concluded, for strip-mining legislation to be effective, all political divisions in the central coalfields needed to be put aside and all interested parties would have to act in concert. The Council also hoped to attract the cooperation of operators by supporting the protection of jobs, reduced freight rates for and research on new uses for coal, and eminent domain for coal pipelines. Unfortunately, this drive appeared to be less successful than hoped. As late as 1964, Ayer lamented the "lack of people from private industry" participating in discussions about Appalachia's problems. The Council, nevertheless, continued to believe throughout the decade that it could influence private interests to act on behalf of even the poorest mountaineer.[22]

In terms of Southern attitudes toward civil rights, Ayer's belief that the Council remain open to all turned into a strong integrationist stance. According to Loyal Jones, the Council's assistant executive secretary, when, in late 1963, Ayer learned that the Asheville, North Carolina, hotel that was to serve as the 1964 conference headquarters practiced segregation, he "hit the ciling [sic]." Using a segregated facility, Jones asserted, would be "compromising our principles."[23]

Perhaps the most significant consequence of the open-door policy and its insistence that the people be involved in each reform effort was the Council's emerging conception of welfare. Reminiscent of New Deal concerns over dependency, this, more than any other facet of the Council's program, belied a purely charity orientation. In a statement to the CSM Board of Directors, Council leaders revealed their concern for both the plight of the mountaineer and what they feared was the Kennedy administration's attitude toward aid. "There was never a time in our history of this country and the Appalachian South," Ayer declared in 1963, "when so many people were in such great need—need of education appropriate to the time, need of earning opportunity, need of hope and realistic aspiration, need of leadership which involves them in the process of their own salvation versus an insidious and growing system of paternal care which results in greater and greater dependency—than at this moment."[24]

Ayer's appeal for responsible welfare was not limited to the Board of Directors. Invitations to the 1962 annual conference again went out to national officials, including those to Commerce Secretary Luther Hodges and Health, Education and Welfare Secretary Abraham Ribicoff, and revealed his apprehensions that the federal government would usurp the Council's role in the region. After the two administration officials declined their invitations, an irritated Ayer wrote to Brooks Hays, complaining that he could not "understand how they can be as concerned as they are about revitalizing the impoverished masses . . . and not jump at this opportunity to discuss some of their principles." After all, the Council had banded together "with the express purpose" of working at this very task "in partnership with the government rather than in a continuing state of dependency upon [it]." For his part, Hays agreed with Ayer's argument that public assistance needed to be linked with efforts at "individual improvement in order to promote individual self-respect."[25]

Failing with the executive branch, Ayer turned his attention toward Kentucky's congressional delegation. Writing to Senator John Sherman Cooper and Congressman Carl Perkins, Ayer once more broached the subject of federally initiated aid to depressed areas. If Kennedy failed to include individual responsibility in his reform efforts, Ayer feared, he wrote Cooper, that, "inadvertently, we will give relief which merely keeps the carcass alive but erodes character." Believing that rural development must begin with "people development," Ayer called on Cooper to ask that a program that addressed the educational needs of a woefully undereducated Appalachian population be added to federal relief programs. Reiterating these ideas to John Whisman of the Eastern Kentucky Regional Planning Commission, the CSM leader argued: "Whatever we do must involve great numbers of individuals and must be something by means of which they can regain some of their individual value and independence, and not merely [create] a palliative situation."[26]

The Council, moreover, was not content to just criticize or make suggestions. It backed up its words with ideas and plans for a comprehensive mountain aid package. First, Council leaders sought, through workshops and speeches at their conferences, to inspire young people from the mountains "to prepare themselves for service" in the Appalachian region. This, they reasoned, would stem migration north and help end welfare dependency. By creating a dedicated core of native mountaineers willing to work for solutions to the region's problems, the Council would realize its hopes for a program that restored dignity and a sense of self-worth. Second, the CSM requested a grant from the Social Security Administration to initiate a project that would prove the viability of a broad welfare concept utilizing human development along with economic aid. Rather than offering simply a monthly check and a periodic visit from a social worker, the Council of the Southern Mountains sought to use a number of people, such as county extension agents, public health nurses, and county school officials, to establish an aid program that truly helped mountaineers. While the county agent would help welfare recipients improve home gardens, the nurse would teach sanitary techniques and birth control, and the schools would conduct classes geared toward making the undereducated more employable. This type of program, the CSM believed, would have three results: mountaineers would realize better living conditions; welfare recipients would face greater prospects for employment; and, most important, children, witnessing that education was the key to success, would gain the necessary motivation to stay in school.[27]

While the CSM itself lacked funds to administer such massive assistance measures on its own, it did what it could to help individual mountaineers, and it was in this way that it most resembled a charitable organization. Because of its many connections throughout the southern Appalachians, the Council facilitated the dissemination of donated material, such as clothes, vitamins, and shoes, to needy mountaineers. While less concerned with these types of handout efforts, the CSM still became the pipeline through which charitable donations flowed. It was not, in most cases, the entity that actually distributed the goods, but it did match requests from individual families or churches in the region with offers from the outside. Prior to the War on Poverty, for example, the Council helped distribute shoes and clothes to a family in Mount Sterling, Kentucky, and vitamins and toothpaste to Wise County, Virginia.[28]

In terms of health education, Ayer sponsored the "talking transparent women," a traveling exhibit that taught about the inner workings of the human female. In June 1960, he dedicated $1,000 of CSM operating revenue to enable a health "field worker" to travel through eastern Kentucky in order to conduct health education lessons. Further, in May 1962, the Council helped host a "health fair" in Wolfe County, Kentucky. At this event, physicians tested for various diseases and administered inoculations to those who needed them. Additionally, there were demonstrations of proper food preparation and first aid along with advice on creating and adhering to a household budget.[29]

Members of the Council also fostered civic improvements in their own hometowns. This reflected one of the Council's most important goals in the area of community development—creating local leadership. As part of its overall emphasis on educational and health improvements, the Council concentrated most of its efforts in or near the larger towns, including Hazard and London, in eastern Kentucky. In Laurel County, Council members worked to expand the county library and to improve the local hospital. They conducted a general "clean-up campaign" and a drive to administer the Sabin oral polio vaccine. Moreover, in the county seat, London, CSM members pushed for street repair and improvements to nearby Levi Jackson State Park. Similarly, in Perry County, Council members worked for a new health center, street and sidewalk improvements, and an upgraded sewage disposal plant.[30]

Underlying this somewhat limited activity was the ubiquitous lack of funds and an awareness of some of the fundamental problems in Appalachia. Though corporations provided the CSM with some revenue, the majority of its funding came from the Ford Foundation and the philanthropic Appalachian Fund. In November 1961, the Appalachian Fund announced a grant of $24,000 to the Council. According to the agreement, the CSM had to use nearly half this total ($10,000) for "economic development" and devote another $7,500 to health education. For its part, in January 1961 the Ford Foundation issued the Council of the Southern Mountains $35,000 to participate in the foundation's "Great Cities–Gray Areas" program. Similar to the urban workshops, this project was supposed to help Appalachian out-migrants, mostly those displaced by the mechanization of the coal mines, who had relocated to Northern cities in search of work. Essentially, the Ford Foundation believed that these transplanted mountaineers, the "fightin', feudin', Southern hillbillies and their shootin' cousins," as the *Chicago Sunday Tribune* called them, were the cause of many of the urban problems in the North. In short, it hoped that the CSM could inform mayors, city councils, and government service agencies how to deal with their new, "culturally unique" residents.[31]

Working with the Gray Areas project may have been more problematic than it was worth. Not only did it draw Council efforts away from the mountains, but the incongruity of the maladjusted mountaineer in an urban ghetto posed a serious question for many in the CSM. Though many, from Bodnar to Harrington, had posed the question, the Gray Areas effort, more than any other, forced the CSM to actively face the issue of a dysfunctional Appalachian culture. Were Appalachians culturally unique? Why did they migrate? What more could be done to halt the flow north? In short, the Council had to ask itself one basic, fundamental question, one that it had not actually confronted thus far: What was the source of Appalachian poverty, and what was the best way of ending it?

After witnessing the unemployment caused by the combined effects of mechanization and the concomitant decline in the demand for coal for over a decade, Ayer and the CSM reasoned: "If opportunities could be made more available locally, many trained young people would stay here in the mountains and contribute their abilities to making a better life for those around them."[32] This conclusion presented the Council of the Southern Mountains with two tasks: creating opportunities and training young people. While one Council enthusiast advocated the development of a tourism industry along with a concerted effort to lobby the federal government to build defense contractor plants in eastern Kentucky, Ayer chose another path, one that allowed the Council to remain focused on areas in which it was already active—education and urban migration.[33]

Perhaps influenced by Eli Cohen, the executive secretary of the National Committee on Employment of Youth, who spoke before the CSM annual conference in 1961, Ayer tended to think that a strong commitment to educational improvement in Appalachian Kentucky would create the trained workforce that attracted industry. According to Cohen, whose address underscored the observations made by such commentators as Bodnar, the technological revolution of the postwar era was "drying up economic opportunity for rural youth" on the farm. Unfortunately, technological advancements also hurt the prospects for gainful employment in manufacturing. Available research indicated that "rural youngsters will be forced to decide between staying in rural areas and operating farms with net yearly incomes of less than $1500 or migrating to urban communities for employment for which most will be unprepared."[34]

Implicit in Cohen's analysis was the inadequacy of the rural mountaineers' lifestyle, echoing a nearly century-old explanation of Appalachian poverty and "otherness." Advancements in technology in the post–World War II era had rendered rural Appalachians "contemporary ancestors." This label, first used in 1899 by the Berea College president William Goodell Frost, implied that the region's rugged terrain had sheltered mountain residents from the influence of modern America and led to their destitution because of how their culture had evolved within the confines of the Appalachian Mountains. As a result, Appalachian residents, particularly those removed from the more urban county seats, retained their allegedly pure Scots-Irish heritage, their strict allegiance to family and clan, and folkways unchanged from frontier or Elizabethan times. This deviant culture, then, contributed to their impoverishment because of the way it conflicted with mainstream American notions of individualism, progress, and acquisitiveness. Ironically, the Council of the Southern Mountains, with its publication of Jack Weller's *Yesterday's People* in 1963, became yet another purveyor of the image of the Southern highlands as a culturally unique and backward region.[35]

Though faced with, and actually part of, a long history that blamed Appalachia and Appalachians for the region's problems, the Council did realize the tremendous obstacle that it had to overcome. Any attempt to create a trained workforce in the mountains, the Council then thought, would effectively eliminate the derogatory label *ancestors*, create employment opportunities, and, finally, attract industry. All these potential results, however, hinged on improving education in the mountains, and the CSM had two alternatives at its disposal. The first of these called into question the efficacy of the school systems themselves. While one Council supporter alerted the organization's leadership to "irregularities" in the Pike County school superintendent's office, other education reform advocates, including important Council administrators, went further. Writing to the noted Appalachian novelist Harriette Arnow in 1961, the Council's assistant executive director, Loyal Jones, broached the subject of education, stating: "With our local county set up we still have the crookedness, graft, and poor instruction which Kentucky has been saddled with for so many years." Jones reiterated this sentiment to Allen Trout of the *Louisville Courier-Journal.* "I am pretty sure that most . . . people do not really understand the political situation here in Kentucky and some of the other mountain states," he declared, "and cannot really understand why we do not do things better than we do."[36]

At the heart of these political problems was the way in which local school officials attempted to manipulate and control their employees. More often than not, the most qualified instructors departed the mountains, not just because of inadequate salaries, a Council newsletter claimed, but because the political machines endeavored to control their votes. Teachers will not be part of a system, the article concluded, "which demands either their votes or their jobs." In Perry County, Kentucky, the Council member Grazia Combs reported, the "schools are staffed with untrained teachers and are kept there by the superintendents who want to perpetuate their tenure in office rather then educate the kids. Every major problem concerning education in Eastern Kentucky can be traced to politics of the very lowest order. Superintendents do not want competent people . . . ; they want . . . 'permit' teachers . . . who can deliver the votes of all the kinfolks on the creek in return for the 'permit.'" Though the region badly needed qualified teachers, they would continue to be difficult to get "until we are able to do something about the type of leadership that is found in the county seats."[37]

Competing with the view that identified political corruption as the source of the trouble were theories of the educational psychology of mountain children. Charles Drake, a Berea alumnus who went on to graduate school in education at Harvard University, carried a tremendous amount of influence with Perley Ayer and popularized these concepts in the CSM. While at Harvard, Drake uncovered research suggesting that mountain children experienced normal mental growth until about age six, when they entered elementary school. It was at this point, the study discovered, that their intellectual development began to slow down dramatically. Thus, the report determined, it was the school *environment* that influenced their ability to learn. If the schools were improved, Drake suggested, educational progress would result.[38]

Perhaps the combined influence of Drake and Cohen was enough to persuade Ayer to select the educational psychology paradigm as pinpointing the source of Appalachia's problems. More probably, it was the way in which the recommendations of these two complemented Ayer's cooperative philosophy that convinced the CSM leader to adopt this particular explanation. In any case, by accepting the reasoning of Drake and Cohen, Ayer made what was in the long term perhaps his most significant mistake. Rather than adopt a more combative or confrontational stance against the mounting evidence of malfeasance in the eastern Kentucky school systems—much of which was produced by Council members themselves, including the associate director, Jones—Ayer adhered to his conviction that all people "could be approached and touched by reason and right and that they would respond." As a result, the Council began to move toward a position that identified Appalachian culture, and the poor educational system that it fostered, as the source of the mountaineers' impoverishment.[39]

Following an established pattern, Ayer was not content simply to define a problem. Action needed to follow definition, and other Council members felt the same way. In 1961, Stuart Faber, a member of the Board of Directors, expressed his fear that the Council of the Southern Mountains was nothing more than a conference sponsor. Ayer himself, a couple of years later, admonished the Board to "get serious and dedicate yourself or quit."[40]

Ayer, for his part, refused to quit. Utilizing Drake's connections in Massachusetts, the Council of the Southern Mountains embarked on a drive to make tangible improvements to the educational environment of Appalachian children. Supporting this venture were the good works of the people of Boston and Harvard University. In early 1961, shortly after President Kennedy suggested the establishment of a "Peace Corps," an international service organization of the federal government that would send skilled, educated Americans to underdeveloped countries, Harvard students organized their own "Peace Team" for similar purposes. Drake contacted them with the hopes of persuading them to begin a book drive for central Appalachia. By providing better reading material in mountain schools, Drake believed, the educational level of the children would soon be elevated, and this would make a significant contribution to solving mountain problems. At its Board of Directors meeting that February, the CSM readily endorsed the proposed book project. According to the minutes of the meeting, the Board maintained that the book drive would improve on the "limited cultural experience" of rural Appalachian schoolchildren. In addition to the Harvard students' efforts, Boston's "Lend-a-Hand" Society also sent books to southern Appalachian schools.[41]

Response to the book drive in the counties in which the CSM worked was equally favorable. According to Loyal Jones, Rockcastle County, Kentucky, was an excellent starting point for the undertaking because those in charge of the schools there seemed "to have the good of their children at heart." Further, students at Caney Creek Junior College (renamed Alice Lloyd Junior College in 1962) at Pippa Passes, Knott County, Kentucky, volunteered their time to distribute donated books. Marie Turner, the school superintendent of Breathitt County, Kentucky, willingly accepted books as well. To the east, across the Tug Fork of the Big Sandy River, the Council member W. R. "Pop" Baley instituted "Operation Bookstrap" in Welch, McDowell County, West Virginia. Baley agreed with the environmental critique of mountain education outlined by Drake. He sought to have indigent mountain children improve their lives by enhancing their educational situation; the children would pull themselves up by their "bookstraps."[42]

Additional Council efforts supplemented the book project. In April, for example, Dr. Louis Armstrong, the director of the Indian Springs School, Helena, Alabama, conducted a CSM-sponsored "youth workshop" at which he discussed the educational goals of the CSM. Of particular concern to Armstrong were the "great problems of bridging the gap between the group which has the knowledge, techniques, and skills and those who do not." Second, the CSM community development specialist, Milton Ogle, in conjunction with the University of Kentucky's rural sociology program, sought to "maximize economic, social and personal development . . . [in mountain neighborhoods] through group action." Again, the CSM stressed its partnership approach. The Council required the development specialist to cooperate with "existing organizational leadership" with the goal of "encouraging community organization for self-improvement," which included adult education classes, public health work, and local leadership seminars.[43]

Keeping contact with the federal government alive, the Council of the Southern Mountains not only asked the Kennedys to deliver the first load of books for Operation Bookstrap but also, in a move that reinforced the perception of Appalachian backwardness, requested the presence of Peace Corps volunteers in the mountains. Actually, the Council hoped for the establishment of a domestic version of the organization that would operate in the southern Appalachians. At the end of 1962, the Council addressed Attorney General Robert Kennedy and his proposed National Service Corps (NSC) directly. This "was a pet project of Robert Kennedy" and exactly what the Council wanted. Kennedy envisioned the service corps to be a domestic type of Peace Corps. NSC volunteers would, after a brief training period, "work for a year in areas where human services were in critically short supply."[44]

Not surprising, the Council's request received a welcome response from Richard Boone, a sociologist in the U.S. Justice Department, whose assignment was to make the NSC a reality. Boone believed that NSC projects should be "conceived by local people and leave behind men and women capable of carrying on by themselves" after the NSC had completed its mission. Recognizing how the philosophy of the Council of the Southern Mountains coincided with his, Boone wrote to Ayer, stating: "[The attorney general's office is] interested in making use of your long personal experience in addressing the needs of the Appalachian South." Further: "We would like to take this opportunity to begin exploration with you . . . possible roles that 'corpsmen' might play in working with local residents in meeting immediate needs and addressing the potentials inherent to the area."[45]

Unfortunately, the House of Representatives failed to pass the NSC bill. Other events, however, served to endear Ayer and the Council to the Kennedy administration. The first of these was the publication of Harry Caudill's *Night Comes to the Cumberlands*. Decrying the horrid conditions in which mountain people lived, Caudill provided the nation with what he claimed were vivid descriptions of Appalachian reality. Following shortly after Caudill's book was Homer Bigart's *New York Times* article "Kentucky Miners: A Grim Winter." As the subtitle made clear, Bigart, like Caudill, detailed the "poverty, squalor and idleness" that "prevailed" in the region surrounding Whitesburg, Kentucky.[46]

"Tens of thousands of unemployed miners," Bigart reported, "face[d] another winter of idleness and grinding poverty." "Replaced by machines," these former miners kept body and soul together by virtue of "government handouts," and three generations of welfare recipients "resulted in a whipped, dispirited community." Sounding like a CSM member himself, Bigart declared that the present system had "eroded the self-respect of the mountain people." He even noted that strip mining had further hurt both the environment and the chances of the people for gainful employment in the region. Moreover, he printed Harry Caudill's statements before a CSM meeting, deploring the "massive doling out of federal welfare money [that had] financed and now sustains a dozen or more crafty, amoral, merciless, and highly effective political machines" that "will oppose by every available means any effort to restore the people to productivity and self reliance." Yet he stopped short of calling for political reform in central Appalachia. Rather, he decided that "the erosion of the character of the people [was] more fearsome than the despoiling of the mountains" and that the abject poverty experienced by rural mountaineers was a "manifestation of . . . government neglect."[47]

Then, echoing Cohen's speech to the Council in 1961, Bigart attacked the educational system in eastern Kentucky and the mountaineer culture. "Escape to the city is not easy," he stated, "for the average miner has no skill for other jobs. He is deficient in education." Bigart noted that, as we have seen, the problems with the education system could be attributed to the enormous political power of the local school superintendents—who controlled the largest payroll in their counties. Moreover, he continued, the mountaineer's "native clannishness makes adjustment to urban life painfully difficult," while "the low educational standards of the people are a major obstacle to the location of new industry."[48]

Bigart, however, did not stop with the indictment of the miners' way of life. He also investigated the conditions of the schools and the politics behind those conditions. On Gilbert's Creek, in Leslie County, Kentucky, was a school so dilapidated that it was "unfit for cattle." Equally disturbing was the failure of the federally sponsored school lunch program. This program, designed to provide a nourishing lunch to schoolchildren who could not afford one, had no impact in the rural schools of Leslie County, for two reasons: the county lacked the funds to collect and distribute government surplus, and few schools had the facilities (kitchens, running water, power) to prepare food properly anyway. In Letcher County, the health officer reported that he had seen children eating dirt and that 85 percent of children in the county were underweight; in Leslie County, three-fourths of the children had intestinal parasites.[49]

Supposedly in response to Caudill's and Bigart's work, President Kennedy, in October 1963, conceived of what he termed a "crash program" to help the residents of southern Appalachia. At last he began to make good on the promises he had made during campaign trips to West Virginia during the 1960 presidential campaign, at which time he had witnessed firsthand the hardships the residents of southern Appalachia had to face.[50] When the then senator entered the West Virginia primary, he faced an enormous task. Not only did he have to diffuse the issue of his Catholicism in this Bible Belt state, but he also had to outmaneuver the well-known Democrat and liberal leader Senator Hubert Humphrey of Minnesota. During his blitz of the Mountain State in May 1960, Kennedy found the issue that endeared him to the people of the state—the unemployment and poverty that he saw among the former Appalachian coal miners. In "a dazzling achievement that assured his nomination" at the July Democratic convention, Kennedy destroyed Humphrey in West Virginia and became the favorite in the upcoming presidential contest.[51]

Eastern Kentucky, not West Virginia, however, was the CSM's focus. Appalachian Kentucky was one of the poorest areas in southern Appalachia in the early 1960s. According to the CSM's own information, one-third of the people living there were on some kind of public assistance, and 85 percent lived in substandard housing. The median education level for adults was 8.05 years of school. While 68 percent of all Kentucky children never finished high school, this figure was even higher for eastern Kentucky. The median family income was also well below the poverty line in 1963 and $3,600 below the national median level.[52]

Kennedy originally placed his program under the guidance of the President's Appalachian Regional Commission (PARC), established in April 1963. Headed by Secretary of Commerce Franklin D. Roosevelt Jr., PARC had as its mandate to formulate a "comprehensive action program" of federal aid for regional economic development. As designed, the commission was to cooperate with state officials in the central Appalachian highlands in the development of the region's tourist potential, natural resources, water power, and human resources through industrial development. These proposals, nevertheless, did nothing to ease the urgency that motivated Bigart's article. More important, especially from the Council's perspective, PARC failed to do anything about Appalachia's problems as late as December 1963.[53]

While PARC busily planned, the Council asserted its leadership role and designed as a winter emergency program its own "Eastern Kentucky Crash Program." The CSM hoped to refurbish rural mountain homes and help impoverished mountaineers cope with the coming winter. Ayer announced that the Council of the Southern Mountains would "continue its major—and historic—role of coordination of voluntary action directed toward the best interests of the people of the Appalachian South." Integral to the Council's view of the crash program was the use of a volunteer labor force. While Kentucky state officials involved in the planning of the winterization effort did not feel that volunteers could be mobilized in time to be utilized effectively, the Council had, by mid-December, already recruited and "made [a] moral commitment to hundreds of students," and Ayer believed that the CSM must "make some constructive use of at least some of [them]." Ultimately, the Council hoped that it could establish, and make available to any future PARC program, a permanent pool of volunteer labor in Appalachia.[54]

Some members of the White House staff agreed that residents who were to benefit from the program should actively participate rather than just be passive recipients. Pursuant to this goal, Richard Boone brought his ideas from his work on the NSC to the CSM community development specialist Milton Ogle. The two worked together to find a way in which continuing benefits could be realized through the efforts of the proposed Eastern Kentucky Crash Program.[55]

Consistent with Council policy, Boone and Ogle believed that a program of charity would be insufficient and possibly damaging to the people of eastern Kentucky, and their proposal called on eastern Kentucky residents to work on their own community projects. This, they argued, would incorporate a sense of self-help and sensitivity to local needs and problems in the program. In addition, as Boone had argued concerning the NSC, they asserted that people who played an active part in the project would be more likely to continue working for improvements after federal assistance was withdrawn. "An emergency program of aid to Eastern Kentucky," Boone and Ogle argued in "A Volunteer Component for the Eastern Kentucky Program," issued in late 1963, "should involve the residents as participants in rendering as well as receiving aid. A program based on the traditional concept of charity—giving aid to enable subsistence, but without requiring a commitment by those receiving the aid—will not be complete. And aid based on the concept of charity tends to drive the poor more deeply into dependency."[56]

The Council had high hopes for its role in the planned PARC effort. While the CSM staff truly believed in the importance of the principle of self-help, the use of volunteers was also high on the list of priorities. Volunteers could make the aid program more economically feasible by providing "sensitive and sophisticated manpower at virtually no cost to the government." In addition, local people helping their neighbors could build into the program a means by which to gain great insight into the needs of each community. Those who could not help themselves, the Council's report continued, could be able to say, "These are our own people who are helping us." Local citizens who saw their neighbors working in the community might motivate some who remained untouched by one aid program after another. Finally, in a statement that revealed its awareness of the "lazy mountaineer" stereotype, the CSM contended that a volunteer program would show the nation that the people of Kentucky felt a vital commitment to their own development and a responsibility to take part in it.[57]

College students from nineteen eastern Kentucky colleges, easily motivated and mobilized, fulfilled the vital role of volunteers in the proposal. Local impoverished Appalachians, the CSM argued, would not consider these students to be outsiders. In addition, it insisted, many college students would have or would be receiving training through their academic courses of study that could benefit the program. Their participation in the effort, moreover, would bring the colleges and communities closer together. "Perhaps most important," the Council concluded, "participation in this effort might encourage some of the students to remain in a region which desperately needs educated individuals." Preliminary contact with eastern Kentucky's institutions of higher learning confirmed the Council's assessment as school administrators indicated an interest and a willingness on the part of their students to contribute their time and manpower. From this initial contact, more than three hundred students (including George Brosi) volunteered their services to the Eastern Kentucky Crash Program during the 1963–1964 Christmas vacation.[58]

On December 20, 1963, the Council of the Southern Mountains issued a policy statement in which it assumed virtual control of any and all Appalachian reform programs. With this, the CSM declared itself responsible for the "coordination of voluntary action directed toward the best interests of the people of the Appalachian South, and the most effective use of PARC services, when and if the PARC program is established." According to its plan, the CSM selected twenty-five eastern Kentucky counties on the basis of three criteria: "the number of volunteers recruited," "the extent of need in each locale," and "the opportunity for success." With the help of the CSM staff, Ogle then informed as many key local leaders as possible—including newspaper editors, politicians, businessmen, and labor leaders—about the proposed volunteer effort in order to "prepare them for contact by students during December" and "request their cooperation." This strategy incorporated every facet of the Ayer philosophy: the program would involve virtually every part of the community, avoid pure handouts, offer local people the opportunity for input, broaden the horizons of rural mountaineers through contact with college students, and, finally, stimulate greater interest in education.[59]

Much of the actual work that took place during December 1963, however, concentrated on organization and preparation. Utilizing its contacts throughout the region, the CSM asked state and local officials in each county to inform Ogle of ways in which student volunteers might be useful. Local county institutions could use student volunteers in either existing or new programs. Initially, the program called for student volunteers to help distribute surplus food, assist in renovating individual homes, serve as tutors for both children and adults lacking needed academic skills, and aid those in need of medical attention. Organized in "county teams" (five volunteers in each of the twenty-five counties), and under the direction of the CSM, students followed the leads provided by the contacts and performed vital reconnaissance work. For five days of their Christmas vacation, they interviewed influential local citizens about possible tasks for a two-pronged (December 1963 and February–May 1964) emergency aid program. It was through the work of these reconnaissance teams that the CSM hoped to convince federal officials—specifically PARC—that a "volunteer component" was feasible and necessary in eastern Kentucky. As a result of this preliminary investigation, the CSM decided that, during the initial phases of the emergency program, volunteers could make the most significant impact by working on improving the physical conditions of rural schools. As the Council later reported: "Those involved in planning the program reasoned that, since a principal source of poverty lay in the schools, and since colleges might be especially sympathetic to a program which attacked poverty at this source, school based projects might be undertaken first."[60]

According to the Council of the Southern Mountains, over one thousand one- and two-room schools accommodating 27,146 children, or 20.5 percent of the school-age population, operated in eastern Kentucky. Its college student investigators further provided a graphic description of the physical condition of these structures: "The typical one-room schoolhouse is a greying, wood frame building with ill fitting windows and cracked floors, which permit a constant rush of cold winter wind. Near the single pot-bellied stove children are uncomfortably hot; further away they must wear their coats. In many instances there is no toilet[.] (Of those 82 schools in Pike County, 37 have no toilet facilities.) There are eight grades in one room, but the 'eighth graders' are already considerably behind eighth graders in other parts of the nation."[61]

Such reports suggested to Council leaders an obvious course of action—one that would, they believed, attract the favorable attention of every potential actor, from the federal government to local student volunteers, in the emerging Appalachian reform effort—a school "winterization" project. Thus, the first program called on students to make emergency repairs—for example, installing insulation and new flooring and applying fresh paint— to Appalachian Kentucky's rural school buildings.[62]

The Council of the Southern Mountains worked vigorously that winter to obtain materials from private sources to realize the first project of the Eastern Kentucky Crash Program. Appeals went out to colleges, interested individuals, and corporations for supplies, services, and financial support. Then, in the second week of January 1964, two groups of students from Union College and the Cumberland Branch of the University of Kentucky, who called themselves "Appalachian Volunteers," went out on the first projects on Upper Jones Creek in Harlan County, Kentucky. The students repaired broken windows and cracked doors and walls and painted the buildings inside and out. The War on Poverty in Appalachian Kentucky had begun.[63]

The initial effect that these student volunteers had on the schools was astounding. A letter from a Harlan County schoolteacher, included in the Appalachian Volunteers' first report, thanked the AVs and asserted that they did "a very good job." "I am sure," she continued, "that my school children and I will enjoy school more. As I look around my school room this morn-ing, I find that it has a pleasant look which it did not have before. I know the children will be able to study better and learn more." The report also contained an excerpt of a letter from a child: "I very graciously thank you for fixing the schoolhouse and painting it. It looks better and I feel better when I'm in it. And I think you should do the same for other schools that are in the position that ours was. I'm sure they will appreciate it."[64]

January was, indeed, an important month in eastern Kentucky, as the Council of the Southern Mountains took an important step in designing a more ambitious program for the Appalachian South. On January 15, 1964, Perley Ayer sent a letter to all eastern Kentucky college presidents inviting two students, one male, one female, along with a faculty adviser, to a Janu-ary 24–25 meeting. This meeting, at which the CSM set up a permanent organization of volunteer services for eastern Kentucky and, eventually, all the central Appalachian coalfields, marked the actual beginning of the Ap-palachian Volunteers.[65]

The attitudes and activities of the Council of the Southern Mountains in the very early 1960s mirrored those it would employ in the initial stages of the War on Poverty. First of all, the Council stressed a volunteer effort that, combined with indigenous support, would alleviate the most obvious manifestations of want in the Southern mountains. Most of the needed volunteers, it hoped, would come from local colleges and universities. By utilizing the talents of local people, CSM programs would motivate mountaineers to help themselves, rather than rely on handouts or the good works of others.[66] This would minimize that aspect of aid that was anathema to the CSM leaders–the tendency, as they saw it, of pure charity to drive recipients further into a state of dependency. In this way, the Council, under Ayer's leadership, resembled a sort of latter-day New Deal organization.

Despite its seemingly boundless energy, however, the Council was restrained by its cooperative philosophy, which served to channel its efforts toward a type of community development that could be more accurately described as "facility development." By improving impoverished mountaineers' health, their recreational facilities, and, most important, their educational facilities, it would, it believed, improve immediately the situation in the region. Moreover, the CSM maintained, these developments would precipitate economic opportunity through the creation of a better-educated, healthier workforce.

Ultimately, however, it was the philosophical implications of the Council's position that proved to be most significant. On a national stage, the CSM's position was congruent with that of those who would plan the country's domestic reform agenda. Rooted in a New Deal approach to the nation's problems, these top-level strategists accepted the analysis offered by critics such as Harrington, Galbraith, Coles, and the emerging pluralist theorists and, thus, failed to consider the possibility that there were major flaws in American society. Harrington went so far as to blame poverty on the fact that the poor had no "lobbies" that could forward their interests and, thus, were effectively invisible. More immediately, the Council's approach signified a cultural basis for the existence of poverty in the mountains. Poverty was not defined simply as a lack of material goods, adequate housing, or sufficient health care. Rather, echoing Galbraith's analysis that poverty was curable, as evidenced by instances of people in remote, isolated areas who have mastered their environment and bettered their situation, it was in

Appalachia at least considered to be the result of the region's dysfunctional society. This society, with its aberrant culture isolated from the mainstream, fostered the undesirable traits, such as fatalism, a devaluation of education, and a lack of community spirit, that the Council of the Southern Mountains hoped to change through its Appalachian Volunteers program.[67]

2

The Shot Heard Round the World

The Battle for Mill Creek, Kentucky, and the Culture of Poverty

> The great national emphasis and interest in Eastern Kentucky, the Appalachians, depressed areas and pockets of poverty largely is a thing of the past. . . . The average citizen in the United States, if he thinks about Appalachia at all this summer, thinks that the problems are being handled—that there is no reason for him to be particularly concerned.
>
> —Thomas S. Gish, editor of the *Whitesburg, KY, Mountain Eagle*, in a speech delivered before the Council of the Southern Mountains on July 14, 1964

Born in Floyd County, Virginia, in the Blue Ridge Mountains, Milton Ogle graduated from Berea College in 1955. Following a short tenure as a math teacher in McDowell County, North Carolina, Ogle returned to Berea to administer the college's broom factory. He enjoyed his job, which allowed him to interact with people from all over the region. It helped him, moreover, appreciate the role that Berea College played in the Southern mountains. "Berea was really good," he recalled in 1991, "at . . . taking in people that had been by-passed by the non-system of education that existed then in Appalachia and helping them to get over the hurdles . . . that they couldn't get over in their own communities." This attitude remained with Ogle after he began, in 1959, to work with the Council of the Southern Mountains (CSM) and, by 1963, the Appalachian Volunteers (AVs). Looking back on his reform efforts in the 1960s, he contended that the overall CSM/AV goal was to show "how people could be involved in things that affected their lives." The question, however, turned on what those "things" were. When

Ogle and the CSM began to send volunteers into the region, he had to answer that very question. Most probably, his view of the region's educational "non-system" influenced his response. Still, though he was born in the region and had a quality education, a wealth of experience, and an impressive array of connections that stretched all the way to Washington, DC, that did not mean that he knew exactly how to initiate effective reform. He should have realized this even before he led the Appalachian Volunteers into the War on Poverty since he well knew that "knowledge and wisdom, far from being the same, often have no connection."[1]

In reality, when those first student volunteers traveled to Harlan County early in the winter of 1964, the CSM had access to many sources seeking to explain the cause of Appalachian poverty. The two most influential and enduring explanations were the "culture of poverty" and the "colonialism" models, both rooted in the late nineteenth century. While the former portrayed the mountaineers' culture, mores, and value system as antiquated and inferior to that of "modern Americans," the latter viewed Appalachians as exploited and victimized by outside industrial giants that extracted the region's wealth and then absolved themselves of any blame for the mountaineers' subsequent problems by citing the mountaineers' own shortcomings as the source of the region's problems.[2]

Not surprisingly, these divergent interpretations of Appalachian poverty suggested their own solutions. On the one hand, the colonization argument contended that the poor must confront the status quo and diligently work to alter power relationships if they ever were to reassert themselves. Conflict was the hallmark of this philosophy. Proponents of the culture of poverty model, however, stressed efforts "to end the ignorance and fatalism of the Appalachian poor, stimulate economic development, and align the region economically and culturally with the rest of the nation." Not only does this imply the superiority of industrial America's values, but it also suggests that, once given the choice, Appalachians would readily recognize that superiority and adopt middle-class ways.[3]

Because the cultural model implied the health and desirability of the American political, economic, and social systems—that poverty was the result, not of inequities in the country's social, economic, or political structures, but of isolation or individual maladjustment—Ayer's espousal of this view placed the Council firmly in line with the thinking of most Americans in the post–World War II era. Indeed, Vice President Lyndon Johnson believed that the "inevitability of the endless cycle of poverty" was grounded in "the lack of specific training, . . . the neglect of the educational needs of our young, [and] the inadequacy of health care." This view dominated those who planned and administered the reform efforts of the Kennedy and Johnson administrations.[4] These national efforts finally began with the Area Redevelopment Administration (ARA).

Though the ARA was not created until the early 1960s, the concept behind it had been in existence in Congress in one form or another since 1955. President Dwight D. Eisenhower, in his economic report in January of that year, suggested that the national government help bring about "high and stable levels of employment in the nation at large." Initially presented to the national legislature by Democrats, including Senator John F. Kennedy, on the U.S. Congress Joint Economic Committee that July, the package originally included a public works program, long-term credit for new industry, technical assistance, retraining of jobless workers, and allowances, similar to unemployment insurance, for those in the retraining program. (Six years later, when the act finally became law, these features were still included, though in a somewhat modified form.) Unfortunately, the Area Redevelopment bill never became legislative reality during the Eisenhower years. Two presidential vetoes and partisan politics prevented its enactment.[5]

One of Kennedy's first acts as president, however, was to reintroduce the Area Redevelopment legislation and appoint a task force to study poverty, dramatize the need for area redevelopment, and cultivate public support for the bill. While endorsing Kennedy's proposal as it stood, the task force also recommended other measures. It argued that distress could be alleviated "through expanded food distribution programs, temporary extension of unemployment benefits and broadening of public assistance." Moreover, it sought special provisions for federal aid to education in depressed areas. In addition, the task force recommended "funds for access roads, supplemental expenditures for [the] development of natural resources, and a regional commission to coordinate the various activities into a 'broad regional development program.'" With forty-three cosponsors in Congress, Senator Paul Douglas of Illinois introduced the measure on the first day of the 1961 legislative session, and, with the popular president's backing, the bill cleared both houses of Congress in early 1961. This act, in essence, was Kennedy's plan for depressed areas, particularly Appalachia.[6] Tragically, the president did not live to see his aspirations for the poor of southern Appalachia put into practice. His assassination in November 1963 elevated Lyndon Baines Johnson to the presidency. Johnson, formerly a Texas senator and Senate majority leader, was a likely individual to continue his predecessor's relief efforts.[7]

On his first day as president, Johnson met with Walter Heller, the chairman of the Council of Economic Advisers. Heller informed Johnson that, three days prior to the assassination, he had spoken with Kennedy about incipient plans for a national poverty relief effort. Kennedy, Heller declared, wanted an antipoverty measure for his 1964 legislative agenda. Heller wished to know whether the new president favored a continuation of such work. After a few moments of thought, Johnson responded: "I'm sympathetic. Go ahead. Give it the highest priority. Push it ahead full tilt." The new president further decided to make the emerging antipoverty idea part of the national, not just the congressional, agenda. Therefore, he took Kennedy's program further, in terms of both rhetoric and action. This "administration today, here and now," he said during his State of the Union address on January 8, 1964, "declares unconditional war on poverty in America, and I urge this Congress and all Americans to join with me in that effort." Moreover, he targeted a specific area: "We will launch a special effort in the chronically distressed areas of Appalachia."[8]

This focus on "distressed areas" marked a shift in the nature of reform liberalism since the New Deal and, because these areas were exceptions to the general abundance characterizing life in the United States, reinforced the perception that equated *distressed* with *aberrant*. In the 1930s, Franklin Delano Roosevelt had faced not an area but a country in economic crisis, and his New Deal sought to bolster American capitalism and, ultimately, create new jobs. In short, the New Deal concentrated on *quantitative* economic issues affecting the entire nation. Johnson assumed the presidency, however, during the relatively flush 1960s. Though the quantitative issues of poverty and civil rights were critical to the president's position, just as important were such *qualitative* issues as educational, cultural, and political institutions and the sense of powerlessness that came from the sense of "anomie and estrangement" that those institutions engendered. In May 1964, speaking at the University of Michigan, Johnson declared: "The city of man serves not only the needs of the body and the demands of commerce, but the desire for beauty and hunger for community." Two years later, he asserted: "In the midst of abundance modern man walks oppressed by forces which menace and confine the quality of his life, and which individual abundance alone will not overcome." Johnson envisioned his "Great Society," of which the War on Poverty was an integral part, as a way to prevail over these qualitative deficiencies. While this focus on quality, coupled with the move toward participatory democracy included in the Economic Opportunity Act, which actually launched the War on Poverty, moved the Great Society away from the much more quantitative focus of the New Deal, it failed to address the realities of life in the southern Appalachians. In this region, one ravaged by poverty and unemployment, the issues were—at least as far as many rural Appalachians were concerned—quantitative.[9]

The federal government did support Johnson's War on Poverty, and, on August 20, 1964, Congress passed the Economic Opportunity Act, a measure designed "to mobilize the human and financial resources of the Nation to combat poverty in the United States." The act declared it "the policy of the United States to eliminate the paradox of poverty in the midst of plenty in this Nation by opening to everyone the opportunity for education and training, the opportunity to work, and the opportunity to live in decency and dignity." "The United States can," it continued, "achieve its full economic and social potential as a nation only if every individual has the opportunity to contribute to the full extent of his capabilities and to participate in the workings of our society. . . . It is the purpose of this act to strengthen, supplement, and coordinate efforts in the furtherance of that policy."[10] In order to carry out these purposes, the act established the Office of Economic Opportunity (OEO) within the executive branch of the federal government. The OEO became the government organization that fought the War on Poverty, and it joined the fight in Appalachia in December 1964 with a grant to the Council of the Southern Mountains for its nascent Appalachian Volunteers program.[11]

Ironically, *conflict* was far from the minds of those who planned for the *war* on poverty. Designed "to be a way in which all important segments of the community would mobilize all available resources to deal with local poverty," the Community Action Program, the centerpiece of the War on Poverty, was, as program planners described it, a "three-legged stool" on

which community consensus rested. The local political structure consti-
tuted the first leg of the stool, civic organizations and social agencies the
second, and representatives of the poor the third. The Economic Opportunity Act mandated the "maximum feasible participation" of the poor, and,
by that means, the OEO hoped to "encourag[e] the residents of poverty
areas to take part in the work of community action programs." In short, the
OEO (again recalling Boone's ideas concerning the National Service Corps)
believed that the impoverished should help design their own programs.[12]

The framers of the Economic Opportunity Act would have been extremely naive to think that this arrangement had the capacity to prevent
any and all conflicts. On the contrary, they saw a certain degree of controversy as "inevitable and, in most cases, healthy." Revealing a belief that friction was inevitable within the context of participatory pluralist democracy,
Sanford Kravitz, the future associate director of the Community Action
Program's demonstration projects, argued that locally administered antipoverty efforts "would 'remain honest' to [the act's] purposes by inclusion
of voices representing the poor." John G. Wofford, who in 1964 became a
staff assistant to the OEO's director of operations, called community action
a "painful, headlining process . . . toward local consensus."[13]

In the CSM's and Ayer's cooperative philosophy, the OEO found the
manifestation of this balance between conflict and consensus. Ayer reinforced his philosophical stance, reflecting the prevailing ideas about how
the country's political system worked, and graphically demonstrating how
the federal government's conception of how poverty should be fought coincided with Council policy. In a letter to the OEO, Ayer stated that the
CSM incorporated "*all segments* of society: public *and* private; dominant
and dependent; . . . affluent . . . as well as poor." He elaborated elsewhere:
"The CSM hopes to encourage people to do whatever they need to do."[14]

Encouraging people to do "what they need to do" was the purpose of
an Appalachian Volunteers organizational meeting held at the Pine Mountain Settlement School at the end of January 1964. Of the nineteen colleges
invited, representatives of sixteen attended. The meeting's agenda endorsed
a permanent regional organization of student volunteers and proposed
short- and long-term plans for the newly formed organization. On the basis of the favorable results of the initial school renovation project, the participants decided to continue working to improve the physical conditions

of the one- and two-room schools throughout the region. However, the Council of the Southern Mountains felt that school refurbishing was not enough, and it argued for a program of curriculum enrichment. Academic enrichment was just as important as schoolhouse improvements. Interesting activities, the CSM reasoned, would attract the community's school-age children and, perhaps, encourage them to complete their education. Thus, in addition to its plans to offer through its enrichment program health education and recreational activities, the CSM hoped to bring in foreign exchange students who attended nearby colleges, such as the University of Kentucky, to describe what life was like outside the United States. While its long-term vision essentially remained limited to school-based programs, the Council did make a few minor adjustments. For example, it included tutors for adults as well as children and Volunteer-operated bookmobiles in its plans. In time, the Council hoped to develop, in conjunction with local leaders, a total community development program that would include public health and sanitation components. Perhaps as a result of the successful school repair project, the participants at Pine Mountain further suggested that students could also help homeowners repair their houses.[15]

Organization and recruitment of the actual volunteers was also important. CSM leaders determined that each college should have a campus chapter of the Appalachian Volunteers. Most probably, they based this idea on an organization already in existence at Berea College—Campus Action for Mountain Progress (CAMP). Concerned Berea College students had created CAMP during the spring semester of 1960 in order "to aid in motivating economic, educational, and recreational development in Southern Appalachia; to study specific problems concerning the mountain region; and to render services whenever possible to civic and religious organizations interested in the mountain region." This purpose, CAMP believed, was very similar to the purpose of Berea College (and, of course, the Council of the Southern Mountains), which was to "contribut[e] to the spiritual and material welfare of the mountain region of the South." Economic conditions were so severe in the Southern mountains, CAMP maintained, that its organization was needed and would exist for a long time.[16]

Led by future Appalachian Volunteer staff member Phil Conn, CAMP was one of the more active clubs on the Berea College campus. Representatives of the organization had attended the annual conference of the Council of the Southern Mountains in Gatlinburg, Tennessee, in early 1963, and, in October of that year, Ayer urged the CSM's Youth Committee to advocate the creation of CAMP chapters on all the college campuses in and near the southern Appalachian region. CAMP members had also initiated a clothing drive for the victims of floods in eastern Kentucky, working closely with the Council of the Southern Mountains when it came time to distribute what they had collected. All things considered, this was the most likely organization for the CSM to use as a model for its campus chapters.[17]

About two months later, on March 14, 1964, the Appalachian Volunteers became official with the adoption of a set of bylaws at the second organizational meeting, held in Berea. According to those bylaws, the AVs' goals reflected the country's assumptions about welfare, dependency, and pluralism. First, the Volunteers wanted to "involve the citizens of the region in the process of meeting community needs by providing capable and highly motivated people to assist in projects in areas such as education, health, recreation, and human welfare." Second, they hoped to establish an organizational base "through which students can assist their fellow citizens." These two goals made possible the third: "to initiate programs which look to lasting solutions of the region's problems." Milton Ogle, who became the CSM's Appalachian Volunteer program director in 1964, condensed the mission of the nascent reform organization into basic terms when he stated: "Deprived people cannot be helped; they must help themselves."[18]

With the creation of a program that so dramatically put into practice the conception of self-help on the local level, the Council further ingratiated itself with the nation's leaders. Even before that first meeting at Pine Mountain had concluded, both the head of the Small Business Administration and President Johnson expressed their support for the antipoverty program. "Your goals," Johnson stated in a telegram to Ogle, "to involve the residents of the region in the development process; to provide a vehicle through which students and others can help those in need; and to demonstrate to the nation the efficiency of the self help process . . . are most gratifying to me." The president also implored Ogle to take control of the efforts to end poverty in Appalachia: "I am looking to you for leadership in demonstrating new and creative ways of using volunteers to help relieve conditions of rural poverty, . . . teaching, providing recreational outlets, better health facilities, helping prevent . . . entry into poverty." While the work already completed in Harlan County impressed the chief executive, more astonishing in his eyes was the inclusion of "the vigor and idealism of youth ... in a great cooperative effort of public and private agencies."[19]

Fortunately for the Council, Johnson's support was not limited to rhetoric. On the contrary, the president followed his words with funds. Even prior to the formation of the OEO, the Council's AV effort received $50,000, spread over a six-month period, from the ARA. Private funding for the AV effort also materialized. That same year, the Ford Foundation issued a grant of over $33,000 to the CSM for "special projects" that would be conducted by the Appalachian Volunteers in the many one-room schools in the Southern mountains. These projects included adult education, tutoring, and scholarships designed to help poor mountain children stay in school. The foundation also provided Ogle and the CSM's Appalachian Volunteer program with about $2,000 in administrative funds. With this money, Ogle could defray the cost of recruiting college volunteers and help pay the salary of a field director.[20]

A brief examination of a few of the activities funded by the Ford Foundation provides a revealing glimpse into how the Council's Appalachian Volunteer project implemented the philosophy that guided its first two years. In Pike County, Kentucky, for example, the Council undertook an adult education program in cooperation with the county school superintendent's office. In addition to its standard instructional aspects, the program contained a motivational component. That is, the CSM hoped "to induce in the adults the desire to learn and become aware of the value of education." It articulated an identical goal for a project in Bledsoe County, Tennessee. Similarly, in Blackey, Letcher County, Kentucky, and Dry Creek, Raleigh County, West Virginia, the Council sought, through adult education and preschool programs, to foster "interest in education" in adults and "stimulate the learning desire" in children.[21]

This attempt to alter the mountaineers' values—instilling in them an interest in and a desire for education—clearly exposes the culture of poverty model underlying the Volunteers' efforts in the early 1960s. It was not so much that the mountaineers lacked a proper education as that they placed no value on learning. This, more than anything else, was what the Appalachian Volunteers hoped to change.

Included in the Ford Foundation program was funding for the placement of an American Friends Service Committee (AFSC)–VISA volunteer in Clay and Harlan counties, Kentucky. Under the VISA (Voluntary International Service Assignment) program, volunteers agreed to serve for a certain period of time (usually a year) in an underdeveloped foreign country. It is interesting that eastern Kentucky qualified for the AFSC-VISA program. Prior to the arrival of the VISA volunteer, two Council-sponsored volunteers visited Mill Creek, Clay County. The Council had high hopes for the Mill Creek project. In their report to the Ford Foundation, the CSM's leaders referred to it as the "demonstration project for the Appalachian Volunteers."[22] Fortunately, much of the record of the Mill Creek project is extant. Rather than revealing an exemplary project, however, that record shows one replete with confusion and conflict. While the friction remained relatively minor, the project should have served as a cautionary tale for the AVs' leaders.

The Council leaders chose Mill Creek because not one of its seventy adult residents had finished high school. Further, of the twenty-five children in the town under the age of sixteen, the CSM reported, most were two to five years behind their grade level. Complicating matters was the status of the teachers. According to Milton Ogle, who presented the Mill Creek proposal to the CSM and the Ford Foundation, all the teachers either had emergency certificates (teaching licenses usually given to less than fully qualified individuals to fill a position in a school where no regular teacher worked) or held regular certificates that had long ago expired. To remedy this deplorable situation, Ogle proposed that the CSM's nascent AV-VISA project "bring to the community through Audio Visual Aids and a wide selection of books and records a modern educational experience that goes far beyond anything that has been attempted in a similar Eastern Kentucky community." To supplement the academic effort, Ogle scheduled field trips to the state capitol at Frankfort, a manufacturing plant, and a state park. Organizations such as Berea College and the Kentucky Library Extension Service had already donated recordings and players, books, and films to the project. Rounding out the effort, a business in Manchester, the county seat, purchased basketballs and goals for the recreation portion of the project, and local families agreed to house the volunteers. Ogle requested that the Ford Foundation provide the last piece of the puzzle—$775 for the volunteers' living expenses, school supplies (paper, paint, modeling clay), and field trip costs. The foundation readily obliged, and, in early June 1964, the Appalachian Volunteers established a permanent presence in eastern Kentucky.[23]

For the two CSM-sponsored AVs, the Mill Creek assignment began on June 8, 1964, and would last until the end of August. Throughout the summer, the Volunteers busied themselves with programs that would, they believed, end the mountaineers' cycle of poverty, namely, running a summer school and leading field trips designed to broaden the experience of the impoverished mountain children. For example, during the week of June 15, 1964, a group of youngsters traveled to Frankfort to meet Governor Edward Breathitt. According to the AVs, this was the first time that many of them had been out of Clay County. Indicating support for the program, Breathitt praised the Appalachian Volunteers for turning their attention toward what really was the "primary target" in the fight against poverty, Appalachia's human resources.[24]

The idea of broadening the experiences of isolated mountain children found adherents throughout the United States. One fervent supporter, Jack Ciaccio, an official in the Department of Health, Education, and Welfare who later joined the OEO, asked the AVs to establish an out-of-town educational camp for the Mill Creek children. Flem Messer, a Clay County native and Volunteer staff member who helped organize the Mill Creek project, objected. Interestingly, Messer grounded his opposition to Ciaccio's suggestion in the culture of the mountaineers. Implying the stereotypical clannishness and aversion to modern ways commonly associated with rural Appalachians, he noted: "I doubt if half of the parents who need to send their children [to the educational camp] would do so, especially if this means sending them to Lexington or other areas any distance from home." Just as important, he argued, if the children's educational experiences removed them from their community, "there would not be enough opportunity to deal with the parents and change their attitude [toward education]." "The parents," he concluded, "need to be able to participate and change as their children do."[25]

Volunteers certainly tried to generate and maintain interest in the project among the parents. In at least one volunteer's eye, however, a cultural and generational gap was always present. "The parents were very cooperative," claimed the AV. "They might not have understood the things I did, and sometimes they found them strange, but they were tolerant. . . . And we talked—*talking takes them out of their environment and gets them interested in the world.*" Children, on the other hand, openly embraced the Volunteers' effort. Nevertheless, this did not make the job less challenging. Calling the children "healthy, intelligent, and enthusiastic," that same volunteer reported that "they responded extremely well" to the lessons offered in the summer school. Yet there were "so many things they didn't know *because of their way of life.*"[26] As these statements reveal, overcoming the deficiencies of the mountaineers was as much the goal of the summer Appalachian Volunteers as was the purely educational effort.

Despite the tremendous cultural obstacles encountered, the Council of the Southern Mountains presented the summer portion of the Mill Creek project to the public as an overwhelming success. Covering the venture for the *Louisville Courier-Journal,* the reporter Jim Hampton recognized that a project such as this was difficult to assess because it produced few immediate results. Rather, the significance would not be felt for some time and would come from the "young minds brought alive, stirring from the lethargy induced by an existence circumscribed by the hills that surround Kentucky's countless Mill Creeks." In the end, it was the Appalachian Volunteers who "kindled the imaginations" of these poor mountain children. Moreover, the AVs pulled back the veil of "isolation and poverty" that kept the "settlement locked . . . in the mold of yesterday." In this way, the Volunteers' summer school was "unique among the efforts being made to lift Appalachia out of backwardness."[27]

What is interesting about Hampton's article is that it constitutes a graphic illustration of the way in which many Americans saw Appalachia, the region's problems, and the solutions to those problems. In short, Hampton provides more information about modern America than about the Southern mountain region and its people. Propagating a view that was by the early 1960s nearly a century old, he characterizes Mill Creek as a "settlement" that was "locked" in the "mold of yesterday" and would clearly remain so until outsiders, representatives of the modern world, intervened to "lift" it "out of backwardness." Clearly, a setting such as Hampton's Louisville represented better than anything Mill Creek had to offer proper American culture and values.

Surface confirmation at least that the community approved of the program arrived in early fall. Between September 1 and September 5, 1964, Messer received five letters of appreciation from town residents. While this alone may not be unusual, the style and form of the letters call into question their honesty. Each adhered to the same formula and addressed the same issues in the exact order. All five correspondents stated how much they enjoyed the teachers, how much the children learned, how all could now write their own names, and how they hoped that the Appalachian Volunteers would conduct a summer school at Mill Creek the next year. Of course, they may, in fact, have felt positively about the program. But it seems just as likely that they were coached and, thus, that their thanks were not sincere. Because the letters were dated after the two volunteers left, it is impossible to determine who guided their authors. Probably it was the emergency teacher who coordinated the effort.[28]

Unlike the first two volunteers, Carol Irons, the CSM-sponsored VISA volunteer, did not enter Clay County until the end of the summer, having committed herself to a year of work in Mill Creek starting early that fall. It is her experience that most directly calls into question the letter writers' candor. Because Irons offered her time and talents to Appalachia, the AFSC relied heavily on the CSM's Appalachian Volunteer program to instruct and guide her while she resided in Clay County. In this way, she was as much a representative of the AVs as she was of the AFSC. Throughout the autumn of 1964, Irons reported that she assisted people with only those things that they could have done on their own anyway, for example, driving them to doctor's appointments in Manchester or helping them around their homes. This, however, was less than satisfying, and she informed Robert Sigmon, the director of the AFSC-VISA program, that she hoped to provide the community with services that they could not get otherwise and that, in order for her to do this, Mill Creek needed a community center. Originally, she had hoped to use the local church as a combination residence and project center, but the preacher balked at this idea. As a result, Irons lived with Amelia Messer, Flem Messer's aunt, and pushed the idea of a new neighborhood center. This center would allow her to conduct what she considered to be two of the more important aspects of her program, a literacy project and instruction in healthier ways of cooking.[29] Unfortunately, controversy surrounding the project—such as where to build the proposed community center and to what uses it would be put—spelled disaster for the Mill Creek project.

Responding to her desire to do more with her time in Mill Creek, Milton Ogle told Irons to let the community people lead, that is, to let the desires of those she was there to help dictate what actions she would take. Her focus, then, remained where that of the two departed AVs had been—on academics. After she finally gained permission to use the local church building, Irons conducted kindergarten classes for two hours each weekday throughout the fall and prepared for a community Christmas pageant. While these efforts achieved acceptable results, by the end of January 1965 problems had surfaced.[30]

On February 1, 1965, Irons wrote to Ogle about Flem Messer, the AV fieldman in Clay County. Her concern was Messer's actions, both as a private citizen and as a representative of the CSM. Apparently, because she had permission to use the local church for her kindergarten classes, she was no longer a fervent advocate of the construction project. Messer, however, vigorously pushed for a community center to be built on land owned by his relatives and with only outside funding. Moreover, according to Irons, he "kept proposing more complicated plans," with the result that the community "got bewildered" and withdrew its support for the project.[31]

While it is true that the reasoning behind Messer's position is not entirely clear, his actions suggest certain motivations. The most obvious is that, should the community center be built on Messer family land with outside funding, the building would belong to the Messer family on the departure of the VISA volunteer. In fact, at the end of May, Irons reported that the community rejected the project for precisely that reason.[32]

Another motivation was Messer's political ambitions. Independently of his work with the Council, Messer had become a political activist in Manchester. Specifically, he was a member of a citizens' action group working toward improved education in the county. As most Council members would certainly attest, this was a worthy cause. Nonetheless, Messer's involvement with it made Irons's job even more difficult. As Loyal Jones described the situation: "The school superintendent and the political boss of Clay County ... accused [Messer] of using his office with the Council to further his own private political ambitions. Thus the word was sent out ... that local teachers and others should not work with the Appalachian Volunteers." Evidence indicates not only that the "word" was sent out but also that it reached Mill Creek. In a report on her activities in late 1965, Irons expressed anxiety about Messer and his presence in Mill Creek. Though working with a "native" was, she felt, instrumental in getting situated at first, associating with that particular native had, "because of his political activities," become a "handicap."[33]

Messer, for his part, did not want to jeopardize Irons's work. Hoping to ease the situation, he suggested to the CSM leadership that it terminate his official duties in Clay County and that he join the staff at the Berea headquarters. Tensions did diminish after Ayer and Ogle met with county officials, but this failed to ease Irons's concerns. "At this time," she wrote to Ogle in early 1965, "I am not sure that there is any value in my remaining in Mill Creek to work not just because [of] what has happened but because the past events indicate a trend in the future."[34]

Irons's troubles forced Robert Sigmon (the AFSC-VISA director) to question the leadership and supervision that the Appalachian Volunteers were providing. Since the early fall, Sigmon contended, "there has been a little confusion about direction and guidance." Responding that he knew that "the indecisiveness in the community" and the "unsolicited 'assistance' . . . created some problems" in Mill Creek, Ogle tried to maintain closer contact with Irons, and she began to submit weekly reports to him. This arrangement did result in an improved relationship between the VISA volunteer, the AVs, and Mill Creek. On February 13, 1965, the community residents finally agreed to construct a "church education building." A committee of religious and lay leaders worked on the details of its specific uses and its location. Moreover, Irons met with the local preacher to discuss her ideas on "certain methods of community development." She also informed him of her objections to the plan for the new church building, yet both agreed to keep the best interests of the community at heart.[35] Yet, from this not very high point, the situation began to deteriorate once again.

While it was not initially clear why Irons had come to object to a community building, her next few reports to Ogle contained a clue. After the townspeople approved the project, they waited for the preacher "to take definite steps for plans and funds." Evidently, Irons feared that, if the structure was on church property, it would be not just part of the church but entirely the responsibility of the church—and, thus, not truly a community center, just as if it had been built on Messer family land. Confirmation that this was the case came in early March. By that time, Irons revealed to Ogle, the community "seem[ed] to have given up." While the people of Mill Creek felt that a community center would solve all their problems, having voted on the issue they wanted to do nothing more than sit back and wait for someone—the preacher—to get the work done. When specific plans and resources failed to materialize, they simply resigned themselves to the project's failure. This resignation significantly eroded Irons's influence in the community. Residents would no longer discuss possible new projects with her, nor did they suggest new ideas. When at one point Irons herself introduced a new idea, "there [was]," she reported, "no reaction, no response." Moreover, her proposal for a second summer school project met with only negative reactions.[36]

Perhaps the reasons why the Mill Creek community development project failed to live up to expectations, despite CSM attempts to ensure a smoothly run program, lay in the fact that neither the Council, the VISA volunteer, nor the townspeople had a clear notion of what they meant by *community development*. It is possible, for example, that Mill Creek wanted improvements made to its church more than it desired a community center. Unfortunately, the record provides no clear answer. In fact, Sigmon wrote to Ogle on this very subject. Revealing that he himself considered community development to be equivalent to educational improvement, Sigmon asked whether "it would be in the best interests of the assignment and the community if Carol could see her objectives extended to include something more than just 'community development'": "That is, would it be possible to define another . . . role to [her], say . . . as a teacher's aide?" In short, the AFSC-VISA director asked the AVs to give the inexperienced volunteer a *specific job* rather than just sending her out into the field with the vague order to "develop the community."[37]

Sigmon's desire that Irons's time in Mill Creek be both productive and rewarding highlighted a challenge facing the entire AV program—how best to utilize the services of young, relatively inexperienced volunteers in admittedly difficult situations. Citing Irons's frustrations with the project, Sigmon added that his suggestion for a more specific job description would profit the AVs, the community, and the individual volunteers "because long term voluntary service among young persons not particularly trained in community development has a history of proving futile for many who have attempted it." According to Sigmon, this was the case with Irons in Mill

Creek. While she did not want to abandon her assignment, she could, Sigmon informed Ogle, "find no valid reason for remaining."[38]

What was Carol Irons's conception of community development? The evidence of her reports suggests that it was more inclusive, more comprehensive than Sigmon's notion of simple educational enhancement. Moreover, coupled with the results of her efforts, it should have provided the Appalachian Volunteers with a guide for future activities.

Central to Irons's efforts, of course, was the kindergarten. She decided to augment her academic curriculum with a drama program, arguing that this would teach the children to speak in front of groups and help them gain self-confidence. While this aspect of her program did reflect the presuppositions on which the project was based—that the mountaineers were shy, reticent people lacking the ability to assert themselves—others transcended purely cultural concerns. Coupled with the academic program was an economic initiative that called on Mill Creek residents to grow cucumbers to sell to a pickle plant that was, reportedly, coming to Manchester. This enterprise, unfortunately, failed to bear fruit. At once the townspeople found reasons to reject the plan. Some, Irons reported, refused to cooperate because they feared that the program would adversely affect their welfare and social security benefits. Others simply manufactured "reasons for not trying it." One resident did, eventually, agreed to plant the new crop. Irons's success was short-lived, however. Antagonism, probably due in part to the residual ill feelings over the building project, grew between Irons and the Messers. Late in the winter of 1965, Irons was desperate to move out of Amelia Messer's house. During the adverse weather conditions associated with the month of February, Irons informed Ogle that "private housing [was] a necessity" and that she was willing to live anywhere, including a small mobile home or even an army surplus tent, rather than in her present quarters.[39]

In April, Irons embarked on a project that involved marketing locally produced crafts, but her influence with the community continued to diminish. When Susan Black, the director of the Crafts Division of the State Department of Commerce, visited Mill Creek that month to offer advice about marketing strategies for homemade quilts, her presentation met with exceptionally poor attendance. Moreover, the "community leader," the local resident who served as the on-site administrator of the CSM-sponsored project, failed to call a meeting that month. Taking matters into her own hands, Irons, during the last week of April, traveled to Manchester to discuss the community's problems with county officials. This action inspired at least one Mill Creek resident, Crit Gambrel, to visit the county Health Department to request the establishment of a dump site for the town's refuse. Not only did the Health Department reject the request, but it also told the townsfolk not to dump their trash in the nearby creek.[40]

While the benefits of a clean stream were obvious, this response did not address the issue at hand. Mill Creek needed a place to dispose of its waste, and the county had failed either to provide such a dump site or to haul away garbage. Again seizing the initiative, Irons proposed a community cleanup project. Nearly everyone in Mill Creek, she reported, understood the need for this type of effort, as evidenced by the fact that they blamed the polluted conditions of their immediate environment for most of their health problems. One person, however, opposed the community effort. That individual was Irons's old nemesis, Amelia Messer.[41]

In her reports, Irons failed to explain why Messer objected to the cleanup project, but it may be explained, at least in part, by yet another shift in the direction of the overall effort. By the end of May 1965, the town's focus had returned to the community center. After an extended period of inactivity, Mill Creek held a town meeting at which Messer agreed to deed land for the building, and the people at first rallied to the cause. Hoping that this renewed enthusiasm would spark interest in the continuation of volunteer work in their community, the people held yet another vote on a second summer school program. Because she believed that there was a "lack of sincerity" in the voting process when she was present, Irons excused herself from the meeting. Unfortunately, this meant that she could not report on the ensuing debate. This information, of course, would have explained why the residents again vetoed the plan (further evidence of the insincerity of the previous fall's thank-you letters). Nevertheless, Irons had her own ideas on the subject. The people rejected the project, she felt, because of the heavy workload that most Mill Creek families faced during the summer season or, more significantly, because of dissatisfaction with the previous summer's program, reasons that she considered mere "excuses."[42]

Irons saw such dissatisfaction as an excuse because, as she contended, the people were free "to alter the summer school program to fit their own desires." More devastating for her was the fact that, in the wake of the rejection of the summer school project, interest in the community center again waned. Irons reported three basic reasons for this turn of events. First, and perhaps most obvious, was the lack of need. Many linked the new building with the summer project, and, without the school, there was no need for a community center. More pivotal, however, was the townspeople's fear that, once the school program was over, the Messers would take over the building and that, "because of her influence," Amelia would "run activities her way, which is not always in the best interest of all." Equally influential was what Irons claimed to be Amelia's evident desire for the building. Irons believed that it should go to her if only to prevent "mean[n]ess" following her, Irons's, departure. "In all good conscience," Irons concluded in her report in early June, "I cannot urge Mill Creek to build and face such unfavorable circumstances." She speculated that fear of this "meanness" prevented offers of other building sites. She had also come to another decision: "Further, without a building to function in or a private place to live, I will not be able to remain beyond the summer." And, in fact, she did not. While she submitted a "terminal report" to Ogle from Charlotte, North Carolina, her June report was the last from Mill Creek. On June 22, 1965, more than two months short of the full year she had originally intended, Irons ceased trying to "develop" the residents and town of Mill Creek.[43]

It would be a mistake to conclude that, while significant, the troubles with Amelia Messer alone caused Irons to abandon her assignment early. Rather, her reasons for leaving reflected Sigmon's concerns of the previous March, in particular, the frustrations of a less than adequately trained person charged with the vague responsibility of developing a community. On June 18, Irons informed Sigmon that she was leaving Mill Creek because of a "lack of understanding with [Amelia] Messer, my landlady and a strong influence on other families; . . . lack of community in terms of unity [and] goals . . . ; inadequate living conditions; . . . no functional place to work." Irons's inability to develop Mill Creek was, as her first two reasons illustrated, the result of her failure to overcome the dominance of one interested party over the rest of the community. This, in turn, prevented the unity that could have made the community center and summer school projects successful. This chain of events led to Irons's frustration and, ultimately, her departure. Had she been better prepared, or had she focused her attention on a couple of specific tasks, the sense of futility she experienced might not have been so acute. Moreover, she could possibly have withstood what must have been the proverbial final straw. Some time prior to her relocation, yet after her final regular report, "[a] person not living in Mill Creek, but related to the Messers, offered $25.00 towards the church building fund on the condition that I and my work be given a bad name and I no longer be allowed to use the church." "The money," she claimed, "was accepted."[44]

Regardless of Irons's personal success or failure, one must question what the Appalachian Volunteers, as an organization, should have learned from its "demonstration project." Certainly, Mill Creek offered more than its share of potentially useful lessons. Unfortunately, what the Council of the Southern Mountains thought of it is difficult to assess. There being no Mill Creek evaluation reports extant, one can only speculate. Taken as a whole—that is, the CSM-sponsored volunteer summer school in conjunction with Irons's later efforts—the program deteriorated from a successful beginning to a difficult, painful end. Considered by itself, the summer school program seems to have achieved much more success than did Irons's efforts at community development.

Such conclusions would, however, be superficial. An evaluation that addresses the question of why Irons encountered so much opposition would be much more instructive. At issue is how the Mill Creek project should have informed the remainder of the AV experience in the Southern mountains and how the AVs could have solved the problems at the root of Irons's trials.

Beginning with the summer school conducted by the Council-sponsored volunteers, the CSM received little in the way of harsh criticism. In fact, other than those questionable letters of thanks, it got very little feedback directly from either the volunteers or the local residents. What responses it did manage to gather, however, reconfirmed the prevailing notions that dominated America in the early years of the decade. Helping bring impoverished mountain folk "out of their environment" and getting them "interested in the world" attracted not just the Ford Foundation but arguably the rest of the United States as well.[45] More important, these types of statements clearly implied the soundness and desirability of modern American culture. Thus, the summer school portion of the program alone fulfilled the basic criteria for success held by such liberal thinkers as the leaders of the

CSM, the various charitable institutions donating to the Council, and the executive branch of the U.S. government. The development work of Carol Irons, on the other hand, taught different lessons.

The most obvious lesson was the inadvisability of the way in which the Council of the Southern Mountains readily accepted nonnative volunteers. Irons's presence refuted the whole idea on which the Volunteer program was based. That is, Irons did not represent the ideal of local people helping each other. As long as she continued conducting essentially the same activities as the preceding volunteers had, however, she had little trouble. In fact, the only complaint came from Irons herself when she made it known that she wanted to do more than just be a helping hand. While she served as the local taxi driver and kindergarten teacher, she experienced a cordial relationship with the entire community. When she placed the idea of a new building before the people, however, problems occurred. The struggle over the community center demonstrated how those supposedly culturally bound, primitive people were not, in fact, locked into a premodern economy in which all were political and economic equals. Rather, throughout Appalachia, as throughout the United States, certain people and interests dominated communities. In essence, Mill Creek was a microcosm of both the region and the nation.

A second lesson was that, at this stage of the reform effort, the concept of community development remained too vague to be of much use. What was a volunteer charged with the task of developing a community to do? Was a community center integral to development, and, if so, how? Was development to concentrate on education, economics, health concerns, or politics? In short, what was the volunteer's job? While the CSM certainly hoped to avoid dictating to the mountaineers, the directive to let the community lead proved insufficient for a volunteer with little or no experience working in central Appalachia. Another argument for the need for a more specific notion of community development was the constantly shifting focus of Irons's ultimately unsuccessful efforts. She repeatedly redirected her attention from the kindergarten, to the community center, to the pickle project, to a cleanup program, back to the community center. Though these course changes could be rationalized as following the community's wishes, they are more accurately seen as a series of attempts by a frustrated and possibly naive volunteer to do something constructive for the community.

Ultimately, neither Irons, the CSM, nor the AFSC had a clear view of the path toward community development. Whether it was a confused volunteer, who had little idea of what the community wanted or what was expected of her, or the CSM, which failed to provide sufficient supervision and guidance, who was at fault, the point remains that the term *community development* lacked sufficient definition in Mill Creek.

Another lesson the CSM should have learned was the role played by the AV fieldman, Flem Messer, both as a CSM employee and as a private individual. Messer's political activism in Clay County and the resentment on the part of local officials that it generated clearly put the CSM-AV leaders on the defensive. In keeping with its "open forum" position, the CSM refused to censure Messer for what he did on his own time, but it did terminate his official duties as a staff member in the county. Early in AV history, then, the CSM leaders became aware of the opposition on the part of the school superintendents and political bosses that could result from the AVs' pursuance of an overt political program. The Council, moreover, did face direct resistance to its efforts in Mill Creek when, as Irons reported, someone offered the town's residents cash to discredit her work. Certainly, the CSM should have realized that acceptance and success—especially in the realm of community development, no matter how vaguely it defined or how poorly it implemented that concept—would not be easy.

Confirming this final lesson were the experiences of the other volunteers who, by the start of the 1964–1965 academic year, began filtering into the Southern mountains. Not long after Irons moved to Mill Creek, the AFSC sent two additional VISA volunteers (who also were nonnatives) to the small mountain town of Decoy, Kentucky. These volunteers did not quit their assignments; instead, the community asked them to leave. When Robert Sigmon traveled to Decoy to investigate, he "found the going rough," as he reported to Jones. Finally, the AFSC leader concluded, the community wanted *teachers,* not *community workers,* and, when the volunteers tried to fill both roles, some of the residents responded negatively. The volunteers tried to rectify the situation prior to Sigmon's arrival, but, after many frustrating attempts to resolve the issue, they left Decoy so that "half-truths" would not become "more distorted" and "suspicious notions" "unduly aroused."[46] Also, after Irons announced her decision to leave Mill Creek, Loyal Jones endeavored to get her a second assignment, this time near Booneville, in Owsley County, Kentucky. Jones wrote to a Booneville minister about the reassignment, but his offer of help was refused. "I will be glad to help if I can," the clergyman replied, "but frankly we have not been too impressed by some of the workers who thus far have been in our area."[47] As this response indicated, locating assignments for all volunteers was decidedly more difficult than most Council staff members had thought it would be. Problems dominated this "demonstration project," and, as Jones himself admitted, these problems were, for the most part, unanticipated and difficult to solve. "Everything seem[ed] to have happened all at once," an apologetic Jones wrote to Sigmon during Irons's initial troubles in Mill Creek, "and by the time we realized that we had a problem, it was almost too late to do anything about it."[48] As future events would show, Jones was not so much apologetic as he was prophetic.

The "Battle for Mill Creek" convinced the Council of the Southern Mountains that school renovation and tutorial programs such as that conducted by the first two volunteers were fundamental to ending poverty. More important, it convinced the Council that these types of efforts would be well received by the targeted communities. Finally, it reinforced for the CSM the culture of poverty model that provided the ideological foundations for the organization's future antipoverty initiatives. The efforts of those first two volunteers in Mill Creek who "brought alive" the minds of the young mountaineers equipped future antipoverty soldiers with the weapons of war. As these volunteers prepared for battle, they armed themselves with books, records, paper, scissors, glue, and guitars. Their enemy was the dark shadow of ignorance cast by a rugged topography.

3

A Splendid Little War

Helping People Help Themselves, 1964

Areas to be stressed will be school renovation and enrichment with
special notice to tutoring. . . . This may sound like a lot but actually it
is not much.
                    —University of Kentucky Appalachian Volunteers Newsletter,
                                                    December 7, 1964

By the time Roslea Johnson entered Berea College in 1961, her experiences had become quite familiar for many Appalachians. Born in Wisconsin in 1943, Johnson was the child of what the historian Chad Berry calls
"northern exiles," people from the Appalachian region who had relocated
to Northern industrial centers in search of employment during World War
II. She was just a year old when her father got a job in a munitions plant
in Tennessee and the family returned to the South. Some time later, when
she was still young, the family finally resettled in the city of Radford, Virginia—very close to Johnson's father's ancestral home. Also closer was her
mother's family, who lived in Caney Valley, near Kingsport, Tennessee. Visits to her mother's relatives, in particular, impressed on Johnson the "differences" between residents of cities such as Radford and those of more "rural"
parts of Appalachia.[1]

    Johnson was in high school, however, in 1956 or 1957, when her father
lost his job and her personal "great recession" occurred. Though the family
was virtually penniless, their financial situation opened the doors to Berea
College. Though Johnson entered Berea as a math major, a friend convinced
her to take a sociology course from Perley Ayer, who at that point taught
one course a semester for the college. So impressed was Johnson by Ayer
that she became a sociology major and, by the end of her sophomore year,
began attending Council of the Southern Mountains (CSM) conferences. It
was as a Berea student, Johnson recalled, that she really learned about "the

mountain culture." Unfortunately, Ayer missed quite a few classes because "he was very active at that time . . . working in Washington in helping to design the war on poverty legislation." Still, to his students' advantage was that fact that "he would come back and tell us all the things that were going on." After attending the CSM's 1963 annual conference, during which she heard "many national speakers, economists, people from Washington, and so on talking about ideas for new programming for Appalachia," Johnson "really got enthusiastic about that."[2]

Toward the end of Johnson's junior year, Ayer, who had just returned from Washington, told Johnson and her class that he and President Kennedy discussed the possibility of a "Domestic Peace Corps." Kennedy wondered "if there would be students interested" in such a venture. "'I don't know,'" Ayer told the president, "'but I'll go ask my students.'" "Talk about being thrilled," Johnson reported. "That really caught my spirit." Excited about this domestic Peace Corps, the students "began organizational meetings for [the] Appalachia Volunteers [AVs]," and Johnson was the Berea College student representative at the first AV meeting. Because they were "really devastatingly awful" and "things like plumbing or electricity . . . were nonexistent" in them, the nearly one thousand one- and two-room schools in eastern Kentucky became one focus of the new volunteer organization. On one of her first projects, Johnson reported, her group of volunteers repaired a school that "had a huge hole in the floor, perhaps four or five feet across." Many other schools, she noticed, had no paper, no books, "nothing for people to use." Because of both the inadequate facilities and the lack of instructional material, Johnson soon realized that "anything that we did was stop-gap, but anything that we did also made a tremendous contribution . . . a dramatic change," whether "[shoring up] flooring, . . . patching up windows, having college students talk with kids at the school." "To me," she concluded, "the Appalachian Volunteers was a very exciting project and I also can see where young people would be drawn to it. You don't have to wait very long to see the results of your efforts, but I think the projects were also designed in such a way too, to give people that sense of accomplishment very quickly." Though these efforts were "minimal in comparison to the immense needs," they "brought people together." For example, through them college students learned about the conditions in Appalachia, and they "made local people aware of another group of people that they had had no exposure to, of people who had been at least a little bit in the outside world . . . through college and through other kinds of experiences."[3]

As important as school renovation was, the AVs' other focus during its first full year of existence was, as Johnson suggested, the recruitment of soldiers for this grand mission. Not just any volunteer would suffice. According to the bylaws, volunteers had to be "highly motivated people" who could "involve the citizens of the region in the process of meeting community needs . . . in such areas as education, health, recreation, and human welfare." Moreover, they had to set an example for the nation by demonstrating the efficacy of "a self-help component in programs aimed at improving conditions of life." The challenge presented to potential volunteers certainly was great. Following the meeting of college officials at Pine Mountain, however, the Council easily recruited college students who met its qualifications. By February 18, 1964, not even one month since the organization's first meeting, the Appalachian Volunteers revealed that it had completed work on ten one- and two-room schools and had organized three hundred volunteers from eight colleges.[4]

Because the need was so great, and because the geography and topography of eastern Kentucky made the task of locating communities in need exceedingly difficult, the CSM determined to establish "self-sustaining," semiautonomous campus chapters of the Appalachian Volunteers. Prior to this effort, Council staff members simply contacted both regional and national construction supply companies such as U.S. Gypsum, Pittsburgh Plate Glass, and Reynolds Aluminum and solicited donations of material. Whenever they had accumulated enough supplies and identified schools in need of repair, a CSM-AV staff member phoned local colleges and asked for volunteers. Campus chapters would eliminate this step. Located on the campuses of those institutions whose representatives had attended the organizational meeting, these college chapters served myriad functions. Most important, they undertook the responsibility of organizing and planning their own projects. Each chapter did its own recruiting, handled its own finances, "did some of the orientation" of new volunteers, and conducted its own follow-up efforts in those places where the Volunteers operated. This organizational structure allowed the staff to "become stimulators and advisers" to the campus volunteers and at the same time to prepare other eastern Kentucky communities for AV activities. Milton Ogle and the AVs placed a great deal of time and effort into the organization of campus units, and, by March 1, 1965, twelve chapters operated under the Appalachian Volunteer banner. Of greatest significance, however, was that the AV staff could now build on previous efforts. With the college chapters managing their own programs, the school renovation projects would, the Volunteer leaders believed, eventually pave the way toward "more than the obvious physical improvement" and bring an "immediate sense of accomplishment" to both the volunteers and the local people who helped them.[5]

Ultimately, however, the goal for the entire Appalachian Volunteer program was the still-undefined concept of community development, but, for the spring semester of the 1964–1965 academic year, AV projects remained focused on rural schoolhouses. In addition to mere repair work, however, the AVs began a program of "curriculum enrichment" as part of the postrenovation follow-up efforts. This decision to augment renovation with educational enhancement adhered to one of the original AV concepts articulated by Boone and Ogle—that college student volunteers would be sympathetic to a program focused on the schools—and, interestingly, embodied a sense of resignation that impoverished adult highlanders were likely not susceptible of improvement. In fact, a form letter designed to recruit additional volunteers explained that, though "the Appalachian Volunteers work with adults, they concentrate their efforts on the children, for [they] can hope to take full part in the modern world someday, whereas their parents can at best learn only to cope with it."[6]

Because local teachers—those charged with the burden of bringing mountain children into modern America—were "handicapped by poor education, inadequate teaching materials, and limited experience of the world," the Volunteer curriculum enrichment program brought "to the rural youth a wide variety of personal experiences as well as educational demonstrations employing the most modern materials available." Included in these demonstrations were science projects, world cultures lessons, art, and music presentations. Arguing that the "education provided in one-room schools [was] usually limited to rote memory work" and that the "children [had] little opportunity to exercise their minds creatively," the planners of this endeavor hoped to make school fun while stimulating in mountain children the desire to continue their education. For example, the Volunteers wanted science majors to construct simple tools (such as inclined planes and levers), demonstrate their use, and then explain how they worked. In addition, they hoped that lessons in animal anatomy (via frog dissections) and the basic principles of electricity would "introduce the children to the joys of logical analysis, . . . [of] learning what lies beneath surface appearances." More important, the demonstrators could impress on the youngsters that these exhibitions were only a "preview" of what they could learn if they continued their education through high school.[7]

By bringing foreign exchange students from local college campuses to the hollows of the central Appalachians, the world cultures presentations aimed to expand the culture and educational horizons of the mountaineers. Notified beforehand, teachers could prepare their students for these expositions by orientating their regular classroom work around the country or culture scheduled for presentation. In return, the CSM reasoned, the exchange students would get the chance to "see a side of American life they seldom meet." This part of the program, then, was as instructive for the foreign students as it was for the children.[8]

Unlike the science and world culture programs, the art and music lessons were more about entertainment than academics. For the AVs, nevertheless, this was fun with a purpose. Because they saw the lives of mountain children as dull and expressionless, they anticipated that drawing and making clay models would "stimulate artistic self-expression." In addition, puppet shows would "introduce an element of the fantastic into lives that are all too close to the grimmer aspects of reality." Equally important, the AVs believed that they could instill proper conduct in the children through these productions. According to the curriculum enrichment plan: "Some skits could be designed to teach elements of good health practices, courtesy, and other *desirable* behavior."[9]

In many ways, these first few months of school refurbishing and curriculum enhancement projects represented an early apex of the Appalachian Volunteers program. First, these efforts adhered to the overarching Council philosophy of cooperation. Successful renovation projects depended on college students for labor, local businesses for donated supplies, local people for aid and support on the job site, and local officials for advice and guidance. The Appalachian Volunteers' first report indicated that "the county superintendent of schools and the teachers themselves" were "among the most effective agents for establishing contact with local citizens."[10]

Just as important, the Council of the Southern Mountains made a considerable effort to implement the idea of local people helping each other. In short, it wanted to make sure that its volunteers were truly *Appalachian* volunteers. Because it was drawing those volunteers from college campuses—which, even in eastern Kentucky, attracted students from outside the region—this was, of course, easier said than done. Still, a late 1963 recruitment campaign targeting students "who live in mountain counties" was remarkably successful, yielding 253 volunteers: 243 from Kentucky, 2 from Virginia, 7 from Tennessee, and 1 from Ohio. Clearly, the CSM attracted "native" volunteers.[11]

Armed with an army of eager native volunteers and a grant from the Area Redevelopment Administration (ARA), the Council-sponsored Appalachian Volunteers program marched into battle against the dilapidated conditions of eastern Kentucky's mountain schools. That winter, in addition to Ogle, the CSM added two more individuals to their staff to work exclusively on the AV program. Flem Messer, a Clay County native and Berea College graduate, and his fellow Berea alumnus, Philip Conn, planned and coordinated the activities of the Appalachian Volunteers in the field.[12]

Because they relied on students to make the actual school repairs, Messer and Conn planned projects for weekends and semester breaks, periods when, of course, students' volunteer work would not interfere with their class schedules. With the surprising number of willing volunteers at the ready, the first couple of months of Volunteer activity proved extremely fruitful. Despite the difficult terrain and the unfavorable weather conditions offered by the late winter months, the AVs' most significant obstacle seemed to reside in Frankfort, the state capital. Evidence suggests that John D. Whisman, the director of the Kentucky Area Program Office and a leading figure in the nascent Appalachian Regional Commission, opposed the Council's Volunteer program. In a letter dated in late December 1963, Ayer informed Whisman that a volunteer-orientated program was not one that could be "structured within, and controlled by, state and federal agencies." Though this letter was not clear as to Whisman's position, it implied that he wished for a greater degree of government control over the emerging Volunteer program.[13]

Council intraoffice communications, however, help clear up some of the mystery. In a memorandum written just prior to the first project, Ogle, the AV director, and Mark Furstenburg, a CSM staff member, discussed ways to generate "local *pressure* against Whisman." This document stated (quite possibly revealing Whisman's take on young volunteer workers) that college students are "an extremely important part . . . of the volunteer effort" and that "any image of students as immature children is detrimental to valuable resources." Finally, it suggested that all Council members and colleges committed to the AV program join "together in a way that will make known the dragging of feet by Whisman."[14]

Whisman did not object entirely to the use of volunteers. But he did favor the use of professionally trained, "technical specialist" volunteers placed "within working state programs of assistance." These technical assistance specialists would meet with county area development councils, created by Whisman's Kentucky Area Program Office, in workshop-type sessions that concentrated on "priority development problems." They would, Whisman argued, help tap local sources of support that were "already committed to action" but "limited by a lack of such technical assistance." This type of volunteer, as opposed to the CSM's college student volunteer, would prove to be of greater help to eastern Kentucky as the region dealt with its "key need," the "shift from traditional small farm and mining communities to the more complex industrial, commercial, and community development patterns required for viable economic growth."[15]

What was actually required for economic growth, in Whisman's opinion, was less concentration on rural schools and more on infrastructure development and efficient resource conservation and utilization. Included under this broad conception were housing loans for both new construction and renovation, a public works program involving road construction, parks, and recreational lakes, and administrative assistance for local communities undertaking such efforts. While Whisman's focus on development centered on upgrading existing facilities and programs or building new ones, he did not completely forget about those whom the Council hoped to help—the existing poor. For these people, he supported such traditionally based charity programs as surplus food and clothing distribution and the nascent Aid to Children of the Unemployed program. Finally, however, taking a position that must certainly have antagonized the CSM, he believed that all such projects should be administered "directly through an appropriate state agency" because such an arrangement would add the "advantage of higher standards of administration."[16]

Whisman's objections notwithstanding, the AVs, in early 1964, established contact with local officials in Estill, Leslie, Harlan, Clay, Knott, and Pike counties and conducted forty-six renovation projects and one enrichment program in a total of twenty-two mountain schools. By the end of March 1964, according to the "Appalachian Volunteers First Progress Report," over 570 volunteers participated in the AV effort. Just as important—since the agreement between the CSM and the ARA called for programs that would foster local participation in antipoverty projects—274 local people joined in the AV efforts in their respective communities. Getting local citizens involved, the CSM and the federal government agreed, effectively developed "local indigenous leadership resources" and avoided the appearance of charity, which, in turn, led to dependency, "a heritage [the AVs] want[ed] to destroy."[17]

In purely physical terms, the renovation projects involved covering the walls and ceilings of the schools with new drywall, painting both the interior and the exterior, installing new flooring, repairing doors and windows, and building bookshelves. Looking beyond the renovations, however, the ARA and the CSM hoped that the Appalachian Volunteers program would circumvent dependency by leading to permanent community organizations that worked on their own toward economic development. The AVs' idea was that the refurbished schools would evolve into community centers. Like the Council's conception of community development, however, the Volunteers' conception of a community center was vague. Only a few programs (school winterization, adult literacy, and surplus food distribution) seemed geared toward economic betterment—and these only loosely so.[18]

ARA criteria for physical improvements notwithstanding, the Council hoped that its Appalachian Volunteer program would lead to "people development." Ayer openly criticized any development plans that simply called for increased industrialization and use of natural resources without consciously including "people as the number one resource." These types of strategies were too simplistic because they did not allow the individual to act as "the designer and creator of his own future."[19]

These comments about development in the mountains are puzzling. Was Ayer arguing that the expansion of an already-dominant coal industry in eastern Kentucky did little to solve long-term needs? It is possible that he thought that industrial expansion (or the increased capitalization of the coal industry) would not fundamentally change anything in Appalachia but simply subject the miner-mountaineer to yet another period of unemployment and uncertainty. Perhaps he was calling for a restructuring of the mountain economy. Or perhaps he believed that, problems in the local political economy aside, any mountain reform effort should center on people exclusively and that industrial expansion was a decision better left to businessmen than to a government agency. Given the direction of the AV program and the Council philosophy, the latter explanation seems more accurate.

Redirecting or altering Appalachian industry in the hope of ending poverty would not reflect the CSM's cooperative approach. Such an alteration, especially one imposed on business by the Council or any other entity, would have assigned blame for the desperate situation in the mountains and identified a culprit. This was not part of Ayer's cooperative solution. Moreover, any attempt to pressure industry to change its practices had the potential to affect industry donations, of which the Council was still very much in need. More to the point, however, was the Appalachian Volunteer program itself. Rooted in the concept of individual self-help, and concentrated on the schools, the AVs quickly became the Council's most significant and visible representatives. Any other effort in any other area would have drawn attention away from this people-orientated venture, and, in March 1964, despite their growing popularity, the Volunteers were still on financially tenuous ground.

As the year progressed, grants from the ARA and the Ford Foundation ensured that school renovation would continue throughout 1964. The work, however, was still far from easy. Because of the remote location of many of the mountain communities, physical contact with mountain residents was extraordinarily difficult. Nonetheless, through the month of April the Council's volunteers persisted in their school efforts. Their contacts with local citizens and county officials, moreover, provided them with a way to stress the cooperative approach and work with individuals. Most counties, the volunteers soon realized, had "development councils," but they were dominated by representatives from the county seat. That they were so controlled was not, as the CSM saw it, the result of any malicious or underhanded intentions. Rather, few rural residents knew of the councils' existence, and, as a result, both suffered. The councils did not get input from all parts of the county, and those residing in the hinterlands did not benefit from the councils' activity. In the end, the development councils were not effective.[20]

With the hope of remedying this situation, the CSM sought to organize rural communities around issues, such as school repair, that were important to them. Council of the Southern Mountains leaders believed that, if local residents became active locally, they would then become increasingly active in county affairs. They also believed that a higher level of citizen participation would result in county officials *inviting* their rural constituents to send representatives to countywide boards. Herein lies everything that the CSM wanted from its growing antipoverty efforts in eastern Kentucky: cooperation among all segments of the population and individuals playing significant roles in the programs designed to help them. With this goal in mind, the Council continued with its renovation and enrichment projects. The school projects, it seemed to believe, would be the first step toward solving "one of the biggest problems in Eastern Kentucky," the lack of mountaineer participation in community action. Little did the CSM realize that this decision would prove to be quite significant in the near future.[21]

At this juncture, the Council of the Southern Mountains was finally well on its way toward a meaningful reform effort in central Appalachia. Ayer apparently recognized that school renovation was not an end in itself but a means toward more significant reform. The Appalachian Volunteers, nevertheless, stayed grounded in such projects for the remainder of 1964 and throughout 1965. Among the reasons for this was Ayer's view of the Council and his philosophy of cooperation. Another contributing factor was the immense popularity of school renovation with political leaders and the public as a whole. At that time, many Americans regarded educational-based programs as the solution to the problem of poverty, and this was reflected in the predominate attitudes of 1960s liberalism.

In 1964, Ayer linked the historical mission of the CSM with its ongoing focus on the educational needs of mountaineers. "The Council of the Southern Mountains," he stated, "is unlike any other institution in this country. In a sense, the Council might be said to combine some of the attributes of a research institute, an extension service, and a learned society. In any event, about one fact there can be no dispute: The Council's business, its only business, is education—the advancement of knowledge." Besides linking the Council with the nation's top universities, this statement also links it with school-based projects.[22]

Because so many in addition to the CSM saw a lack of education as the major cause of poverty—and not just in Appalachia but nationwide—school-oriented efforts appeared to all as the solution to the problem. At a meeting with Kentucky state officials in Frankfort concerning the proposed Economic Opportunity Act, Jack Ciaccio of the Department of Health, Education, and Welfare argued that "education was the answer" to Appalachia's cycle of poverty. Having the nation's attention focused on eastern Kentucky would further highlight the region's educational deficits, but, should the pending antipoverty legislation receive congressional approval, Kentucky "schoolmen" could show that they could do a fantastic job if given the appropriate financial resources. For any war on poverty to be successful, agencies such as the state Department of Education must "take the initiative . . . and work closely with the Council of the Southern Mountains and Kentucky's colleges and universities." Ciaccio urged Kentucky to start formulating plans immediately so that, if and when the antipoverty legislation passed, Kentucky could take advantage of it instantly. Most important, he hoped that the state would provide assistance to local school boards in their efforts to develop antipoverty projects. This would ensure that education would be given priority in local community action programs (CAPs).[23]

Support for the school renovation projects was not limited to federal bureaucrats, however. The program also received highly favorable publicity, especially from the *Louisville Courier-Journal.* In a March 15, 1964, article, the columnist John Fetterman referred to the Appalachian Volunteers as "young Samaritans in Appalachia." So popular were the first few renovation projects, Fetterman wrote, that "pleas have come from" the superintendents of Knott, Floyd, and Leslie counties for the AVs to come to their districts. Less than a week later, a *Courier-Journal* editorial stated that the Volunteers "have done more good per dollar spent than any group, governmental or private, in the history of depressed areas." This "domestic Peace Corps" should serve as the model for the national War on Poverty. Even the AV leader placed significant weight on school repair (implying, at the same time, his resignation toward the situation of the region's adult population). According to Ogle (as quoted by Fetterman), it was "vital 'to get at the pre-school and primary ages'": "'They haven't become exasperated and hopeless about the future. [The AVs] might just make a big difference between what they are now and what they could be.'"[24]

As the Appalachian Volunteers prepared to close out the 1964 spring semester, they attempted to organize communities around issues other than school renovation. Despite these efforts—which succeeded at Persimmon Fork, in Leslie County, where the people expressed a desire for a new road into their community—most activity still centered on local schools. Even Persimmon Fork residents placed education high on their priority list. At Big Willard, in Perry County, residents and AV members sought ways to raise money in order to send their children on a field trip to the state capital. In short, while the AVs did find that the mountaineers certainly had concerns beyond their schools, education was never far from their minds. Even road repairs, which for the AVs gained in importance as the summer approached, were part of an overall school-oriented outlook. Improved roads translated to school bus service for rural children. What was ironic was the fact that the school-based projects were supposed to create a desire for education among rural mountaineers. Clearly, those impoverished people already had this aspiration. Yet the AVs failed to see it.[25]

AV plans for the coming summer called for an "exclusive concentration on community action programs." The Volunteers claimed that, because of the work completed during the spring of 1964, they had "gained acceptance" in forty eastern Kentucky mountain communities. Through school renovation projects, the Appalachian Volunteers believed that they had demonstrated to rural mountaineers that they could improve their lives if they all worked together in an "organized" manner. Because the summer allowed student volunteers to spend more time in the mountains, AV leaders advocated weeklong, in addition to weekend, projects. Also, the AVs allotted time during the summer months to conducting follow-ups in those places where they began renovations and to solidify plans for the 1964–1965 school year.[26]

Despite their plans, the Volunteers got off to a relatively slow start in June 1964. AV leaders spent much of that month in consultation with Kentucky college officials, hoping to ensure their support for the AV program in the upcoming school year. The Council called two additional meetings that June. Because they still operated on a tight budget, CSM officials invited the state's business leaders to support the Appalachian Volunteers' efforts through donations of virtually any type. Finally, the CSM board of directors met with the AV board. Though the AVs were part of the Council, they did have their own board, which consisted of a student representative from each member college and eight adults "whose experience and backgrounds enable them to make positive contributions" to the AV organization. The purpose of this third meeting was to establish policy guidelines that the Appalachian Volunteers would follow "when the Council's administrative responsibility to the effort has ended." Ever since the start of the Appalachian Volunteers, nearly all those involved operated with the understanding that, after one year, the program would become, as Flem Messer stated, "a separate and action oriented organization." Now, with campus chapters functioning and projects in various stages of development, it appeared as if the Appalachian Volunteers, at a mere six months of age, were all but ready to fend for themselves.[27]

With plans for the short-term future seemingly set, the Volunteers turned their attention back to the mountains. As their reports illustrate, they made an effort to get beyond school repairs and address other issues. At Upper Thousandsticks, in Leslie County, for example, the AVs helped local residents dig a new well to improve the clean water supply and worked on repairing the road into town. Leslie County, in fact, became a focal point for the Appalachian Volunteers that summer as workers descended on the communities of Lower Thousandsticks, Hurricane, and Persimmon Fork, among others, focusing on similar road and water projects. Slone Fork, in Knott County, also noticed vast improvements. Volunteers renovated twenty-one houses and collected and disposed of trash that lay about the town. At the small hamlet of Red Bird, near the Red Bird River in Clay County, the Appalachian Volunteers reported that the people held a succession of community meetings to determine a set of priorities for Volunteer work. In what was, perhaps, the high point of the summer, AVs cooperated with the people of adjacent Saylor and Spruce Pine to build a small picnic area and park.[28]

The road and water projects in no way replaced the school programs. A significant amount of AV time and energy went into the Mill Creek summer school program. Moreover, the Volunteers utilized a group from the central Kentucky–based Wilderness Road Girl Scout Troop to conduct a two-week educational program in Leslie County. After a short training period in Berea, the scouts arrived in Leslie County on August 10, 1964. Dispersed to eight different communities, the girls spent the first week of their stay managing recreational activities for the rural children. Their second week was also the grade schoolers' first week of classes. During this period, the volunteers acted as teacher aides by distributing textbooks and doing other jobs that made the instructors' tasks easier. Other mountain locales received Volunteer enrichment or renovation projects. AVs at Urban, in Clay County, virtually rebuilt the local school, while other volunteers treated the youngsters in Bear Creek to both a recreation and an academic enrichment program. In total, of the thirteen communities identified in the AV reports of June and July 1964, nine had at least some part of the programs offered them rooted in the local school. The impression that the key to abolishing poverty in Appalachia was education was still very much alive in the summer of 1964.[29]

As the Girl Scouts returned to their Bluegrass region homes, the Appalachian Volunteers, as an organization, began to get ready for a return to the weekend projects that characterized their modus operandi during the academic year. Part of that preparation included promoting the Volunteer program on college campuses again. Interestingly, those returning Girl Scouts provided the Appalachian Volunteers with another strategy for gaining student support. Reflecting on their experiences, one scout stated that she thought the AV program was "one of the best ever": "I wish everyone could have this wonderful experience." Another "found this project one of the most rewarding, enjoyable, and educational opportunities ever offered by the girl scouts." A third echoed these sentiments, which focused, not on what the girls had *done* for the poor in Appalachia, but on what they had *gained* from this type of volunteer work: "I wouldn't trade these two short weeks for anything in the whole world. The experience gained by working with the people [was] greatly appreciated and every girl who didn't get to go ... miss[ed] a great opportunity."[30]

While it would not be accurate to argue that each Girl Scout who participated in the Leslie County program did so for purely self-centered reasons, Council leadership recognized that many potential volunteers would need something more than just an altruistic desire to help the poor to sustain their interest in the Appalachian Volunteers. Students should be involved "in the planning and administration of the program," the Council declared, and they must develop a "system of rewards so that they can be made to feel that they are part of a 'movement.'" Further, according to one AV, part of the success of the school renovations was the sense of immediate satisfaction and accomplishment that went with seeing a previously dilapidated schoolhouse transformed into one fit for habitation.[31]

While a certain degree of personal satisfaction, especially in a program as demanding as the Appalachian Volunteers, may have been necessary, the AVs needed to be careful so that personal satisfaction did not become the primary goal of the program. Unfortunately, it appeared as if this happened. While those charged with administering the program wanted to believe that these "young, flexible, energetic" students were "motivated solely by a personal concern for the conditions they are combating," this perception was not quite accurate. Even the AVs themselves, in a statement that contradicted their own ideas about the students' activism, declared that "for them the work is not a job, but a *duty.*"[32]

In other ways, mountain reform leaders reasserted the importance of the individual volunteers, but not because they gave freely of themselves. Rather, the students were important for what they represented. By exemplifying success, college students, the Appalachian Volunteers board declared in August 1964, raised the mountaineers' expectations for their children: "When the [mountaineers] see girls like the Volunteers and look at their girls that are the same age, . . . they will see a new example which they want their girls to follow." So impoverished were the rural Appalachians, this attitude implied, that they had no idea that a better life was possible. Simply by going into the mountains, the Volunteers provided them with previously unknown aspirations.[33]

When the Appalachian Volunteers went back to the mountains in the fall of 1964, they abandoned development projects in favor of a renewed concentration on renovation and enrichment. Still, they initiated the Books for Appalachia project when they realized how inadequate libraries in the local community schools were. Some, they reported, had no books at all. One AV, Roslea Johnson, remembered trying to write a note for a mountain teacher whose school the Volunteers had earlier repaired. While searching for a piece of paper and a pencil, she noticed that this particular school had virtually nothing with which to work—no paper, no writing utensils, no books. As she visited other mountain schools, she noticed that they were in like circumstances. This, she later recalled, was "an eye opener." Arguably, other student workers felt the same way, and these experiences gave rise to the school library project. The AVs collected books donated by publishing companies, schools from outside the region, and the national Parent-Teacher Association and shipped them by the boxcar to places such as Berea and Barbourville for distribution to rural mountain schools.[34]

Ultimately, the book project resulted in a great deal of publicity and prompted the expansion of the overall AV program. In order to help distribute the books and to provide shelves in those mountain schools that had none, the Volunteers convinced the industrial arts classes at the region's colleges to construct interlocking "book boxes." These boxes allowed the AV workers to pack the donated materials in containers that, after delivery, could be converted to stable bookcases. One effect of this aspect of the book project was to allow those college students involved in the construction of the book boxes to become "Volunteers" without ever leaving campus. Another was that the nationwide appeal for books—one volunteer claimed that the organization collected nearly 1.5 million—made people from every corner of the country aware of the Appalachian Volunteer effort. Jack Rivel, one of the first college volunteers and later an AV field man, claimed: "National PTA people from all over came down [to Barbourville] and spent a day or two days helping us sort books." By November 21, 1964, Knox County alone gained thirty-one "libraries" in its mountain schools. The next week, schools in Leslie and Jackson counties also acquired AV book boxes. Financial support for the program came from the National Home Library Association, which donated $15,000 in early 1966 to purchase encyclopedias for the schools. With the library project, the Appalachian Volunteers took a significant step toward becoming a national program.[35]

The success of the Books for Appalachia project was not the only boost the AVs received in the fall of 1964. That August, Congress passed the Economic Opportunity Act. Though this act benefited the Council of the Southern Mountains and its Appalachian Volunteer program in terms of economic resources, in other ways it served to limit and delineate the CSM's thoughts and actions. Speaking before an AV Special Advisory Committee meeting in Berea, Ralph Caprio, representing the newly created Office of Economic Opportunity (OEO), stated that, in order for the AVs to secure federal funding, their plans must be "crystal clear." In addition, college administrators needed to declare their commitment to the Volunteer project, and county school superintendents must proclaim their desire for and need of Appalachian Volunteers. Just as important, echoing the requirement for cooperation expressed in the act, the Volunteer organization and the local officials had to announce that they would work together in the fight against poverty. This was of primary importance because the county superintendents' offices were the agencies through which the AVs operated.[36]

For their part, the Appalachian Volunteers certainly were "crystal clear" in their plans to continue renovation and enrichment programs in the mountain schools. As their reports of the previous spring illustrated, these efforts brought the local people and the student volunteers together, and "the success of the school renovation [was] virtually assured." Anything more complex created the potential for failure. Failure was anathema because it would "return [the mountaineers] to their former apathetic state." Further, the AV Board of Directors reiterated the necessity of working with the elected county officials, especially school superintendents. "You must work with the school superintendents," a board member declared, "and make sure the programs are desired in the school[s] . . . and do not come in unwanted." Another board member, the *Louisville Courier-Journal* columnist John Ed Pearce, urged the Volunteers to meet with county officials so that each would know the others' plans.[37]

Specifically, those plans called for curriculum enrichment. After eight months of concentrating on renovation work, the AVs decided that enrichment would, as much as any other Volunteer program, "influence more and more youngsters to stay in and finish their schooling." Additionally, the Volunteers, by submitting one of the first proposals for an OEO demonstration grant, moved to take advantage of the newly passed federal antipoverty legislation. Though it would be about six months before the AVs learned the fate of their proposal, they still had time and money left from the original ARA grant. With these funds, plus the reinforcements of the lessons from the Mill Creek summer school project and a belief in their own ability to end Appalachian indigence, the little army of Appalachian Volunteers again marched off, in early autumn, to vanquish poverty.[38]

During September 1964, Milton Ogle contacted numerous local superintendents and announced that AVs would be available for work in their rural schools. Generally, the responses were favorable. David Craft, the head of the Letcher County school system, embraced the enrichment concept but dissuaded the Volunteers from doing renovation work because of the county's plans to consolidate its smaller schools. William Gilreath of the McCreary County system and George Alice Motley, the superintendent of the Menifee County schools, heartily encouraged AV participation in their mountain schools.[39]

September, unfortunately, also witnessed the beginning of a relatively quick process of change within the AV organization itself. Along with creating CAPs and a funding base for them, the Economic Opportunity Act had created the Volunteers in Service to America (VISTA) program. This invention was a national version of that domestic Peace Corps that the AVs, up to that point, had emulated in eastern Kentucky. When the Volunteers requested OEO funds, they also requested VISTA volunteers to conduct a "health project" for residents of the Red Bird Valley, near the border of Bell and Clay counties. This represented a departure from the original conception of what an "Appalachian Volunteer" was. First, the VISTA volunteer was required to *stimulate the interest* of the people of Red Bird in the project. In other words, the volunteer, not the community, had to take the lead. Most important, however, was that the the Appalachian Volunteers program began to move away from its Appalachian constituency—at least when it came to the recruitment of volunteers.[40]

Some of the same conditions, including massive unemployment and the resulting poverty, that motivated the AVs spurred others—local Appalachians more concerned with quantitative issues, particularly income—to action as well. Commonly referred to as the "roving pickets," the Appalachian Committee for Full Employment traveled from nonunion mine to nonunion mine protesting the high levels of unemployment and the loss of United Mine Workers union health benefits. Because individuals associated with Students for a Democratic Society (SDS) joined the picketers as they moved through eastern Kentucky, it was easy for many of those local officials with whom the AVs hoped to establish close working relationships to associate the student AVs with the SDS members. Apparently, this was a concern of the Volunteers as well. One AV member actually wrote the AV office asking advice about how to deal with that "supposedly communistic" group known as the "Appalachian Volunteers for Equal Employment (or something to that effect)." For their part, the Appalachian Volunteers, fearful that they had "become confused in the public mind with another footless, pointless aggregation of 'rousers' . . . who had caused considerable confusion in some mining towns," assured local county officials that, while they "hoped to change the bad conditions in which some people live," they did not intend to "enter into every . . . embroglio that may arise out of people's reactions to those conditions."[41]

Nevertheless, the last few months of 1964 saw a flurry of Volunteer activity. AVs held enrichment projects in Knott, Knox, Clay, and Leslie counties. At a school in Knox County on October 17, Union College students dug a drainage ditch for the playground and a well, installed siding on the building, and performed enrichment demonstrations. AVs repaired the playground at Rye Cove, in Leslie County, and managed a general enhancement project at Lick Branch, in Knott County. During October alone, student Volunteers executed twenty projects, prompting the AV staff member Jack Rivel to assert that the Appalachian Volunteers "continue to provide new experiences in the rural school areas for the culturally deprived youths."[42]

This intense period of work put a strain on Ogle and the Volunteer staff. In order to ease the pressure, Ogle again looked outside the region. Moving yet one more step away from his original position, he asked the president of Antioch College for help. Founded in 1852, and located in Yellow Springs, Ohio, Antioch was one of the first institutes of higher learning to establish a work-study program. Designed to provide real-world experiences that would enhance classroom work, the program had, by 1964, already sent Antioch students to work with the civil rights movement in Mississippi. Ogle believed that "the participation of [Antioch] students would be of immeasurable value to the Appalachian Volunteers program." Coming directly on the heels of the recruitment of VISTA volunteers, the solicitation of Ohio students dealt another blow to the philosophy of local people helping their neighbors.[43]

To say that the Council of the Southern Mountains felt good about the school projects would be an understatement. The same could be said about the student volunteers and the federal government. According to a Volunteer report, the organization took for granted the receipt of OEO funds, and the Council began hiring additional staff solely for the AV program. That same report claimed that, on November 21, the AVs reached their participation goal for a single weekend when two hundred student volunteers conducted school-centered activities in the mountains. Elliott and Jackson counties saw the bulk of Volunteer activity that month. The Lower Blaine, Roscoe, and Wright-Watson schools in Elliott all hosted enrichment efforts. Escorted by two Americans, two Morehead State College foreign exchange students—one from Iran and one from Hong Kong—traveled to Roscoe and Wright-Watson to enlighten the children there about life in the Middle East and the Orient. In Jackson County, AV workers brought art supplies (clay, crayons, paint, construction paper, and glue), teaching aids (dictionaries, maps, and globes), and playground equipment (bats, baseballs, jump ropes, and basketballs and goals) to the Adkins, Hisel, Huff, Kerby Knob, and Letterbox schools. Tom Davis, who participated in the Letterbox project on November 21, took particular interest in the school's bell. Because it lacked proper housing, its axle had corroded, making it extremely difficult to ring. The volunteer greased the bell, but he encouraged the Volunteer staff member Gibbs Kinderman to construct a belfry and to apply a more durable lubricant. "I think you will agree," he wrote to Kinderman, "that a schoolhouse bell is an important part of the school's total function."[44]

Other counties also commanded Appalachian Volunteer interest late that autumn. At Jones Creek, in Harlan County, twelve Cumberland College students and twenty local children cleared the school's playground of debris, built a slide, hiked the neighboring hills, sang songs, and played games. Six students from the University of Kentucky's South East Center in Cumberland, Kentucky, went to Persimmon Fork, in Leslie County, on November 28, where they installed a basketball goal and then grouped about twenty-five locals into teams. They also brought one hundred books in AV book boxes. Volunteers from Lees Junior College and Alice Lloyd College treated seven other Leslie County rural schools to similar programs. In short, the War on Poverty as conducted by the Appalachian Volunteers included basketball games, singing, tape recorder demonstrations, and foreign culture presentations. Though the more tangible projects, such as the renovation of a lunchroom at Lower Polls Creek, in Leslie County, and the distribution of books, continued, AV efforts were, in late 1964, becoming increasingly focused on enrichment.[45]

The onset of winter did little to slow the Volunteers' enthusiasm or work effort, and they received tremendous news in the form of a letter from

Sargent Shriver, the OEO director. Writing on December 15, 1964, Shriver informed Ogle that the federal government had granted the CSM's Appalachian Volunteers program $299,242 and assigned fourteen VISTA volunteers under Title II of the Economic Opportunity Act. Under the terms of this grant, the AVs agreed to "demonstrate the efficiency of an intense volunteer effort in inspiring disadvantaged people to work for the betterment of their condition through self-help projects in home management, sanitation, improving school buildings and libraries, tutoring, developing recreational and cultural activities, and motivating people to discover their needs and develop their potentials." While the Volunteers interpreted this mandate as allowing them to continue handling the book drive and renovation efforts and presenting science, world cultures, and music programs, the VISTA volunteers focused on helping rural teachers, developing community leaders, defining a community's problems, and organizing the people around those problems.[46] Though the grant created specific jobs especially for the AVs, the charge to "[motivate] people to discover their needs" was as vague as the desire to develop communities—creating a large loophole through which the Appalachian Volunteers and their VISTA allies would eventually jump.

Along with ensuring the continuation of its weekend programs, the OEO grant convinced the CSM that its Volunteer program was on the right track. Federal funding, moreover, allowed the Council to give serious consideration to expanding the program to the neighboring states of West Virginia, Virginia, and Tennessee. Also, the Appalachian Volunteers established four Kentucky field offices, in Barbourville, Manchester, Morehead, and Prestonsburg. Each was responsible for eleven different counties. Of immediate consequence, however, the AVs began to make plans for weeklong projects.[47]

The Volunteers, nevertheless, did not abandon their weekend ventures. During the weeks prior to Christmas break, they worked feverishly. Adding a director of field operations and a library specialist, they again took to the battlefield. In the first week of December, five University of Kentucky volunteers and one adult supervisor went to Salt Rock, in Jackson County. In addition to building a bookshelf, the students cut down a nearby evergreen, moved it into the school, and made Christmas ornaments to hang on the tree with the paper, glue, and other art supplies they had brought.

Then the AVs hosted a "punch and cookies" party for the local children and sang carols, told stories, and distributed balloons. The following weekend, Tom Rhodenbaugh led over thirty volunteers back to Jackson County for projects in five additional schools. A Christmas program monopolized the Volunteers' attention at the Letterbox school, while basketball reigned supreme at the Huff school. At New Zion, the children had both, but the Adkins kids had to settle for spelling lessons. After no locals appeared for the planned Christmas program at Kerby Knob, the Volunteers went through the community and "rounded up" ten children to take part. In McKee, the AVs sponsored a production of *Amahl and the Night Visitors* the week of December 14.[48]

At a conference intended to assess their first year of operation and make suggestions for the next, the Volunteers closed out 1964. Held in early December, what was designated as the "Fall Conference" was a forum to discuss the overall effort and plan for the next year. Almost immediately, AV members voiced their concerns. Some complained about the escalation of enrichment as opposed to renovation efforts. One volunteer who took notes during the conference reported: "The typical volunteer tends to get greater feelings of accomplishment from actual physical labor projects such as school renovation, rather than intangibles such as school enrichment." These anonymous notes also revealed a growing concern over the planning and organization of AV projects. Such complaints may have been the motivation for the creation of the four field offices. Most interesting, however, was the apparent focus of the convention. When asked, the volunteers responded with comments about themselves and their organizations, and about their sense of satisfaction, but not about those people they were supposedly trying to help.[49]

The conference was, however, more than just a gripe session. In the hope of improving the overall project, the organization sponsored a series of workshops geared toward the improvement of the volunteers' skills. Addressing such topics as storytelling, science demonstrations, arts and crafts, and recreation, these workshops indicated the direction the AVs would take in the next year and reflected the agreement between the OEO and the CSM over the proper way to attain the goal of ending Appalachian poverty.

If the reaction of the University of Kentucky AV chapter is any indication, the Fall Conference certainly made an impact. Two days after the meeting, on December 7, 1964, the University of Kentucky chapter circulated its newsletter, which announced a Christmas vacation project scheduled to take place at the Lick Branch school, near Ary, Kentucky, between January 2 and 9, 1965. With less than a month until the project's scheduled beginning, the newsletter urged those who wished to participate in the effort to make immediate plans, yet tried to minimize the sense of urgency. "This [project] may sound like a lot," the announcement reassured potential participants, "but actually it is not much."[50]

With the construction of a basketball court, the organization of recreational activities and science demonstrations, and the installation of a sink in the local school as the major accomplishments of the University of Kentucky Christmas program, the reality of the newsletter's last statement was more real that any Volunteer would, or could, admit.[51] The CSM leaders', the OEO's, and the Volunteers' own conceptions about America conditioned the University of Kentucky students to believe that this was the way to solve the region's problems. The schools were dilapidated because the people were removed, physically, politically, and culturally, from the achievements of modern America. Their task, their *duty,* as the AV leadership phrased it, was to bring those quality advancements to the mountains. Once they introduced even just a few antiquated, isolated mountaineers to, and integrated them with, modern, urban America, those left in impoverishment would readily embrace what the Volunteers offered. The mountaineers would then make demands of the political, social, and, most important, political systems, and rural Appalachia's problems would end.

As the AV Board of Directors reflected on this mandate and reflected on the organization's efforts in the mountains during 1964, they expressed a great deal of satisfaction. The greatest benefit that the people of the mountains gained from the Appalachian Volunteers was, they felt, not repaired schoolhouses, but a sense of community and a desire for a better education. Further, the volunteers themselves were good examples—excellent role models—for mountain children. Also, because the volunteers were college students, they were not a threat to local adults, which resulted in a good rapport between the two groups. Some Board members, nevertheless, expressed reservations as to whether they were really helping the poor or merely covering up the outward signs of poverty. A second concern was the effect that the Appalachian Volunteers would have on mountain residents. Would it be positive and long lasting, or would it cease when the AVs had completed their work? With these reservations and expectations, the Appalachian Volunteers prepared for 1965.[52]

4

The War to End All Wars

A National Quest to End Appalachian Poverty, 1965–1966

The mountain people, like all chronically poor people, are fatalistic—
life is something that happens to a person, not an adventure to be
undertaken and enjoyed.... The people living in these isolated
mountain settlements have little knowledge of and almost no
personal experience in the outside world. The Volunteers, through
their enrichment program, their libraries, and their very presence,
bring the world to these people, show them something of what their
lives (or at least, their children's) might be like. Most important, they
provide a model for the children to compete with that offered by the
local school drop-out. Bringing the world to these children in such a
personal way makes it seem nearer, something they themselves might
someday be a part of.
—Appalachian Volunteers: The Gift of Hope

Jack Rivel and Flem Messer make an interesting pair, especially in the context of the War on Poverty in eastern Kentucky. Though both were Appalachian Volunteers (AVs) and were involved in some of the organization's
earliest projects, their experiences and backgrounds highlight a transformation that the AVs underwent by the summer of 1965. While the organization still held to its philosophy of local people helping each other, that ideal
was, by late 1965, becoming increasingly untenable. With the involvement
of Volunteers in Service to America (VISTA) in the antipoverty effort in the
region, the Appalachian Volunteers underwent, within a year of its founding, a significant demographic shift, one that would remake its identity by
the end of 1966. In fact, the presence of the New Jersey native Rivel, the first
"president" of the AVs, undermined the ideal of local people helping each
other from the very beginning. This is not to argue that Rivel, a graduate

of Union College, in Barbourville, Kentucky, was in any way a detriment to the Volunteers. Nevertheless, unlike Messer, a Clay County native and Berea College graduate, he was not a Kentuckian, let alone an Appalachian. Another difference between the two, and perhaps a more intriguing one, was the manner in which these two related to the Appalachian Volunteers and the people they were then working to help.[1]

Because he was from Clay County, Messer claimed that he "had a better 'feel' . . . for the area [than outsiders did], . . . an ability, perhaps, to relate to some of the [mountain] middle class that some of the outsiders didn't." Though he claimed that this "ability" did not automatically translate into a completely different point of view, his "refusal to idealize poor people" and his desire to include "discontented middle-class people" in the reform program—something that was in keeping with the overall, inclusive approach of the Council of the Southern Mountains (CSM)—made Messer, as he later asserted, "the conservative of the group." Perhaps this is how he "created" problems for Carol Irons in Mill Creek; his attempts at inclusion resulted only in confusion and animosity. Still, despite the fact that he believed himself more sensitive than outsiders to local concerns, Messer was not necessarily opposed to their presence among the Appalachian Volunteers. On the contrary, he argued that they can benefit any reform effort. "There is a point," he contended, "when local control is concentrated in such disproportion between the poor and non-poor that you have to have outside influence, and it can be missionary."[2]

Rivel fulfilled both of Messer's change-agent criteria. As a graduate of the Methodist Church–affiliated Union College, he had at least been exposed to some degree of the "missionary" zeal of that organization. As a student at Union, Rivel participated in "church camps" and led a youth group that, even before the onset of the War on Poverty, undertook reform-activist activities similar to those that characterized the early AV projects. Though he was committed to such activities, he later recalled: "As we took projects out, the hardest thing we had to do . . . was to get kids from east Kentucky to participate. Guys from Ohio and New York . . . wanted to go, but we couldn't get many kids from the eastern part of Kentucky. . . . Students from the mountains just didn't seem to want to go back." Was it Rivel's failure to recruit enough Appalachian students that precipitated the influx of VISTA volunteers and nonnative AVs—those with "personal experience in the outside world," as the AVs' own literature described them—that descended on the mountains?[3]

Just as the biblical Walls of Jericho came down on the Canaanites, "the outside world" certainly did crash down on the mountaineers in 1965. Buoyed by extreme confidence and a federal grant, the Appalachian Volunteers entered an eastern Kentucky that they saw as an unspoiled, untapped, primitive reserve in which they could build a brave new world. As the text of a proposed Council fund-raising brochure promised, a vast region "designed, built and developed in accord with Space Age concepts is within reach." Even the stereotypes that characterized "yesterday's people" and originally motivated the Volunteer effort were somehow dismissed. "Training centers and industrial establishments turning on the concept of automation are possible here without the handicaps of traditionalism in either the minds of the people or the architecture and tooling of production facilities." Ignoring the steep hills and narrow valleys, the Council argued: "The wheel-hub type city . . . need not be brought over into the mountain region. Instead the city of modern design that responds to present-day living conditions could characterize the region." The CSM proposed other theoretical developments that reflected both an idyllic Appalachian past and an unfettered future: a high speed rail system would not have to deal with preexisting rights-of-way, and a mountain multimedia broadcasting network would produce "quality programming" of "artistic excellence and intrinsic value." In short, Appalachia was the artist's blank canvas, and the Volunteers could, with the aid and support of the rest of America, turn the region into that elusive city on the hill.[4]

Growing support among both private concerns and Kentucky college students bolstered this vision. Corporate contributions also increased. The Voit Rubber Company, for example, donated one hundred basketballs, one hundred softballs, fifty playground balls, six footballs, and six soccer balls to the Volunteer enrichment program. Furthermore, the AV chapters at Ashland Community College, Georgetown College, and Transylvania University (the latter two in the Lexington–Bluegrass region area) reported increased interest in the program. Believing that the AVs were the answer to the problems outlined in Michael Harrington's *The Other America*, Ogle invited the noted journalist to address the Appalachian Volunteers at the organization's spring meeting.[5]

Underneath this exuberance, however, was growing doubt about the cause of poverty in the Southern mountains. Soliciting the donation of vehicles suitable to the difficult terrain, Ogle attempted to explain the conditions the Volunteers encountered in eastern Kentucky to the Ford Motor Company. "The mountaineers," he wrote to Henry Ford II, "long ago drifted away from the main current of American life and were subsequently forgotten by the bustling world outside the hills." While this sentence reveals that Ogle remained firmly positioned in the culture of poverty camp, the one that follows offers a new explanation for the situation in which the mountaineers found themselves: "Their traditional mode of life *has been destroyed by the inroads of the machine age;* now they must learn the ways of the twentieth century." The mountaineers' "traditional mode of life" was, at one point, viable—but *only* until the introduction of automation. The solution, nonetheless, stays the same. The mountaineers' must "learn the ways of the twentieth century"—from the AVs. In the end, the methods through which the Appalachian Volunteers hoped to end poverty in the hills were unchanged.[6]

This consistency translated into the continued focus on ending Appalachian poverty through school renovation and enrichment. Reporting to Ayer, the AV staff member Thomas Rhodenbaugh reiterated the organization's stance. Renovation continued to be important, Rhodenbaugh argued, because the horrid conditions of the schoolhouses reinforced "the handicaps inflicted on the children by their background and surroundings," while curriculum enhancement improved "the mountain children's chances of taking part of the modern world."[7]

On January 4, 1965, three AV members arrived in Knott County for a five-day renovation and enrichment program at the Lick Branch school. They began the project with a basketball game to "break the ice." Following the game, they divided the schoolchildren into three groups, with each volunteer serving as a leader, for a "current events" discussion. After this, one volunteer played banjo while the others danced with the children. This first day did contain an academic component—a wall map was hung in the school. The second day was much like the first. It began with a basketball game, but, because errant play usually resulted in the ball rolling into a nearby creek, the AVs spent a good part of the remainder of that day and the next constructing a fence around the court. In terms of enrichment, the children listened to classical music and then their own voices recorded by a tape recorder and then played back. The project ended with the installation of a washbasin in the school and a party for the community.[8]

Both the AV representative, Joe Mulloy, and the student volunteers concluded that the Lick Branch project was a success. Everything, from the attitude of the town's adults to the number of volunteers, worked in favor of the project. According to the college volunteers, the community's adults eagerly shared their time, energy, tools, and equipment to help with the re-furbishing efforts, while the small number of volunteers allowed the people to get to know each student visitor.[9]

As with the previous school enrichment efforts, the apparent success of the Lick Branch project reinforced the Appalachian Volunteers' belief in such programs. Their efforts, consequently, continued unabated for the next few months. Moreover, they began to plan for a weeklong project to take place over the upcoming spring break. Nevertheless, as the AVs gained in numbers over the winter months—averaging two hundred students per weekend in January—local participation dropped. When twelve Southeast Christian College students held an enrichment program in Jackson County, for example, only ten local children attended. Despite the low turnout, the Volunteers led games of "farmer-in-the-dell" and "hot potato," and, through the use of picture books, posters, and costumes, the "deprived" children went on a "tour" of Mexico. Afterward, the children performed a bullfight reenactment and listened to their visitors tell stories. Volunteers canceled enrichment activities in February 1965 at Hunting Fork and Vortex, both in Wolfe County, owing to the lack of local involvement. Also that month, at the Dry Fork school, again in Jackson County, Milton Ogle, who attended this planned enhancement project, had to search for children to see a slide show on South America.[10]

Despite these setbacks, the Appalachian Volunteers remained undaunt-ed. Criticizing their own project, Southeast Christian students suggested that the AVs play games of more interest to the mountain boys and that the children be grouped according to age during the storytelling period. Rob-in Buckner, a Georgetown College volunteer working at the Blue Springs school in Rockcastle County, reported a waning of interest as her enrich-ment program, which involved paper chains, storytelling, and a microscope demonstration, neared its end. She suggested that the AVs conclude each project with a "hootenanny" in order to keep the children's attention levels high. Despite the drop in local interest, the Volunteers refused to give up on their efforts to enhance the experiences of those attending a "culturally deprived one-room school."[11]

In keeping with this commitment, the Appalachian Volunteers began to use Office of Economic Opportunity (OEO) funds to hire additional staff, including an education consultant, J. Hoge T. Sutherland. At last, the Council had the organizational structure with which to fight the War on Poverty in the forty-four Appalachian counties of Kentucky. Yet, while a native of Appalachia, Ogle, continued to run the Appalachian Volunteers, the vast majority of his staff came from outside the region. Selected as Ogle's assistant director was Gibbs Kinderman, a Harvard graduate and a Student Nonviolent Coordinating Committee worker in Mississippi. The new director of field operations, Dan Fox, came to the mountains via Harvard's Psychology Department. Of the four field office directors, only one—Flem Messer, from Clay County—was a native mountaineer. Of the others, Jack Rivel of the Barbourville office was, as we have seen, a New Jersey native, William Wells, who operated out of Morehead, hailed from California, and Thomas Rhodenbaugh, the administrator of the AVs' western Appalachian district, came from Akron, Ohio. Even as, throughout the year, the staff grew with the addition of fieldmen (each responsible for a few counties within each district), the Volunteers undercut the original premise of the institution—that of local people helping each other. For example, Mike Kline, Joe Mulloy, Steve Daugherty, and Doug Yarrow all joined the AV staff in 1965, and not one was from eastern Kentucky. Only one, Mulloy, was from anywhere in Kentucky, and he hailed from the state's largest metropolis, Louisville. This "strange conglomeration of people," as the CSM associate director Loyal Jones called them, represented an AV organization that was no longer indigenous to the mountains. More important, during 1965, the Appalachian Volunteers became larger and more visible than its parent body, the Council of the Southern Mountains.[12]

While the high visibility of the Appalachian Volunteer program had a significant impact on the number and origins of those hoping to take part in the effort, it did not change, at least at this point, the AV approach to poverty. During the first quarter of 1965, fifteen University of Kentucky volunteers went to Hunting Fork and Vortex in Wolfe County and taught "the dirty and scantily dressed boys the fundamentals of basketball." Volunteers from other college campuses held even more basketball games as well as "valentine making" parties; they read stories, "toured" such places as New Jersey, and sang French and Spanish songs. Enrichment activities such as these, the AVs believed, remained the answer to the region's poverty.[13]

In order to ensure that their program met the needs of the impoverished mountaineers, the Appalachian Volunteers sent Sutherland, their AV education consultant, into fourteen of eastern Kentucky's counties to ask the people directly about their wants and concerns. Though traveling was difficult, especially during the winter months, this retired school superintendent from Virginia visited more than 130 homes in about fifty mountain communities. He contacted at least two families in each school, and this, Sutherland claimed, represented approximately 25 percent of the families in the target locales. Through this interview process, he discovered what the people wanted and made trenchant observations on the conditions that future volunteers would face in the Southern mountains.[14]

Prior to their arrival in any particular county, Sutherland and his assistant, Roslea Johnson, queried the county school superintendent about which schools and teachers to visit and obtained directions to the school. By meeting rural teachers at their job sites, the two had an opportunity to examine the physical condition of the school as well as to get advice about which families to interview. These visits alerted the pupils that their parents and families might be interviewed and provided Sutherland with firsthand knowledge of each local school. Most disturbing to the former school official was the lack of sanitary facilities, which he emphasized in his written report: "[I] DID NOT FIND A SINGLE URINAL TROUGH IN BOY'S TOILET. . . . a few schools HAD NO TOILETS." Interestingly, he made no mention of other items, such as leaky roofs, drafty windows, decaying walls, or the lack of teaching materials, that remained high on the AVs' priority list.[15]

As Sutherland moved from the schools to the homes, he apparently missed the worst of Appalachian poverty. Rather than speaking with unemployed miners, he spent the majority of his time with farmers, many of whom supplemented their income with jobs in nearby towns. In particular, they worked as school bus drivers and lunchroom cooks, jobs that the county school superintendent controlled. One family Sutherland interviewed actually employed four farmhands. Moreover, even though most of the adults had never attended high school, they still placed a high value on education for their children. "Many had children in high school or intended to send them [there]," Sutherland reported. "Some children were in college."[16]

Though Sutherland failed to come in contact with Appalachia's poorest, his findings revealed that, despite his contention that the mountaineers needed to "learn what is most important—to *put first things first*," their long-term concerns were remarkably congruent with those of the Appalachian Volunteers. "Interviews with Eastern Kentucky parents in small schools," he wrote, "revealed some of the things they consider important [such] as education, . . . moral training, . . . [and] homemaking." So too were their more immediate, short-term concerns: the need for improved schools, more playground facilities, improved roads (to facilitate bus service and, thus, education), and more jobs.[17]

In certain ways, the Sutherland survey was a self-fulfilling prophecy. The Appalachian Volunteers began almost a year earlier with the hypothesis that mountaineers were undereducated and that, given the opportunity and the example, they would warmly welcome a better school environment. To test this supposition, the organization sent agents first to the county school superintendents, who were already quite familiar with the program, and then to the schools themselves, where the AV representatives told the teachers and students about the purpose of the visit. When he finally introduced himself to his subjects, Sutherland "stress[ed] the Appalachian Volunteers and school connection." Even during the interviews themselves, as his assistant observed, "he became [the] *teacher* . . . more than [the] *interviewer*." Furthermore, because the superintendents directed him to specific households and those households had prior warning of his visit, those individuals whom Sutherland interviewed probably told him exactly what he wanted to hear or, more probably, what the superintendents wanted him to hear.[18]

Ignoring the extremely poor did not necessarily reflect suspicion on the part of the local superintendents toward the AVs. Rather, their hesitancy to send Sutherland to the most impoverished areas of their counties was probably a reaction to the growing national attention being paid to the region and its problems. In late December 1964, CBS News produced two special reports on impoverishment in eastern Kentucky, *Depressed Area U.S.A.* and the more famous *Christmas in Appalachia*. Both set out to find the worst that eastern Kentucky had to offer, and the powers that be in the region apparently became increasingly concerned about how the region and they themselves were being portrayed.

Hosted by Charles Kuralt and filmed on Pert Creek, Letcher County, Kentucky, *Christmas in Appalachia* juxtaposed the immense poverty of the Appalachian coalfields with the spirit of joy and giving felt by most Americans during the holiday season. It showed many hardworking people who "lived in a country far removed from ours" and struggled to survive. Kuralt interviewed a number of local residents, asking them about, among other things, the local school. Again, *all* claimed to recognize the value of education and affirmed that they wanted their children in school. Despite scenes of coal cars "carrying the wealth of Appalachia away" and the "tour" of the abandoned town of Weeksbury, once "the trading center for this whole valley" where jobs could be had, the report never attempted to explain the cause of poverty, which, as Allen Batteau has pointed out, "was due to the coal-buying policies of the Tennessee Valley Authority, or how the electricity powering the viewers' television sets came from cheap coal." "[The report] showed a run down schoolhouse," Batteau continued, "but it failed to explain that the inadequate fiscal structure of Letcher County was due to its domination by some large mineral interests." Equally mystifying was the continued discussion of the mountaineers' attitudes toward education. The report implied that all that was needed to bring these poor mountain folk out of that "country far removed," rebuild the town of Weeksbury, and keep wealth in the region was a proper education. This belief, already embraced by the Appalachian Volunteers, took hold of the rest of America as well.[19]

Much more biting in its criticism, *Depressed Area USA*, in which the Council of the Southern Mountains took an active part, did attempt to provide a more comprehensive analysis of Appalachian poverty. According to the suggested story line submitted by CBS to the Council of the Southern Mountains, the report sought to develop the theme that, "while many can be accused, all of these people we see and hear are the victims of history, an oversight on the part of the body politic." Rather than contrasting poverty in Appalachia and the Christmas spirit in more prosperous areas of the country, *Depressed Area* first showed the Clay County resident Odie Mills "accusing the school system of taking more than a year of her life," followed by the faces of "local big wigs" claiming "'We're doing the best we can'" and local bankers revealing "that they are minions of larger banks in Lexington and Louisville, which set credit policy." Though the script did not specify in what way the mountaineers were "victims of history," it claimed that the problems in Appalachia lingered because of a national "failure of nerve" and "fear of risk."[20]

In the proposal submitted to the CSM, *Depressed Area USA* did not offer any tangible solutions. Rather, it focused on the problems and allowed locals to make accusations. Much like *Christmas in Appalachia, Depressed Area* called on all Americans to take responsibility for remedying the national oversight of Appalachian poverty. The implicit message was the need to educate Appalachians so that they might take part in the wealth and prosperity of the modern United States. This, of course, was the message of the Appalachian Volunteers.

There was a second implication in *Depressed Area* that the Council openly exploited—the lack of leadership in the Appalachian region, as demonstrated by the report's depiction of the "local big wigs" as powerless "minions" of outside forces. In contrast to those powerless flunkies, the Council of the Southern Mountains saw itself as the source of a renewed mountain authority. "The desperate region-wide material poverty and poverty of the mind and spirit and inadequate resource development throughout the entire Appalachian South," Ayer wrote to the OEO, "is fundamentally based in a lack of specific and interrelated information, a lack of social and organizational 'savvy' and a lack of competent leadership in this new day as differentiated from the power structure group of so-called leaders under whose domination and control the situation came to be as it is." Because of this dearth of local leadership, he continued, those involved in implementing the OEO's community action programs (CAPs) must "come from outside the community." Finally, he argued that only the Council was in a position to provide any reliable information on the conditions in Appalachia and that the OEO should consult it before approving any CAP there. Though Ayer claimed that he sought only to ensure that the OEO developed programs on the basis of accurate data, his argument that the Council "need[ed] to have the authority . . . to act as OEO's emissary" in Appalachia clearly translated to a desire for control of federal dollars.[21]

Interestingly, these harsh words about the "power structure" did not produce any fundamental alterations in the AV focus. The publicity that

Appalachia gained as a result of the national news coverage was, however, a boon to the AV cause. Donations of all sorts poured into the region (and not just to the AVs), and the organization opened its doors to the flood of young Americans who wanted to do their part for the less fortunate. By this time, Appalachian Volunteer chapters existed on three college campuses outside the region: at Earlham College in Indiana, Queens College in New York, and Harvard University in Massachusetts. With the addition of the VISTA volunteers who filtered into Appalachia in early 1965, the War on Poverty exploded on eastern Kentucky. The *Appalachia* in *Appalachian Volunteers* now referred more to where the AV members worked than to where they were born—though most were still volunteers.[22]

This transformation was intentional. Ayer suggested that the CSM attempt to attract sociology students from places such as the University of Wisconsin, Columbia University, Cornell University, and other "far flung campuses on which there are people orientated to and concerned about this area." In addition, the AV staff member Gibbs Kinderman informed an interested student from Louisville that the organization was "most interested in involving colleges outside the Eastern Kentucky area in our work." Before the spring was over, his wish was granted.[23]

In late 1964, the Council's assistant executive director, Loyal Jones, had "encourage[d] Peace Corps returnees to check with the Council" about working in the mountains following their overseas assignments. Further, he worked with the United Church Board for Homeland Ministries to find suitable "work camp experiences" for interested young people. This was but the beginning of a massive influx of nonnatives into the Appalachian Volunteers. In February 1965, Flem Messer began making arrangements for a church group from Elkhart, Indiana, to conduct a school project in eastern Kentucky, and, during the summer of that year, Beloit College in Wisconsin sent two female students to the Appalachian Volunteers through the school's social service program. In November, volunteers from a student church group at Pennsylvania State University held a weeklong project at Quicksand Hollow, Knott County, while volunteers from Saint Pius X Interracial Council, located in Uniondale, New York, provided manpower for the Volunteers in April 1966. Not all the new volunteers, however, came from so far away. By 1965, University of Louisville students actively participated in the AV program. Nevertheless, extant in the Appalachian Volunteers files

are letters to and from virtually every state in the Union either from individuals requesting information about the AVs or from the Appalachian
Volunteers themselves seeking new volunteers and asking former students
to return for yet another tour of duty. By mid-1965, the AVs were a national
organization.[24]

Not only were the Appalachian Volunteers more than willing to accept
participants from outside the region; they also were ready to abandon that
sense of selflessness that they originally hoped to infuse in the project. From
Annandale-on-Hudson, New York, Bard College asked to send students to
the Appalachian Volunteers so that they might gain knowledge that would
supplement their classroom studies. Even certified teachers expressed a desire to spend time in the rural mountain schools. Representing a group of
teachers in New Jersey, Richard Blass wrote to the Council about arranging
a "teacher exchange" program between the rural instructors and those from
the Northeast. Such a program, Blass argued, would be of great benefit to
the Jersey children, who were very interested in learning more about the
"romantic Appalachian area."[25]

Ironically, the Appalachian Volunteers' overwhelming confidence in
their own abilities prevented yet another group from turning the fight
against want in the Southern mountains into a lab course for its students.
Clarke Moses of Pomona College in Claremont, California, wanted to form
a "social action seminar" in which students would work with reform efforts
such as the Appalachian Volunteers and read prescribed texts, assigned by
Pomona faculty as a supplement. This seminar, he believed, would successfully combine academics with actual experience. Responding to the proposal, the AV fieldman Thomas Rhodenbaugh informed Moses that his idea
was an admirable one but that the Volunteer staff was the better judge of
what academic work should supplement the "action" part of the course.[26]

Rhodenbaugh's response is interesting on many levels. First, he was
open to the possibility of a group using mountaineers as research subjects.
Second, he must have understood that the primary objective of the proposed
seminar was not the improvement of the mountaineers' condition but the
education of the college students. Finally, his reaction to the professor's attempt to control the reading material for his own class again illustrated how
sure of themselves the Volunteers were and how they believed they were the
ones most prepared to initiate change in the Appalachian coalfields.

By the end of 1966, the Appalachian Volunteers began to suffer the consequences of both the national publicity and the changing composition of its work groups. After the *Depressed Area* film crew completed its work in Clay County, the county school superintendent, Malie Bledsoe, was so incensed that she refused to allow the Appalachian Volunteers to undertake any additional school renovation projects in her district. William Miller, a member of the AV Board of Directors, subsequently urged the AV staff to evaluate the methods used by the Volunteer groups to contact local officials. Many superintendents, he warned, were "disturbed at the Volunteers [for] ignoring them." Ayer, somewhat uncharacteristically, believed that the "push" from the national media would lead only to progress in the region. "We cannot alleviate any of these great social problems by sweeping them under the rug," he told an NBC reporter, "and if we offend some of the dominant 'leaders' in the area this may result in positive action which would not otherwise have been aroused."[27]

In spite of these early warnings, the Appalachian Volunteers continued to bring work groups from all over the country into the region. Three of these were from Earlham College, Wilmington College (in Ohio), and Queens College. Prior to the students' scheduled arrival on January 29, 1965, the Wilmington Project was already in trouble with the AV staff because of an article that had appeared in the *Louisville Courier-Journal* on January 20. In a letter written the same day the article appeared, Gibbs Kinderman chastised Tim Sword of the Wilmington College Appalachian Project because, as he saw it, the article implied that the Wilmington students sought "national recognition" for their efforts. Kinderman reminded the Ohioans that the AVs worked "with" and not for impoverished mountaineers. He also pointed out that there was no mention of the Council of the Southern Mountains in the article and that, as the agency that actually administered the AV program and sponsored the Wilmington group, the CSM had to be included in all statements issued about the project.[28] Still concerned about its financial position and its fund-raising potential, the CSM wanted to maintain the level of visibility that it had achieved with *Christmas in Appalachia.*

Putting this incident behind them, the Ohio students conducted a combination curriculum enrichment and renovation project at the Kerby Knob school in Jackson County. The work must have been more difficult than anticipated because the students failed to complete all they had hoped to do. They did, however, write to Otis Johnson, the superintendent of the Jackson County schools, requesting permission to return later and finish the job. Johnson refused the request. In a letter to the AV fieldman Rhodenbaugh, Johnson stated: "At our regular board meeting . . . the letter from Wilmington College requesting their return to Kerby Knob School to finish their job was refused by the board. The reason was because of all the unjustified publicity." It is uncertain whether Johnson meant the earlier *Courier-Journal* article, but it is clear that one more superintendent began to curb Volunteer activity in his county.[29]

The Queens College and Earlham College projects were also significant in that they spurred a change in AV operations. Taking place in the early spring of 1965 at Decoy in Knott County and at Wright-Watson in Elliott County, the Earlham College program adhered to the Appalachian Volunteers' curriculum enhancement program to the letter. The twenty-seven Earlham students held dances and sing-alongs and presented dramatic skits and arts and crafts classes. They attempted to teach nutrition and health. They also served as teachers' aides, instructing the local children in nearly every subject. According to the fieldman Bill Wells, few volunteer groups embraced projects with such energy. Unfortunately, this enthusiasm nearly ruined the project. Wells reported that the "zeal and almost revolutionary spirit" of the Earlham students stationed at Wright-Watson disrupted the daily routines of the community and the school. According to the local teacher, the volunteers were one step away from disaster because they had little regard for local sensibilities until confronted with their insensitivity. Bill Marshak closed his report to the AV staff with the cryptic statement: "Reminder that all people are human beings and are just like us."[30]

Though no reports or evaluations of the Queens College project are extant, a questionnaire used to prepare the New Yorkers for their summer visit to Appalachia remains. Though problematic—there is no indication who composed it or why—the language used provides insight into the participants and their perception of eastern Kentucky, illustrating the gap between the "monotony of daily routine" in the mountains and the "sophisticated culture" of New York City. Among other queries, project organizers asked whether students could endure "smelly clothes" and "do without washing for an extended period."[31]

Most interesting, however, were a series of preproject statements that questioned the rationale behind the project: "Tutorials [were] ineffective since the children will return to their inadequate education in the fall. Whose idea was this recreation stuff anyway? In a poor society recreation is irrelevant." One student even declared: "Community development is a joke. Renovation programs cannot be accomplished with our limited resources, . . . and even if minimal achievements are accomplished they will not be maintained." Certainly, recreation is not irrelevant, and even short-term improvements are just that—improvements. So one wonders why the New Yorkers made such statements. The prompts directed at the students were, most likely, designed to make them say that any improvement, no matter how small, was beneficial. In many ways, such a position was correct. Nevertheless, as future events would soon indicate, the direction of the Queens College project questions was more prophetic than rhetorical, foreshadowing the future of the entire AV program. Further, because it recognized the possibility of failure, however remote, it also suggests that cracks had formed in the AV foundation of overwhelming confidence and self-assurance.[32]

That foundation, nevertheless, was still strong enough in 1965 to withstand the weight of the continued influx, in the form of the AV Spring Break and Summer 1965 projects as well as additional VISTA volunteers, of non-Appalachians. These three developments further undercut the notion of local people helping each other and solidified the change in the meaning of *Appalachian Volunteer*.

Scheduled to take place from March 15 through March 20, 1965, the AV Spring Break Project had as its "primary concern" "the growth of an enrichment program whereby the students of the one- and two-room schools can gain new insights into their world." Prior to the start of the program, however, the AV staff requested that all participants (most were from the University of Kentucky) meet in Berea for one day of "orientation to Eastern Kentucky and to Appalachian Volunteer techniques." Only after the volunteers were properly trained did the AV staff send them into the hills.[33]

The weeklong effort followed the pattern of virtually every other Appalachian Volunteer project in that it was designed "to bring the outside world . . . to these children." At the Spruce School in Knox County, for example, a group of volunteers made much-needed repairs to the school building. They patched the leaking roof, glazed the windows, and painted the entire structure. They also constructed a rock wall around a flower garden and laid a stone path from the school to the water pump. One AV member, Larry Qualls, used the telescope he brought to the community to teach an astronomy lesson, and foreign exchange students spoke about their countries. Similarly, volunteers at the Ligon School in Floyd County and the Bruin School in Elliott County focused on the basics, including spelling, geography, history, and science, because, as one volunteer argued, that was what was needed.[34]

An examination of some of the Spring Break Project's participants reveal emerging structural problems within the Appalachian Volunteers and the increasingly resistant attitudes of some of the mountaineers themselves. One of the exchange students who did foreign culture enrichment programs at a number of schools reported on the parents' lack of involvement with their children's education. "They sent their children to school," he stated, "but they weren't bothered by the happenings [there]." A second exchange student lamented the fact that the constant travel the project involved prevented him from meeting local people and also told the AV leaders that the parents were "terribly indifferent." Unfortunately, he did not indicate whether they were indifferent to the school itself or to the Volunteer program. Still, given the information the Appalachian Volunteers had already gathered on mountaineer attitudes (including Charles Kuralt's interviews), it is likely that their indifference was to the Volunteer program, especially since fewer and fewer AVs were themselves Appalachian.[35]

Within the organization itself, reports indicated that the Appalachian Volunteers came up short in preparing the students for their weeklong projects. "I think if we had more information on the program," one student volunteer exclaimed, "we would have absorbed more. In fact information on the whole project [was] needed especially as to what the community expects of the volunteers." Other spring break volunteers echoed this sentiment. One declared that the Volunteers placed too much emphasis on the physical environment and not enough on the "socialogy [sic]" of the mountaineers. According to this individual, potential volunteers needed to have a better understanding of the norms and mores of the people with whom they would be working. Another added that the program would be more beneficial if the volunteers knew the education level of the children and what the teachers really wanted in terms of help.[36]

All three who criticized the orientation program indicated that they had no idea what was expected of them once they were on the job. Equally important was the question of the mores of the mountaineers. Because they were operating under the assumptions inherent in the culture of poverty model, the AV staff may have ignored the rural mountaineer culture since that was what they ultimately hoped to change. In addition, very few of the AVs understood mountain culture because so few of them were Appalachians themselves.

Located in the Appalachian Volunteer papers are biographical data sheets for twenty-seven volunteers from the Spring Break Project. These forms clearly illustrate that, by March 1965, the organization had abandoned its founding concept of local people helping each other. Of the twenty-seven, two were from Tennessee, and seven were Kentuckians. The rest—the majority of whom were University of Kentucky students—listed hometowns such as Rockville, Maryland, Bay City, Michigan, and Syracuse, New York. More interesting, only one listed an Appalachian county, Sullivan County, Tennessee, as his place of origin.[37]

Compounding this demographic change was an attitudinal shift that also went against the founding principles of the Appalachian Volunteers. By this time, there were many AV members who turned the focus of the projects on themselves rather than on the mountaineers. "I would like to help the unfortunate people of Eastern Kentucky," answered one volunteer when asked why he wished to join the AVs, "because I feel that it is part of my responsibility as a human being. . . . I will provide them with a broader education and better facilities which will make their everyday life much more enjoyable and prosperous. . . . I will *be a missionary*." Echoing this statement was a native of Bay City, Michigan, who wanted to change Appalachia into a "better and happier [region] through a little understanding, friendship and hard work": "For those of us who are rich in essentials . . . it is not foolish to say that it is *our duty to share*." A third participant saw the Volunteer experience as an opportunity for selfless action. She complained that all her life she thought only of her self but that now, through the AVs, she could finally do "for others."[38]

Though many saw the AV experience as an opportunity to cleanse their souls, others, like the Pomona College group, saw it as an opportunity to learn themselves. One University of Kentucky student, for example, wanted to do anthropological research in eastern Kentucky, and she looked to the Volunteers as a means to this end. Implying that genetics explained the region's limitations, she hoped that the AV experience would enable her to complete her tentatively titled thesis "The Consequences of Genetic Lines in Eastern Kentucky." Still others hoped simply to bring a ray of sunshine into the bleak world of the central Appalachians: "I see myself trying to penetrate their world and trying to make them smile where before they may have had sad, dismal faces." Finally, two participants fell back on the Appalachian Volunteers. One had been rejected by the Peace Corps and, thus, settled for the AVs, while another, possibly hoping to avoid the same fate, decided that the AVs could provide him with a quality Peace Corps training experience. Though the reasons for wanting to participate in the program varied widely, what was important was that many applicants had little connection with the mountaineers. Indeed, concepts of missionary charity and a sense of noblesse oblige began to emerge within the Appalachian Volunteer organization.[39]

Their place of origin and attitudes concerning the mountaineers notwithstanding, the participants in the Spring Break Project were but a small part of the outside world that descended on eastern Kentucky. By the summer of 1965, the Appalachian Volunteers had VISTA volunteers in fifteen schools in twelve counties, and, with the Summer 1965 Project, they brought in nearly 150 additional volunteers. According to the AVs, the VISTA volunteers had the responsibility to make sure that efforts—particularly school renovation and curriculum enrichment—continued in those places where Volunteers had already started the work.[40]

Accompanying the Volunteers that summer were "VISTA associates," the product of an interesting combination of the Volunteer and the VISTA programs. Rather than spending a year on assignment like regular VISTA volunteers, the associates signed on for an eight-week tour of duty over the summers. Of the 150 volunteers for the Summer 1965 Project, half were out-of-state VISTA associates from thirty different states. These volunteers worked for eight weeks in forty-three eastern Kentucky communities. Despite their widely dispersed geographic origins and the fact that, technically, they were Volunteers, VISTA volunteers and VISTA associates should be considered as part of the AVs. While some VISTA volunteers worked in eastern Kentucky in other capacities, those who came to the mountains under the AV banner operated, Loyal Jones declared, "under the direction of the Council" and worked "solely on the Appalachian Volunteers Project." In this way, the Council truly considered VISTA volunteers to be AVs. In fact, the two programs—VISTA and the Appalachian Volunteers—were so closely linked that the Volunteers distributed VISTA applications and told those interested in the Southern mountains to specify that they "want placement with the AVs and AV training" on their VISTA application. The AV staff member Tom Rhodenbaugh told one VISTA associate: "You will be, as far as we are concerned, an Appalachian Volunteer." Equally important was the attitude of the VISTA volunteers themselves. One AV-VISTA, as they frequently labeled themselves, described himself and his fellow VISTA volunteers as "full time A.V.'s." This individual was not unique. A careful reading of the AV correspondence reveals that those who wrote to AV headquarters, either during their tenure in the mountains or after, constantly referred to themselves as Appalachian Volunteers or "AV-VISTAs," as opposed to just VISTA volunteers, and the *Appalachian Volunteer* label always came first.[41]

Prior to their departure for their assigned communities, the VISTA volunteers underwent a ten-day training program under the direction of the Appalachian Volunteer staff. Utilizing such sources as Jack Weller's *Yesterday's People,* a book that embraced the culture of poverty perspective, the new recruits prepared for their mountain tasks under the direction of an "AV professor." These professors, actually AV staff members, conducted three-hour sessions twice a day for the first four days of the week and then took the new volunteers on orientation field trips to counties such as Clay, Jackson, and Rockcastle. According to Fox, the director of AV field operations, fieldmen prepared a two-page description for each community in which volunteers were to be assigned. These descriptions included population figures, income, social structure, teacher qualifications, welfare roles, and the "extent of isolation" of each town. These reports, along with a series of hypothetical case studies called the "Library of Community Action Styles" and Weller's book, became the basis of the training sessions. The last three days focused on the tasks of actually getting the summer volunteers to their assigned communities and settled in their "new mountain homes."

In most cases, the AV staff arranged for the summer workers to board with local mountain residents. Therefore, with about twelve hours of preparation and a brief tour of the region, the Council of the Southern Mountains released 150 summer volunteers, in teams of four to six, into forty central Appalachia communities.[42]

Unfortunately, responses to the first summer project training session are not available. The Earlham College volunteers, however, did respond to a similar training experience that they had just prior to their Spring Break Project in March 1965. Because the Earlham project had a similar thrust as the Summer 1965 effort (enrichment and renovation), the preparation probably was similar. In any event, the Earlham students' reactions to the AV orientation were decidedly negative. One student considered it "adequate but dull"—the most positive of the responses—while another claimed that it was poorly organized. "The talks of the supposed orientation were extremely superficial," a third argued, "[and] seemed only [to] give us unrealistic ideals." More important, the Appalachian Volunteers provided "very little about [the mountaineers'] attitudes."[43]

John Hogarty of Antioch College echoed this negative response. He was in Berea that March to help with Volunteer training and to establish a permanent work-study program that would improve education in the mountains. In a letter to Milton Ogle about the spring training session, Hogarty remarked: "In short, there was a lot of verbiage, but I don't really sense that there were too many creative and different ideas which might be used by you in the program . . . that you are planning."[44] If the summer orientation was anything like that offered the Earlham students, the training sessions taxed the whole AV program terribly, and the unprecedented number of volunteers undoubtedly made it more difficult to administer. Still, instructing volunteers for work in the field, especially those volunteers coming from outside the region, was vital to the long-term success of the AV effort.

Just as the training sessions failed to impress many of the volunteers, the volunteers failed to impress many eastern Kentuckians. In fact, complaints arose even before fieldwork began. Two female employees of Berea College who helped run the orientation sessions complained to Ayer about the demeanor of the potential volunteers. "I hope there is a second screening of persons before they are sent out into the area," Minnie Macaulay wrote. "I cannot believe mountain people would welcome some of the girls . . . in the AV group. [They are] demanding, pushing, [and] most unkempt in dress." Echoing these sentiments was Florence Brooks, who believed in the AV program but not the people it attracted. "I have observed these people on campus and in the boarding hall," she informed Ayer. "I strongly urge that no one of the AV group be allowed to leave for the mountains without a final evaluation."[45] The gap that had opened between the AVs and those they wanted to help had widened beyond place of origin to include attitudes and community mores.

Despite the warnings, the summer of 1965 brought an influx of VISTA volunteers, VISTA associates, and AVs into Berea and eastern Kentucky. The Appalachian Volunteer leadership and people from outside the region saw great promise in the new corps. The Harvard University faculty member and psychiatrist Robert Coles, who joined the AV consulting team in 1965, told Fox that he had never witnessed a "so well organized, sensible and tactful approach based on really sensitive appreciation of the delicate relationship between people and those that come to 'help' them." Even the lawyer Harry Caudill, a vocal critic from the mountains, wrote to the Council office praising the work of the AVs. Exhibiting a belief that the region's infrastructure contributed to its problems, Caudill declared himself "delighted with the work the Volunteers are doing in so many places in eastern Kentucky": "Highly paid government officials have spent much time endlessly grubbing about our problems and writing expensive study reports. They have cost America enormous sums of money and have not yet laid one brick upon another." In Caudill's estimation, the Volunteers "have rolled up their sleeves and have come to grips with" the problems of the region. Even an OEO representative referred to the Appalachian Volunteers as "one of the more successful programs" of the War on Poverty.[46]

The Appalachian Volunteers maintained that, by "reaching more people in more communities," the student workers, coupled with the VISTA volunteers and the VISTA associates, "achieved fuller participation in community action." In many ways, the AV program began to show signs of effecting real change in Appalachia. Focusing on the schools, the CSM reported that the combined AV-VISTA effort demonstrated to the mountain folk that "their combined power, as delegates to county officials," has "produced improvements needed for years, ranging from replacing windows for the school

house to cutting a new road." The people of Elkhorn, Leslie County, picketed the State Highway Commission until the county graded the road to
the town, and one particular one-room school in Wolfe County received its
first visit from the school superintendent in twenty years. In Joshua, Knott
County, unemployed fathers built a new lunchroom on the local school,
while, in Breathitt County, the fathers in Quicksand constructed a bridge
across the creek. Other reports indicate that the Volunteers convinced children to stay in school and that they organized community improvement
associations. In its summation of AV activities through 1965, the Council
argued: "In the field of what Washington Community Action Program people call 'resident participation' Appalachian Volunteers and VISTA workers
. . . have taken the lead in Eastern Kentucky."[47]

The Council, however, may have gone too far in its claims of "resident
participation." According to the CSM report, it was the Volunteers who organized town meetings and convinced the county CAP director to attend
the "up-the-holler community meeting." The CSM's own documentation
actually downplayed the role of the people in community development,
and the Volunteers, not the local people, were the "developers."[48]

Not everyone viewed the AVs' work so positively. For example, the
Knott County school superintendent attempted to discourage the addition of a lunchroom to the school in the small town of Joshua because,
according to an AV report, he did not want "the added bother of delivering
food, keeping accounts, etc." As the project neared completion under the
direction of a VISTA volunteer, the superintendent, "apparently alarmed at
the unexpected progress," told a community leader that "no surplus food
would be available until certain unrealistic health code requirements were
met." The community vowed to fight for the lunch program, and a group of
residents confronted the superintendent in his office. His response was to
inform the group's leader that, if he wanted to discuss anything, the "crowd"
would have to stay home.[49]

Then there were those county officials who, instead of trying to ob-
struct the AV effort, attempted to control it. This was, most likely, a reaction to what had become the continued AV presence—in the form of the
resident VISTA volunteers—in the region. That is, a contest had developed
between county-administered CAPs and the Appalachian Volunteers over
who would control the funding supplied by the federal government for the

War on Poverty. For example, in Morgan County, the AV fieldman, William Wells, discovered that the county superintendent removed encyclopedias donated by the Volunteers to the White Oak Branch and Peddlers Gap schools and transferred them to the county seat of West Liberty. Neighboring Elliott County also became a trouble spot for Wells. The local superintendent refused to give his consent to a proposed AV project and denied the AVs access to any school property in the county. Perhaps he did not want the Volunteers using his schools for community organizing centers as they had done in Joshua. Flem Messer also complained about the way in which county school systems spent OEO and Elementary and Secondary Education Act funds. This money, he contended, was supposed to provide for an improved remedial education program in the mountains, but teachers requested "such items as stoves and refrigerators" rather than educational materials.[50]

These incidents were not limited to Morgan and Estill counties. When the Appalachian Volunteers again tried to evaluate their educational programs, the testing administrator, Charles Shedd, reported that local superintendents discouraged visits to rural schools. According to Wells, local superintendents in his area told Shedd that the poor attendance in those schools would make the trip and the test less than profitable. Shedd, Wells maintained, discounted the officials' assertions and claimed that the superintendents "attempted to delay testing because . . . they [felt] threatened." Curt Davis of Elliott County, another school official in Wells's area of responsibility, expressed concern over the attention being paid to these one-room schools since they were slated for consolidation. More significant for the Volunteers, however, was Davis's attitude toward the AV effort. Wells reported that the superintendent saw little good in the work performed by the Volunteers and referred to the plight of the poor in his county as "a disease." This so-called disease, Davis further informed Wells, was just "plain laziness."[51]

City officials and local CAP administrators also objected to AV plans and projects. In late May 1965, for example, the mayor of Pikeville met with the Volunteer staff member Flem Messer. Messer concluded that, while the mayor had given him "three hours of his philosophy and said he was interested in our program," his "main interest [was] centered on the physical needs of Pikeville and the surrounding area rather than human resources."

In Rockcastle County, an AV-VISTA spoke frequently with public officials who always asked how they could help her. "I tell them to help," she reported to the Volunteer leaders, "by not condemning the OEO program." The director of the Knox County CAP, James Kendrick, reprimanded the Volunteers because he had not been informed that a VISTA volunteer was being sent to his county. The volunteer had been at work for three weeks, he claimed, before he discovered her presence. "It seems appropriate," Kendrick wrote, "for VISTA volunteers to be introduced to the local Community Action Agency."[52]

In 1965 and early 1966, Volunteer reactions to these problems ranged from counterattacks on those now seen as obstacles to declarations of frustration and resignation from the AV ranks. "I did my best in Kentucky," Sue Leek, an Oregon native, wrote to Milton Ogle and Dan Fox after she quit the Volunteers and returned home. "I was so tired of having [the community people] say 'show us where to go from here' and then having my gov[ernment] and theirs say 'sorry can't help you.' I was tired of having to fight dirty people with clean hands." Leek was clear just who those "dirty people" were. "I wanted to fight the school board like they fight, but the AV name had to be held up high [and] the bad publicity it would have got would have hurt. So I [and] the other VISTAs [and] AV's are to be in a community to look good for Shriver."[53]

Unfortunately, Leek failed to illuminate just how the school board fought "dirty." Other AV workers, however, suggested that local public officials were more concerned with perpetuating conditions in eastern Kentucky than with changing them. "I still say," Loren Kramer, an AV "teacher" stationed in Ary, Kentucky, wrote, "that we have much to learn and preserve in Appalachia that is great and beautiful, while at the same time changing, gung-ho, the status quo." Echoing the theme that the AVs were the sole change agents funded by the OEO, Kim Hashizumi, an Appalachian Volunteer operating in Glade, Kentucky, commented that the Volunteers worked hard, "unlike a certain CAP Dir[ector] I know who [spent] more time [and] energy trying to convince certain feds that he's concerned about poverty—(he is—his own)."[54]

A volunteer in Leslie County decided to take a more confrontational approach to the emerging AV problems. Instead of simply complaining to his AV supervisors, P. D. Merrill made his complaints public. "What are we fighting," Merrill wrote to the *Leslie County News*, "poverty or the poor?" He went on to attack those who believed that the poor could not work effectively in the poverty program because they were either too lazy or too unintelligent to prevent themselves from being "manipulated by the power hungry politicians." Merrill's meaning was clear. It was not a lack of intelligence that precipitated the political manipulation of the mountain people but ignorance, an ignorance perpetuated by politicians. Offering an example, Merrill claimed that the Leslie County Development Association Board of Directors failed to provide all association members with copies of the articles of incorporation and, thereby, prevented the poor from comprehending how the organization operated. Moreover, the board also initiated projects that were not "sensitive to the feelings of the people with whom they were dealing."[55]

Even if the individuals who ran the county CAP had the real interests of the impoverished at heart, Merrill concluded, their practice of excluding the poor from participating in the administration of their projects was wrong. With the aim of remedying this, Merrill took the unprecedented step, especially in light of the Council's cooperative philosophy, of trying to tell a local agency how to operate. The articles of incorporation of the Leslie County CAP should, he contended, be amended so that it would be "mandatory" for there to be on the board representatives from each neighborhood in the county, representatives "whose annual income is less than $4,000."[56]

In a letter to Dan Fox, the AV director of field operations, Merrill confessed that his statement to the newspaper was "calculated to affect the more educated leaders of the county." "Though it was not the success that I hoped it would be," he lamented, "it did create quite a bit of conversation." Given the AVs' conception of the lack of education in the mountains, there was no doubt that the "more educated leaders" whom Merrill targeted were public officials and business leaders in the county seat.[57]

Though the Appalachian Volunteers experienced mounting difficulties with local and county officials in 1965 and 1966, this situation was not unique to eastern Kentucky. As Allen Matusow has illustrated, local officials in cities such as Philadelphia, New York, and San Francisco fought tooth and nail to maximize their own control of and minimize the input of the poor into antipoverty programs. Matusow's account does not consider the action of the poor themselves or any group, such as the Appalachian Volunteers, that worked on behalf of the poor, but it does raise important issues of self-interest.[58]

While certain powerful local individuals may have sought to enhance their own positions, evidence suggests that some county superintendents were genuinely less than pleased with how participants in the AV program depicted eastern Kentucky. In a national magazine, the Volunteer field representative Thomas Rhodenbaugh described the educational system in the region as a "dull, dry, and monotonous" experience that failed to address the needs of the people. He also suggested that the political system in the mountains failed to live up to the American ideal. "The [AV] program is a vehicle," he claimed, "upon which people can begin seeing their own needs in the light of the twentieth century and co-operatively work together to satisfy some of those needs." "This process," he concluded, "has as a goal co-operation and the restoration of grass roots democracy."[59]

Rhodenbaugh's comments may have reflected the position held by many on the AV staff, but such publicity did not endear the program to county boards of education. By 1965, AV leaders required that all publicity issued by any individual or group operating in the mountains under the AV banner be cleared with the Berea office. This decision was made in reaction to experiences with "people coming into the area who mean well but because of published articles in newspapers and magazines, some of the good that they did . . . was more or less undone by the negative reaction toward publicity concerning conditions in the area." Because of all the national attention already focused on the Appalachian region, this sort of unofficial publicity "tends to take the extreme, leaving the impression that somebody or some particular school system or county officials are to blame." As the Appalachian Volunteers were beginning to discover, an antagonistic county government spelled trouble for their reform efforts.[60]

Unwanted publicity, as the January 1965 Wilmington College project illustrated, was already a source of friction between the Appalachian Volunteer organization and some county superintendents. Moreover, it caused problems between AV leaders and the campus chapters. In March 1965, the University of Kentucky's campus newspaper, the *Kentucky Kernel*, published a story about the antipoverty efforts of its campus chapter in Knox, Elliott, and Floyd counties. After recounting the work they had done renovating buildings and improving playgrounds, the participants assigned blame for the conditions they encountered, singling out, for example, the "unqualified" teacher at the Bruin School in Elliott County and "apathy on the part of the teachers at Ligon School" in Floyd County. It was the latter, they contended, that "allowed the new concrete building to become run down and filthy." Without follow-up work, they concluded, their work at Ligon School "will have accomplished little."[61]

Reaction to the *Kernel* article—by both the Volunteer staff and Floyd County—was swift. While the Volunteer staff member William Wells criticized the tone of the piece, the Floyd County superintendent Charles Clark informed Flem Messer that the Ligon staff no longer welcomed the Volunteers. Though Messer recognized that the "teachers were not appreciative of the negative publicity given to their school," he urged Clark to meet with them and ask them to reconsider their stance. Clark agreed, but Messer reported that the AVs could only hope that Clark and the teachers would "come to a positive decision."[62]

Problems with the state's flagship university continued. Just over a year later, undoubtedly inspired by both the efforts of the War on Poverty in Appalachia and the activities of her fellow students, Judy Grisham, a *Kernel* columnist, visited southeastern Kentucky. What she reported and photographed angered the Volunteers. The people, she wrote, "live in a world of their own—a world consisting of themselves and their neighbors just over the hill": "They know nothing else. Nor do they seem to care." Outsiders, she continued, were "sickened by the unspeakable stench and unbelievable filth" that characterized the mountain homes she visited. The real tragedy, as one of her picture captions made clear, was the fact that the "children stay."[63]

Though no one—not even the Volunteers—disputed the nature of Appalachian poverty, the images created by the article implied that the problem could not be solved—or that no one was seeking a solution. Grisham's remarks particularly angered the AV staff member Jack Rivel. In response, Rivel wrote Grisham:

> I cannot reach very far for the words necessary in explaining my feelings and that of others . . . here who have read the article but I suggest that maybe [y]ou can find them in the gutter. . . . We do

not feel that you gave many [people] a chance when you visited the creek you wrote about. Sure it makes beautiful copy but how much greater a contribution could your words of wisdom have been if you had experienced more than just that which you wrote about—possibly a community meeting, using more of the sweat of your brow, . . . working with rural people as they renovate their school, as they improve their roads.[64]

Rivel intended his words to express his anger at one journalist, but they also illustrate the AV leaders' frustration with their inability to control the dissemination of information about their own program. As the number of participants, particularly non-Appalachians, increased, the organization's ability to control its members decreased. Such unwanted or ill-advised publicity was symptomatic of a much larger problem.

The experiences of two VISTA volunteers in Dorton, Bell County, Kentucky, are indicative of the AVs' lack of control. Though the exact circumstances are a mystery, the volunteers discovered, in March 1966, that the more influential citizens of Dorton did not want them present. "There are about 5–8 families out of 40," Judy Thomas wrote Dan Fox, "who really want to push us out. But these are people who do carry weight and fear us because they are afraid we might upset their 'safe' position." She also expressed her sense of abandonment when she indicated that VISTA volunteers "*rarely* have any outside [support] . . . in such situations." Because Thomas's fieldman, Jack Rivel, instructed her and Julia McKeon, Thomas's fellow volunteer, to play it "very cool," they remained but accomplished little.[65]

Two months after writing Fox, Thomas and McKeon contacted VISTA headquarters in Washington, DC, and asked to be released from the AV program. "We are now under the Council of the Southern Mountains (Appalachian Volunteers)," they informed the national office, "and wish to transfer to the Bell County Economic Opportunity Council, Inc." They listed three reasons for their request: the "lack of communication with [their] present sponsor"; the fact that their work in Dorton was "blocked by the power group's hostility"; and the belief that they could be of immediate use in the nearby city of Middlesborough.[66]

As the summer of 1966 approached, the Appalachian Volunteer program expanded dramatically in terms of participants but not necessarily in terms of their base of support. By early 1966, the patronage of local governments that the AV program enjoyed during its initial months of operation began to erode. As volunteers entered the mountains and assumed (or tried to assume) leadership roles by becoming teachers or serving as go-betweens connecting the local people with the county seat, indigenous local leaders both in the towns and in the outlying communities began to move against them.[67] School superintendents in particular stalled if Volunteer initiatives did not in some way benefit them.

Much more disturbing, however, were the problems emerging within the AV ranks. The failure to control information about the program and the Volunteers' perception of abandonment by the Council of the Southern Mountains hurt morale. At best, some volunteers, including those who wanted to continue their assignments in the mountains, sought other sponsors. At worst, they abandoned their assignments. The CSM's War on Poverty in eastern Kentucky faced serious challenges on nearly every front, and the poverty warriors' responses to those challenges created even greater conflict.

5

The New Model Army

The Appalachian Volunteers Splits from the Council of the Southern Mountains

Never have I seen so well organized, sensible and tactful an approach, based on really sensitive appreciation of the delicate relationship between people and those who come to "help" them.... [Do not change a thing, only] worry about losing what you have.

—Harvard psychologist and AV consultant
Robert Coles to Dan Fox, July 13, 1965

Thanks a lot. Until last week I was in a county with a lousy sponsor and eleven lousy Vistas. Then came along the four from Berea. We now have a lousy sponsor and 15 lousy Vistas. Let's cure poverty by teaching remedial physics, weaving baskets and flirting with boys. Add that to a sponsor who is going to cure poverty by building art colonies in ruined coal towns and you end up with lousy letters from a depressed Vista.

—Clay County, WV, VISTA volunteer
Ellen Weisman to Dan Fox, October 11, 1965

By May 1966, Loyal Jones, the assistant director of the Council of the Southern Mountains (CSM), faced a serious conundrum. On the one hand, their accomplishments sparked in the Appalachian Volunteers (AVs) a desire to get closer to the heart of the mountains—by moving their headquarters to the city of Bristol, which straddled the Tennessee-Virginia border. From the organization's founding, Jones admitted, the Council considered the idea of an independent Appalachian Volunteers. Moreover, recent experience had led some AV members to question the leadership of Ayer and the CSM. On the other hand, should the AVs leave, the CSM could lose control of its most visible, most notable effort in its long history. "As the War on

Poverty heated up, and as more people became involved in it, . . . as projects became more controversial, particularly the Appalachian Volunteers," Jones recalled, "I counseled the Office of Economic Opportunity to separate them from the Council." Jones "didn't believe" that, should the AVs relocate, "it would be possible . . . for the [CSM] to administer that project."[1]

This was, unfortunately, not the only problem Jones faced at that time. A long-standing Council employee, Jones—a native of western North Carolina and, like many of his counterparts, a graduate of Berea College—first came to the CSM in 1958 to run the organization while the director, Perley Ayer, went on leave to study rural sociology. On Ayer's return, Jones took up the position of assistant director. Though he may have been more sympathetic to the Volunteers' emerging frustration with the War on Poverty than was the rest of the "far more conservative" CSM, Jones still had sympathy for Ayer's administrative style. More just a naively "neutral stance," Ayer's "call to partnership," Jones contended (paraphrasing David Lilienthal), got "everybody . . . involved . . . in a certain political sense and in an educational sense and at the end . . . they would feel that it was their program rather than somebody else's." Thus, the "call to partnership" actually "democratized programs" and gave all levels of society a sense of ownership, which, Jones believed, would ensure success. In the end, because Ayer had hired him, Jones threw his support behind the partnership philosophy. For its part, the Office of Economic Opportunity (OEO) favored having one of its signature programs attached to a relatively stable, "church-related, . . . old-line liberal organization." These two decisions—one by Jones and one by the OEO—proved fateful for both the War on Poverty in Appalachia and the Council of the Southern Mountains.[2]

Jones, however, was not the only poverty warrior at a crossroads. As the epigraphs to this chapter illustrate, the Appalachian Volunteers as an organization was in the midst of a metamorphosis. Contrary to Coles's warning not to change a thing, by the start of 1966, it did not have to worry about losing what it had—that was already gone. The Volunteers were, as we have seen, no longer truly Appalachian, and the consequences for reform efforts in the region were profound. For one thing, the inclusion of more and more outsiders meant the importation of more and more ideas and mores that were foreign to Appalachia. Also, the Volunteers were increasingly willing to confront, rather than (as the CSM advocated) cooperate with, the local political establishment as they sought "to help adults in forming a community organization so that they may be better able to participate in their County Economic effort." As county officials balked, the reformers faced a choice. They could accept the Council's philosophy and follow the lead of county officials, or they could reject it and gird themselves for battle. As the AVs faced increasing opposition in the field and the CSM lost control of its young poverty warriors, the choice grew easier and easier. Change, then, was at the center of the Appalachian Volunteer experience in early 1966.[3]

Up to this point, the AVs believed that nearly every rural Appalachian welcomed them with open arms. Certainly, they maintained that this was true, despite growing evidence to the contrary of the Appalachians' actual opinions. Some AV members began to feel that the inclusion of VISTA volunteers jeopardized AV efforts. However, individual VISTA volunteers were not the problem. The problem was the inflexibility of the "administratively centered program" that sponsored them. VISTA imposed on impoverished communities, one AV wrote, a set of "predetermined ideas from D.C." The Volunteers' efforts, by contrast, were characterized by their "understanding and feelings for the worth of every man," while "government controlled programs view people by statistics." Linking the AV and VISTA programs threatened that understanding. Further, few mountain residents recognized the Appalachian Volunteers as a government program. "Even though our major source of funds is OEO," an unnamed AV concluded, "we are still separated from their failures. It would be awkward for me to work in Eastern Kentucky if people realize that I was just another government employee there to help them." This volunteer also worried about AVs training VISTA volunteers. If there were any "failures" on the part of these federally supported volunteers, the fault, the AV reasoned, would be perceived as resting with the Appalachian Volunteers. Ultimately, the AV member felt that the Appalachian Volunteers could continue to utilize federal money and VISTA personnel only as long as the tie between the AVs and VISTA went unrecognized.[4]

As AVs and VISTA volunteers worked through 1965 and into 1966, more and more AVs came to feel the same way, soured, perhaps, by experiences similar to that of Bill Wells, who in the spring of 1965 reported on an Elliott County woman who cooperated with the VISTA program because she expected monetary compensation. She had worked with the Volunteers, Wells believed, in the hope of getting herself out of financial difficulty (her own self-centered War on Poverty) and had become "dissatisfied with the community and with the Council for not showing her more material appreciation for the work she had been doing." Such self-interest was hardly what the Appalachian Volunteers wanted motivating their acceptance by local communities.[5]

One observant AV member, reporting from the Leslie County community of Trace Fork, spelled out the damage inflicted on the organization by the inclusion of so many non-Appalachian Volunteers. "The very fact that a volunteer goes into a community to assist, a fact which is realized by everyone no matter how much it is avoided and played down by the [volunteer], degrades, threatens, and sometimes angers the mountain people." The "college outsider," the volunteer continued, "is viewed from the start as having a superior education and wider background." In conclusion, the writer claimed, the mountaineer, "burdened by a feeling of inadequacy," "tends to feel ill at ease, talk only when necessary—volunteering nothing—and feel disinclined to accept the outsider's suggestions or his friendship."[6]

A second critic of the move toward nonnative volunteers echoed the Trace Fork reporter's remarks about the resentment felt toward outsiders and restated the connection many AV workers made between poverty and the problems in local governments. Writing from Thousandsticks, Leslie County, the volunteer Judith Allcock related how local teachers resented the work of every outsider who came to the community to improve it. In fact, the present teacher "harangued . . . the Volunteers for coming in and promising to send supplies and do things and then not come back": "She also resented that they considered Thousandsticks poor." In her report, Allcock related how one volunteer commented to the teacher that the children were "really culturally deprived." This "must have confirmed [the teacher's] feeling that outsiders look down on the community." According to Allcock, two local teachers reported that photographers came to the community with their own mules, on which they placed children for publicity pictures. Those same teachers claimed that the journalists asked one mother "to take off her kids shoes" before they took pictures and asked other people "to claim they were hungry." These incidents, Allcock concluded, led the locals to think that all proffered aid, including AV aid, was an attempt either to exploit the mountaineers for personal gain or *"to get votes for the superintendent."*[7]

Allcock's report highlights the two fundamental problems that the

Volunteers faced. First, they had to determine what role, if any, outsiders should play in the AV program. Second, they had to determine how to deal with those local officials whom they—and a significant number of local people—considered to be corrupt. The solutions to these problems—which came quickly—had long-term consequences.

Allcock provided the AVs with part of the solution. Of particular concern to most rural mountaineers, she stated, was the overtly missionary attitude held by so many who came to the region to "'help the poor.'" The Trace Fork AV concurred. Throughout the report, she repeatedly warned against exhibiting any type of behavior that could in any way be interpreted as a demonstration of superiority. Few Volunteers heeded the warning, however—not even Allcock herself, her reports (which described "a dull routine way of life" in Thousandsticks) exuding an air of superiority and missionary purpose.[8] More important, the AV organization never adequately addressed this issue, focusing instead on relations with local officials.

Augmenting this dilemma was the AVs' growing fear that their efforts addressed only the symptoms of poverty, not the root cause. Already by early 1965, this perception had gained credence. In Pike County, Kentucky, a school renovation project yielded disastrous results. According to the AV fieldman Flem Messer, not only did the local community fail to take part, but the project proved to be "a waste of materials, and more importantly a great waste of enthusiasm for . . . the Appalachian Volunteers program." Certain unknown individuals "vandalized and [broke] the windows" in the newly refurbished building.[9] Though the AVs never determined who was responsible for the vandalism, it convinced some of the activists that simply repairing schoolhouses and broadening the mountaineers' cultural horizons through curriculum enhancement did nothing to change local attitudes or empower local people to deal with their problems on their own. In addition, this event echoed a warning that Tom Gish, the editor of the *Whitesburg, KY, Mountain Eagle*, had issued to the CSM as early as July 1964. Though he contended that education was "the only way out [of poverty] for Eastern Kentucky," Gish also claimed: "The existing political and economic power structure in the mountains [did] not really want change and will oppose any real reform. . . . Those who wish to bring about change—those who want community development—are going to have to go beyond the political and economic leadership to the people themselves, and deal directly with them." Following this vandalism episode, the AV organization began to seek a new direction and began to question the inclusive, nonconfrontational approach championed by the Council.[10]

Appalachian Volunteer problems, however, went beyond incidents of vandalism and the questions of an influential eastern Kentucky newspaper editor. As the Volunteers continued their work in the field, they again encountered recalcitrant local county officials and failed projects. One particularly problematic area was northeastern Kentucky. Carter, Elliott, Greenup, Lewis, Morgan, and Rowan counties were part of a multicounty community action program (CAP) known as the Northeast Kentucky Area Redevelopment Council, and, as early as mid-1965, when the Redevelopment Council was not yet two months old, the Appalachian Volunteers experienced difficulties with that agency's director, Lee Taylor. It appears that the AVs failed to inform Taylor of their activities and coordinate them with those of the Redevelopment Council. For example, on September 21, 1965, Taylor told his Board of Directors that two VISTA volunteers assigned to the CSM's AV program currently worked in Elliott County. He had "not been able to find out their specific duties," but he had "learned that the community was in a turmoil because of something related to [their] presence." In an attempt to resolve the problem, Taylor tried to get the volunteers recalled and told the CSM "that it would be wise and certainly helpful . . . if their VISTAs were withdrawn from our area."[11]

Taylor's complaints did not end there. He also reported that the Redevelopment Council had four of its own VISTA volunteers placed in neighboring Lewis County but "discovered that they were not free to *perform* the tasks given them": "Representatives of the Council of the Southern Mountains consistently countermanded the direction of . . . our director in that [county]." Taylor claimed that the Redevelopment Council VISTA volunteers confronted their CSM "tormentors" and informed them that they would follow the instructions of the Redevelopment Council, not the CSM. Later that morning, after the confrontation, "a representative of the Council of the Southern Mountains childishly stole a distributor cap" off the automobile of one of the Lewis County volunteers.[12]

Taylor also believed that CSM-AV training of VISTA volunteers biased them against the area councils. Along with a few fellow Redevelopment Council employees, Taylor attended an AV training session in Berea in the hope of "getting some of these people assigned to our Area Council." "We had the distinct impression," he reported, "that these people [the VISTA trainees] had been trained to believe that the members of an Area Council and its staff were their worst enemies." The CSM, moreover, "knowing that all young people do not subscribe to this philosophy," would not allow anyone to personally interview the potential volunteers and would allow CAPs to have VISTA volunteers "only as the [CSM] assigned them."[13]

Though the CSM staff member Alan Zuckerman tried to pacify Taylor, the Council of the Southern Mountains faced an uphill battle. "You should realize . . . that your organization has made a very unfavorable impression on me," Taylor wrote Zuckerman. For any agreement to be reached, he continued, the CSM would need to understand that, though it had "certain facilities and services available," they must be "offered to and not forced upon" other agencies if they are to be "of any value." Additionally, Taylor noted, the CSM could expect the full cooperation of his (or any other) agency only if he was "fully informed, consulted with and ha[d] prior understanding of the program" in terms of how it would fit into the Redevelopment Council's own activities. Before he and Zuckerman could even meet, Taylor indicated, the CSM would have to remove its workers from his region "so that the turmoil and resentment [could] subside."[14]

Both the letter and the spirit of Taylor's statements explicitly placed the functions of his and all other CAPs ahead of those of the Appalachian Volunteers. The Volunteers, Taylor argued, were to support and aid the CAPs, which, in his view, had the primary responsibility for solving Appalachian poverty. Equally important, his reaction to Volunteer activity confirmed Gish's warning about dealing directly with the people. Nevertheless, if the AVs bypassed or ignored the many CAP directors, school superintendents, and other local elected officials, they would violate the CSM's philosophy that all segments of eastern Kentucky's population be included in reform efforts.

Oddly enough, it was representatives of the OEO who came to observe and evaluate the Volunteer program that provided the mountain reformers with additional incentive for moving further from the CSM's traditional position of cooperation. Following his visit to eastern Kentucky, the OEO evaluation team member Frank Prial wrote: "The poverty program in Eastern Kentucky is in trouble and unless some drastic changes are made rather rapidly, there is a good chance it may never get off the ground." Describing the region as a place where "none of the standard rules of democracy apply," Prial articulated the growing concerns of many of the Appalachian Volunteers. "There is a hostility to outside assistance," he wrote to the OEO's mid-Atlantic regional director Jack Ciaccio, "unless the power structure can use it to turn a profit." The powers that be, moreover, were "resisting strenuously the threat that the poverty program will alter the status quo in their areas."[15]

Supporting the local political leaders, Prial reported, were the coal operators. In fact, he declared: "The coal operators are closely allied—often literally related to—the political powers in these counties. Together, they have no intention of permitting Federal poverty program money to upset the delicate economic balance they have maintained for many years." After detailing the nepotism inherent to this corrupt political system, Prial hit on what he perceived as yet another key factor underpinning the widespread political corruption—the absence of an articulate opposition to the ruling oligarchy. "The absence of any middle class is one of the factors contributing to the perpetuation of poverty in Eastern Kentucky." Doctors, lawyers, all the "better teachers," and even the United Mine Workers have "vanished from the scene." Only those too old, too young, or too sick to fight back, and "those who prey upon them," Prial argued, were left in the mountains.[16]

As a result, according to Prial, those who administered the OEO programs, in particular the county-run CAPs, in Appalachian Kentucky "evidenced in some cases little or no sympathy for the poor." At best, the local program directors had "not the faintest notion of what is expected of them, of the meaning of social action, or of the import and content of the Economic Opportunities Act." Prial went so far as to include in his attack the Council of the Southern Mountains because its personnel were "overly conditioned to working through the established power structure." The Council's executive director "would rather not jeopardize the outfit's prestige by tilting at windmills."[17]

Prial asserted that most county CAP officials "expressed considerable disappointment" in the training sessions administered by the CSM. Reflecting the "delivery of services" attitude of most county politicians, one local program director informed Prial: "We need hard-nosed information about preparing programs and submitting them, not a lot of vague stuff about

how to deal with people." For his part, Prial believed "that the Council people had not really prepared an agenda or thought about what they wanted
to say." Though he admitted that the CSM's lines of communication were
"invaluable" in establishing contacts in the mountains, he found virtually
all leadership in the mountains, whether that of the Council or local elected
officials, wanting. "I believe that someone is going to have to strongarm the
power structures in the poor coal counties," he summarized, "if anything is
to be accomplished in the war on poverty." Finally, because the political situation in the mountains precluded the replacement of the ineffective, uncar-
ing local CAP directors, "they should be superceded as soon as possible by
trained regional directors." This regional director, responsible for three or
four counties, would provide the OEO with "extremely close surveillance"
of federally funded antipoverty projects in Appalachian Kentucky.[18]

Jack Ciaccio, the head of the OEO's mid-Atlantic office, which was responsible for the Kentucky programs, refused to take Prial's evaluation at
face value. Ciaccio claimed that the report echoed the voices of two of the
mountains' most persistent critics, Harry Caudill and Tom Gish, and did
"not tell us anything we did not already know." Moreover, while Prial made
sweeping generalizations about the people and politics of the region, Ciaccio warned against such a practice: "There are differences among E. Ky.
counties, among the people who make up the power structures, and among
the people who live in the hollows. We have to get the facts on a county-
by-county basis." Though Caudill and Gish sounded the "clarion call . . . for
sweeping and massive changes," they had, Ciaccio felt, "little interest in the
day-by-day changes that will add up to solid progress over the long run." To
caution against the ready acceptance of Caudill's (and Prial's) views, Ciaccio
argued that Caudill represented the "opposition" that Prial maintained was
missing in eastern Kentucky. In fact, this opposition was vice chairman of
the Letcher County CAP. Indicating that Caudill had a disagreement with
other members of the Letcher County agency, Ciaccio revealed that he had
"threatened . . . to resign his position." "Must the articulate opposition have
a voice," Ciaccio asked, "or complete control?"[19]

Ciaccio did not, however, reject Prial's report in its entirety. On the
contrary, he readily admitted that the representatives of eastern Kentucky's
public and private agencies—two of the three legs of the OEO's "stool"—
on the local CAP boards were either "identical with the power structure in

E. Ky. communities, or . . . controlled by [it]." He further recognized: "If existing services are not improved, the war on poverty will be just a series of political plums for the local power structure. And existing services will be improved only if the poor are organized, and protest—*long and loud*— about the lousy job that is being done."[20]

With the goal of circumventing the local power structures in the region, Ciaccio cited OEO policies that would, he hoped, lead to a "*diffusion of power*" in the Appalachian poverty program. Included in this plan was the funding of the Council of the Southern Mountains, the formation of multi-county CAPs (which the OEO believed would actually dilute local control), and the insistence that poor people be included on those programs' boards as a requirement for federal funding "even though we realize that in many cases the [poor] people selected are probably controlled." These moves, Ciaccio maintained, would prevent a monopoly of antipoverty programs in the mountains and would help establish the "missing ingredient" or the third of the three legs of the stool—"organized opposition." If need be, Ciaccio stated, the OEO "should be prepared to recognize a *neighborhood* organization as a CAA [community action agency], where the local power structure refuses to go along on resident participation."[21]

In fact, Ciaccio did just that. According to an AV report, the Volunteers' organizing work in the community of Verda, in Harlan County, was so successful—even across racial lines—that the OEO funded the fledgling community organization independently of the already existing county CAP run by the county school superintendent. Though the Volunteers reveled in their accomplishment, the superintendent, they claimed, was determined to gain control of the Verda program. Ciaccio, nonetheless, supported this sort of action. "It is essential," he argued, "to get meaningful resident participation in the development and conduct of CAP's in Eastern Kentucky. We want to go all out on this not only because it is what the law says and the agency preaches, but because it is the only way the cycle of poverty in Eastern Kentucky can be broken."[22]

As the AVs continued their projects in the mountains, however, evidence supporting Prial's and Gish's perceptions trickled in. For example, near the middle of August 1966, a volunteer working in Fonde, Kentucky, wrote radiantly of the AV effort. "The AV program," she stated, "is simply people—people getting to know people so that each is better off." It was not so important that the children of the community attain academic excellence or that adults learn better sanitary practices: "What matters is that in the exchange people come to have more confidence in themselves and in their own abilities to bring about beneficial change." After returning to college for the fall semester, however, the Fonde volunteer's attitude changed dramatically. Responding to a questionnaire given to those who worked in the Kentucky mountains that summer, she expressed regret that she learned about the community's problems too late to help. She recalled "the anger and frustration that builds up inside of you when someone shares a problem with you—a problem that everyone says has no solution—but a problem that still eats into the joy of living: a lousy school teacher, a coal leasing company that in no way recognizes that human beings are living on its land[,] in its houses[,] in its town."[23]

As AV members attempted follow-ups in counties where they had performed work, they came across schools that had in a very brief period of time become run-down again and communities no better off than before. After the Fonde volunteer revisited that community, she issued a statement that evidently reflected the thoughts of many AVs in 1966:

Fonde can be a pretty rough place; in three hours I learned: One boy flew off in the mines and hit his father with a board . . . ; one of the girls is pregnant and unmarried; Richard still beats Christeen; Dave . . . received the results of the Health Department's test—all three wells were unsafe . . . ; kids still don't have shoes; the people aren't holding community meetings any more; Mr. . . . still drinks up the welfare money. Another 6th grade girl has "quit coming" to school. . . . There's not a lot of surface joy in Fonde. . . . Sometimes I wonder about the real value of AV's in places like Fonde. There are so many problems we're not the solution to. I see Dick's point when he says we by-passed the big problems . . . and threw a lot of time, money and effort into little things that don't amount to no more than memories of good times spent together. . . . I get discouraged when I think of places like [this] because you know what we're doing? We're supplying candles when the house needs to be wired for electricity.[24]

Fonde was not the only community to experience hard times despite the War on Poverty. When asked by the Volunteers what could be done to improve their community, residents of Weeksbury, in Letcher County, revealed how Appalachian landownership patterns perpetuated poverty. "One thing hurts here," one community member announced, "that the companies owns a lot of land. Like where someone would want to clear out a pasture land to raise cattle, well these [coal companies] owns most of them and they won't agree to sell at no price, so thats holding up things that could happen."[25]

Another critic of the present state of the War on Poverty in Appalachia, the AV-trained VISTA volunteer Ellen Weisman, stationed in Clay County, West Virginia, decried the OEO guidelines that required resident participation in CAPs: "Its what we call a farce. Resident participation! Who writes the . . . programs?" she asked rhetorically. Insinuating that the poor with whom she worked had no idea how to conduct themselves at a board meeting or how to formulate an antipoverty plan, she informed Dan Fox: "If the poor knew how to eliminate poverty they wouldn't be poor." Ignorance and apathy born of the fear of the powerful characterized West Virginia's impoverished people, she believed, and the reformers needed to strive for real, fundamental change. "To attack poverty," she wrote Fox, "means to attack the status quo[,] meaning an attack on the local power structure! Does the local power structure want this?"[26]

Even her attempts at organizing the poor, Weisman declared, were "farcical." Highlighting the quiescence she found among the mountaineers, she noted that, when she told the people they "'must all work together,'" "they wonder what the hell for because if [the local politicians] don't profit by what they want they don't get it anyway because they have no way to apply pressure besides a petition that will be filed away." Her frustrating experiences finally caused Weisman to leave her assignment a month early. She did not feel that she had accomplished much during her time in Clay County: "Certainly 4 weeks will not make any difference . . . [and] I do feel guilty about staying. . . . I don't feel honest to myself wasting all that time [and] energy. As for Wash[ington] or the Clay Co. Dev[lopment] Corp[.] is concerned," she closed, "I am . . . car[e]less. They never lived up to their commitment to me."[27]

Others went even further, condemning the Band-Aid approach of not only the Council but the OEO as well. Reporting from Verda, the AV field coordinator Steve Daugherty decried the "obvious paradox" of trying to end poverty "without disturbing the present situation." Frustrated by the county superintendent, who also ran the local CAP and controlled the allocation of federal funds in Harlan County, Daugherty reasoned that, to be effective, the War on Poverty required a "basic reorganization, an abolition . . . of those institutions which initially led to the impoverishment . . . of the Appalachian people." According to Daugherty, James Cawood, the superintendent and chairman of the Harlan CAP board, and Claude Dozier, the CAP's director, wrote OEO proposals for Verda that ignored the community's expressed wishes and concerns. Further, the extended system of patronage provided by the school system, Cawood's and Dozier's positions with the county CAP, and their ability to weave their way through the OEO's bureaucratic obstacles limited the choices available to the people of Verda when, for example, Dozier ignored requests for better roads and instead sought to build a community center that no one wanted. "Persons with a vested interest in the status quo," Daugherty concluded, "have a notoriously poor record in initiating change." The federal antipoverty effort, he continued, simply "strengthen[ed] one of the most insidious forces of oppression in eastern Kentucky." These experiences, according to one activist, "radicalized" Ogle and the AVs, who now realized that school repairs only made the situation more profitable for a corrupt system. Volunteer renovation projects did nothing but save local politicians money.[28]

Having come to the position that the horrid situation in the mountains could be attributed to the local political system, the Appalachian Volunteers decided to change course and organize the people around such issues as school system reform, welfare rights, and anti-strip-mining legislation. Confrontation became the new AV strategy. Through this new approach, the AVs sought to undermine the entrenched interests in eastern Kentucky—the coal companies and the political system—in order to effect substantial structural change.[29]

Warning against abandoning the traditional Council philosophy of cooperation, Ayer informed all members of the Council staff: "Our service projects are possible mainly because donors and authorities trust our wisdom and integrity. These, in turn, rest firmly on the basic concept and philosophy of the Council. If this is abandoned or adulterated we will have disqualified our Council for public trust." "This can happen," he cautioned, "by carelessness, by credit seeking, by surrender to expediency." The desire to confront rather than to cooperate with local county officials was such a "surrender to expediency," straining the overall CSM approach to reform, and, in Ayer's mind, jeopardizing the overall effectiveness of the Council. While Ayer recognized that the county judges and school superintendents were "rogues," he also understood that, with the OEO's "three-legged stool" approach, "you've got to deal with them."[30]

The Appalachian Volunteers wanted to "deal" with county officials, but not in the ways Ayer thought appropriate. Believing that nearly absolute political control by a few public officials rendered the majority of mountaineers voiceless, the AVs maintained that the oppressed could not effectively fight for their rights without "the necessary aid coming from outside the county." This aid was the AVs and their VISTA allies. As new VISTA and AV recruits entered the activists' ranks, this attitude toward mountain county governments became part of the training they received. It also became a source of conflict between the Appalachian Volunteers and its parent organization, the Council of the Southern Mountains.[31]

The disagreement over how to effect reform in the mountains was not the only source of friction between the CSM and the AVs in late 1965 and early 1966. Some Volunteer members thought that the operation's headquarters in Berea was too far from where the AVs did most of their work. In April 1966, the AV leadership proposed to the CSM Board of Directors that Volunteer headquarters move to a place more centrally located in the Appalachian region. Though associated with the mountains for over a century, Berea was on the fringe of the mountain region. A more fitting location, many volunteers felt, was the city of Bristol, Tennessee. Though a move would prove costly in both time and money—the Volunteers would need to move office equipment, recruit and train new office staff, and lease office space—the advantages, many believed, far outweighed these drawbacks.[32]

On the positive side of the relocation equation, the move would save considerable sums of money in terms of purchasing and distributing supplies to the workers in the field. In addition, the size of the AV operation, it was argued, "strain[ed] the facilities of Berea and the tolerance of its inhabitants." The CSM board chairman Donald Fessler informed the other members of the Board of Directors: "[These] idealistic, highly dedicated men and women . . . have had their problems and their brushes with the more staid thinking of the Berea College faculty." More important, especially in light of those Dorton (Bell County) AV members who defected because of what they believed was a lack of support from the CSM, the Bristol region would permit the central staff "to provide much assistance to the limited field staff." The move would also "demonstrate our willingness to live in and be part of the area we are committed to serving." Most significantly, for both the Volunteers and the Council, this physical separation "would force [them] to work out relationships—both administratively and policy [*sic*]—between the AV program and the CSM central office."[33]

The proposal to move the Appalachian Volunteers far from the Council's watchful eye should have come as no surprise to Ayer. Since its inception, the Council had entertained the possibility of a separate, independent AV program. One of the first alternatives discussed by the Council of the Southern Mountains concerning the formation of an antipoverty group was the establishment of an independent organization. Under that plan, the CSM would have provided only temporary professional leadership. Ultimately, the Council, of course, placed the Appalachian Volunteers and its staff under its direction. Nevertheless, the existence of an independent AV organization, even in 1966, remained a possibility. Evidence of this dates as early as August 1964, when a Council special advisory committee stated: "At the time when the Council of the Southern Mountains ceases to perform administrative services for the AVs, they should then become full fledged members of the Kentucky Development Committee." The question before the CSM board now was whether the Council should grant the Appalachian Volunteers administrative independence.[34]

For his part, Ayer believed that the Appalachian Volunteers should remain in Berea and that the organization still needed the CSM's guidance and direction. Writing to Fessler that April, he claimed that in his "honest judgment such a move would not be in the interests of the Council or the AVs." Ayer stated that the only reason he submitted the idea to the board was because he had promised Ogle that he would do so. Implying, however, that Ogle engaged in less than honest behavior, Ayer told Fessler that Ogle refused to recommend a course of action when the CSM director and the AV leader first discussed the proposed move. When the two met with the board, however, Ogle presented a strong recommendation for administrative independence. Believing that this subject was only in the "discussion" stage, Ayer felt himself, he indicated, to be at a disadvantage when the board proceeded to weigh the matter.[35]

This apparent administrative end run was not Ayer's sole concern. As he wrote to Fessler: "[The] AV program . . . , as magnificent as it is . . . , is being implemented by a group of eager young enthusiasts whose standards and judgements are not always consistent with what the Council stands for." Should the Volunteers relocate, Ayer contended, problems with the AV program "will get worse rather than better." Arguing that, if the Council expected "a responsible, high degree of leadership . . . in terms of character standards and behavior," as opposed to a "merely enthusiastic organization," the board needed to keep the AV headquarters in Berea, where the young people "will be benefited by our leadership."[36]

Despite Ayer's protests, the CSM board voted to approve the AVs' move to Bristol. According to Fessler, it determined that, if the Volunteers resettled, the question of complete independence, still a future possibility, could be easily settled without arousing "ill feelings or reflections on the soundness and integrity of either organization." Moreover, there "was little evidence that relations between the A.V. leaders and the executive offices of the Council would improve under present conditions." Therefore: "Moving the A.V. headquarters to [Bristol] at least offered the possibility that a better modus operandi could be worked out."[37]

The exchange between Ayer and Fessler revealed more than the AVs' desire to move their offices. Ayer's concerns about character and the AVs' disregard for the Council's philosophy were not superficial, aired merely in an attempt to sway the vote toward his position. They were, in fact, well grounded in what he considered to be disturbing developments within the ranks of the Appalachian Volunteers. Through confrontations with the Volunteer staff, Ayer demonstrated his obsession with publicity and how that influenced Council funding. His opposition to the more freewheeling Volunteer program, therefore, centered on the AVs' personal behavior and how it affected publicity and funding.

Tension between the two organizations had, in fact, surfaced soon after the founding of the AVs. In a memorandum dated March 19, 1964, only five days after the AVs adopted their new bylaws, Ayer reprimanded Milton Ogle, the AV director, after reading a *Berea Citizen* article that announced the first federal grant to the new reform effort. Ayer noted that the article ignored the Council's responsibility for the Appalachian Volunteers program. Referring to it as an "intolerable, senseless, and unjust situation," he pointed out that the Area Redevelopment Administration awarded that first grant to the CSM, not the AVs, as the article suggested. In defending what he believed to be the Council's role in the reform program, Ayer told Ogle that he resented being "purposely and deliberately disregarded as one, if not the basic, factor in the success of what has happened to date."[38]

Unfortunately for Ayer, his tirade had little effect. In yet another memo that same month, he reproached the AV staff member Phil Conn, a Berea College graduate, for not being a team player. Conn, the memo disclosed, neglected Council staff meetings and failed to inform Council leadership of his activities. Ayer had a similar problem with another CSM-AV staff member, Jim Blair. Blair, who worked out of an AV field office, had a "notice in his window saying 'Appalachian Volunteers' only." Again referring to this as "intolerable," Ayer demanded: "If the Council is going to have an office . . . anywhere . . . , it needs to be a Council office." Ayer was adamant, he wrote in a communiqué to Ogle, that anyone who worked for the Council "clearly publicizes the fact that they represent the Council, with specific assignment in AVs." Ayer experienced a similar problem when he tried to call the CSM staff member Bill Wells. Wells's assignment at that time was in the AV program. The telephone company in Cincinnati, where Wells was located, had no listing for the Council of the Southern Mountains and, in fact, had never heard of the Council. When Ayer requested the operator look it up under Well's personal name, the response was: "'Oh, yes, the AVs; we know them.'"[39]

Ayer failed in his attempts to force the AVs into line, and he soon became frustrated over yet another article about the Volunteers in the *Berea Citizen*. This piece said that Ayer "spoke about the Council of the Southern Mountains and its relationship to Appalachian Volunteers as if [he] had spoken about the University of Kentucky or the Leslie County School Board or the National Council of Churches and the relationship between any one of these and the [AVs]." Having checked with the *Citizen* and determined that the printed statement was not an "editorial misunderstanding," Ayer blamed Ogle for the misrepresentation and took him to task: "I cannot tolerate repeated references to the Appalachian Volunteers as an agency which has only a tolerant and friendly relationship to . . . the Council." Expressing his special concern, he continued: "I have been subject to a 'ground swell' of comment from within your own [organization], . . . indicating an attitude of impatience with the Council as if it were a cumbersome and unnecessary partner, tolerated by necessity. It would seem that for the overall philosophy of the Council itself the field staff could not care less."[40]

Ayer probably did not realize just how accurate his statement was. On two fronts, personal morality and reform philosophy, the Appalachian Volunteers differed dramatically from Ayer's vision of the Council. Most disturbing to the CSM was that many AV workers openly expressed these attitudes. As young men and women from all over the country poured into Berea for AV training for the 1966 summer project, they challenged the moral sensibilities of the CSM. With the hopes of preparing the new recruits for their stay among the mountaineers, the Council issued a document entitled "You Are Responsible: Some Thoughts on the Appalachian Volunteer Summer Project." Council leaders tried to impress on their new soldiers that it was the people in the local communities in which they would spend the summer that would "be left with the results—and consequences" of the summer project. While in the mountains, the CSM leaders informed the potential AV workers, they would be "neither a member of the community . . . nor an unwanted intruder." Nevertheless, the directive went out: "Act like you were a guest of some pretty particular and somewhat conservative people you wanted to impress." "If a Volunteer is to have maximum rapport with the community," it was further stipulated, "he should try to live up to the expectations of the most particular residents, but not hold himself above associating with the least particular."[41]

In order to give each volunteer the greatest opportunity for living up to mountaineers' expectations, "You Are Responsible" provided a sort of "code of conduct." "You shouldn't dress ostentatiously," it warned, "but try to be neat." In addition, rural people "tend not to respond too quickly to fads in dress, hair, beads, makeup, etc." Girls, moreover, should "do a little asking around before appearing in shorts." The "training manual" also addressed drinking and dating. "In some cases," it explained, "a drink or two with the boys may be a necessary step to establishing rapport . . . but *nobody* respects a drunk Volunteer." Finally, because "new standards of dating behavior are not adopted so quickly in many rural communities," and because the Volunteers themselves "should realize that they will be glamorous people to their contemporaries in the community," relationships between volunteers or between volunteers and local people should be "conducted in a manner respectful of community standards."[42]

As helpful and appropriate as these suggestions were, it is intriguing that the leaders of the program believed it necessary to put them in print and distribute them to all potential volunteers. Ayer and the Council must have received complaints, in addition to those concerning the summer training, concerning the personal behavior of some of their volunteers from the people with whom they were working or suspected that certain undesirable situations had occurred. An examination of a series of memos between Ayer and the two top AV officials, Ogle and Fox, suggests that the latter explanation is accurate. In the spring of 1966, Ayer felt it necessary to question Ogle's and Fox's stance on the social conduct of the AVs. He told the two: "I have before me two written statements and I have, in addition, oral confirmation that we did badly on this score." He then quoted what information he felt most fully illustrated his point:

> "From the standpoint of the job that we committed ourselves to do . . . there is no excuse for drunken sex parties in Lexington or anywhere else. If we . . . truly seek to help the people of Appalachia, then we better give some serious thought . . . to what we mean by 'help.' . . . [I]f we mean immorality, drunkenness, vulgarity . . . we are not here to help Appalachia, but will help destroy it." "The Lexington weekends were the worst part of the AV [1965] summer project. There were drinking parties that the staff were involved in, not only in Lexington but here in Berea. . . . [S]ome of the AV staff brought in liquor so it was available to the kids who wanted it in one last big fling before they left for the mountains." One VISTA bragged "about the amount of liquor consumed and said the place could have floated away with booze, and girls were available if desired."[43]

This information had a profound impact on Ayer. Maintaining that this type of conduct was damaging to the Council of the Southern Mountains and its attempts at reform, he demanded of Ogle and Fox "a statement in black and white" of their "commitment to an overall Council approach which will set a high standard of moral purpose." In addition, he required, "of all people, officially sponsored and directed by us, leadership which neither by example, tacit permission, nor neglect allows moral disintegration to occur." "I am so deeply concerned about this," Ayer concluded, "that unless we can achieve some unanimous commitment on this issue and some practical plans to do better, I shall feel it necessary to discontinue sponsorship of the whole program."[44]

Ayer's admonition was a result of a disagreement with Fox over the degree of authority that the CSM and AV leaders should exercise over the personal conduct and morality of the volunteers. While Fox never denied that incidents such as those mentioned in the report had happened, he took the position that "[the] attitudes I have acquired about drinking, fornication, smoking, [and] birth control . . . must be as irrelevant as possible in the process of making the decisions which fall to me as a working professional." He argued that "whether the men concerned [were] alcoholics, teetotalers, swordsmen or celibates" was not his concern, as long as they performed their jobs. As in the U.S. Army, "Saturday night, away from the front, belongs to the private man." Unless the actions in question harmed the Volunteer program, he concluded, "I cannot, as a professional, call forth a moral code and lay on its wrath."[45]

Ayer disagreed. A person's attitude, he believed, was inherently relevant to his job, especially when that job was as a Council employee. "The personal character values by which all these people are guided," he claimed, "have a direct relationship to their responsibility and effectiveness and therefore their employability by the Council." Ayer asserted that the Appalachian Volunteers were, by the very nature of their work, on the job every hour of every day, and he insisted that the leadership must "take firm and uncompromising steps" to ensure that further "moral disintegration" did not occur.[46]

While the debate over Volunteer morality raged, Ayer's concept of the Council's philosophy was hit with yet another broadside. This second blow not only breached the CSM's morality standard, but it also violated the call for cooperative efforts in reform. Following their AV training, two VISTA volunteers (and former Berea College students) "of unquestioned integrity and personal dedication" presented the CSM with five pages of grievances against the AVs. These complaints ran from charges of graft to Volunteer advocacy of revolt against local governments. According to these volunteers, their trainers told them that "Berea [College] treats its employees as servants and that the poor are held in servile stations in order to enrich the college coffers." In addition, the trainees noted that, while the college administration controlled the local CAP and excluded the poor, they, under their AV supervisors, were to "purge the rottenness that now existed": "The poor, under direction of the AVs, were going to revolt and overthrow the powers that be. . . . We also learned that we must hate (1) VISTA Washington Feds, (2) our CAP's, (3) the professionals in our area." Finally, the Volunteer trainers informed their charges that "all CAPS were rat finks and were to be worked against." No such program was "worth spitting on, much less merit cooperation."[47]

Learning whom to hate was only the beginning, according to these two unnamed sources. The Volunteers, they claimed, also wanted the funds allocated to the VISTA volunteers for training purposes: "We were asked to sign a statement saying we used all the money VISTA Washington allotted us for training and then turn the money over to the Appalachian Volunteers so that they could do their good works. . . . They over looked the fact that the money was scheduled to go back to Washington." After being called "money grabbing bigots" by their AV trainers, the two "conceded to put the money in a trust fund for un-wed mothers—in the name of the wife of one of the AV staff members, of course": "Whether the project is good or bad, there is still the element of misappropriation of funds. . . . The money was supposed to go back to VISTA Washington."[48]

Alcohol played a role in this indictment as well. "Then came Saturday and the beer blast," the volunteers reported, "held in a private home in Bristol." Admittedly, "a few" VISTA volunteers had beer. More to the point, however: "The AVs arrived with bottles sticking out of every pocket. . . . They marched in and proceeded to drape themselves across every girl in the room. . . . From there on they really impressed Bristol." According to the complaint, the volunteers "paraded through the hotel [lobby] swinging their bottles and slapping the gals on the fanny." This sort of debauchery continued at the trainees' "graduation." The AVs forced a party on the VISTA volunteers, singing "bawdy songs" while "the kissing of the VISTA girls by the AV boys proceeded with vigor." "We were really glad," they announced, that this finally "ended our little tour de farce with AVs."[49]

While these statements offended the sensibilities of Perley Ayer, equally disturbing was the undercurrent of superiority that the two VISTA critics noticed in the Volunteers. As they put it: "The poor folks' children were there watching [the volunteers on an unspecified project] but the AVs treated them like lepers or something." The VISTA trainees claimed that they did not want to degrade the AV organization but warned that it needed more careful supervision and that "the quality of the person and their motives" required a greater examination "before turning them loose on the defenseless mountain folk." At one training session, the informants recalled, the Volunteer instructor began "to expound and glorify the AV field work as Christ-like and all goodness and mercy." "Another facet I did not appreciate," the trainees continued, "was that all through our training the AVs were set up as the great and glorious saviors of the economically crucified." In the end, they summarized, "[we] can't help but be critical of our training."[50]

Swayed by such evidence, Ayer not surprisingly believed that the situation would only deteriorate if the Appalachian Volunteers relocated to Bristol. He repeatedly asked Ogle not to move AV headquarters despite the board's approval, but Ogle persisted with the move regardless. Further, not one of the Volunteers made any attempt to address Ayer's other objections. This increasingly antagonistic situation came to a head as the AVs prepared for the 1966 summer project. On May 2, 1966, after he learned that Ogle and others "met secretly with members of the Board of directors to try to get [him] 'retired,'" Ayer accused Ogle of "organizing a general staff rebellion." Because of this, and "for the sake of the Council and its present and future effectiveness within its philosophy and total program," Ayer fired Ogle and Fox. "Your first responsibility," their original letter of appointment read, "will be to the philosophy and overall current purposes and program of the Council itself." Their conduct in the recent past, Ayer informed them, breached the terms of their contract. The two top AV officials, Ayer believed, reneged on this most important obligation.[51]

Unfortunately, Ayer's actions did not resolve his troubles with the Volunteers. As a professional courtesy, he kept both men on the payroll until the end of the month, but both resigned the next day—along with the entire AV staff. The thirteen staff members who resigned did so in support of Ogle and Fox but also in protest over Ayer's administrative style. "Mr. Ayer has violated the free and inquiring spirit implicit in the Council philosophy," the staff contended, "by attempting to impose upon the rest of the staff his own exclusive system of values and his highly individualized conception of the Council's role." Then, on May 3, 1966, Ogle, Fox, and their thirteen staff members created a nonprofit corporation called the Appalachian Volunteers, Inc.[52]

Initially, support for the independent Appalachian Volunteers appeared less than unanimous. Ayer informed the CSM Board of Directors that at first he believed Washington "would not fund the Appalachian Volunteers independent of the Council." In a surprising move, however, Ayer immediately took the initial steps to ensure that the AVs would receive federal funds. He did everything in his power, he later claimed, to "expedite the transfer in order that their program [would] not be destroyed or damaged."[53]

According to Loyal Jones, the CSM associate director, the OEO had hoped to keep the Volunteers under Council direction but was "forced" to fund the highly visible and successful program after Ayer relieved Fox and Ogle of their responsibilities. Jones, moreover, counseled the OEO to separate the AVs from the CSM immediately after the board approved the Volunteers' request to relocate to Bristol. He "didn't believe it would be possible . . . for the Council of the Southern Mountains to administer that project and be responsible for what they did" after the Volunteers transferred their headquarters. As amicably as possible, Ayer agreed to relinquish Council funds earmarked for the AV program.[54]

Public support among the Appalachian people for the Appalachian Volunteers, Inc., was, nevertheless, less than certain. Joe Barker, a native of Louisville, Tennessee, and longtime associate of the Council of the Southern Mountains, deplored the actions of the AVs. According to Barker, the focus of the War on Poverty should be on education, as the Council believed: "What can you do for young people with only some grade school education if you can't get them back in school? . . . I'm disgusted with poverty programs. And the actions of the volunteers disgusts me some more [and] opens a question whether such a group is capable or qualified to spend . . . public money. . . . The Council is one group I do believe in."[55]

Beliefs, especially those that concerned the United States, its place in the world, and the nature of the country's democratic institutions, were important to many citizens in the mid-1960s. As politics became increasingly radicalized in the late 1960s, many young people who were exposed to such influences permeated the ranks of the Appalachian Volunteers. New AV staff members and VISTA volunteers from across the country entered the mountains of eastern Kentucky, and their attitudes concerning the Vietnam War and their perceptions of American democracy influenced their feelings about the War on Poverty. As a result, the Appalachian Volunteers came in contact with other more militant groups, such as the Southern Conference Educational Fund (SCEF), that operated in the mountain South. The SCEF issued a statement in September 1967 that was indicative of a new Appalachian Volunteer attitude. "So far the only answers the government has come up with," it announced, "are make-work ('weed cutting') programs that have no meaning, shipping people off to low paying city jobs, or sending them to Vietnam."[56]

His socially and politically conservative background, particularly when it came to matters of personal behavior, along with the fact that his job involved administering and protecting the Council's fiscal health, prevented Ayer from embracing—or really understanding—this new attitude. He sought to continue his policy of political neutrality, which dated to the late 1950s. Had he adopted the AVs' new stance, perhaps the split between the two groups might never have happened. Given the demographic makeup of the AVs in 1966, the national attention focused on Appalachia by the War on Poverty, and the creation of VISTA, however, to have expected the group to remain unaffected by outside influences was naive at best.

6

Operation Rolling Thunder

The Political Education of Mountaineers and Appalachian Volunteers

The message should be one of reform, self help, determination, and a
vigorous fighting stand such as that assumed by the Southern Negro
in his struggle for civil liberties.

    I hope the Appalachian Volunteers will carry out this possibility
and that they will become a great new force struggling for reform for
the region's institutions and attitudes.

—Whitesburg attorney and CSM Board of Directors
member Harry Caudill to Milton Ogle, May 4, 1966

The Louisville native and University of Kentucky student Joe Mulloy, much
like his counterpart, George Brosi, was unusually attentive for a Southern
college student in the early 1960s. Though he did not readily recall President Johnson's declaration of a "war on poverty," he was impressed by the
civil rights movement, the Freedom Rides of 1963, and Freedom Summer in
1964. "That's the kinda stuff," he later recounted, "I was listening to or paying
attention to." Then, at one point in 1964, Mulloy heard the Appalachian Volunteers (AVs) field representative Jack Rivel speak on campus. Rivel "made a
good case for getting involved with things in our society and trying to be a
part of the solution instead of being part of the problem." Because its "focus
. . . was working with school children," the "student oriented program" about
which Rivel spoke "impressed" Mulloy. As he remembered: "It was something
I could do on a weekend and I could connect, somehow, with what was going
on in the world." Further, because, by the end of that calendar year, the federal
government, through agencies such as the Area Development Administration
and the Office of Economic Opportunity (OEO), looked to the nascent AV
program as a model for reform efforts across the country, Mulloy "felt as if
we were part of something bigger than just going out there on weekends."[1]

Mulloy constructed a number of recreational areas and basketball goals, installed new windows and drywall, and painted a number of schoolhouses on these weekend projects. The Appalachian Volunteers, he stated, "assist[ed] local school boards, . . . supplying some things that everybody else in the state had, but because of the unemployment . . . counties in eastern Kentucky didn't have." In addition, these relatively quick weekend efforts allowed the student volunteers to see the "concrete . . . physical result" of their work, and, thus, as other AVs recalled, it "provide[d] a meaningful experience" for the college students.[2]

After gaining some experience, Mulloy recalled, "we, the younger group of AVs," began to disagree with the tack taken by the Council of the Southern Mountains (CSM). While the Council followed the course prescribed by those "conservative church-related" folks that Loyal Jones described, the AVs, who worked at the "furthest out places, . . . the most remote 'head-of-the-holler,'" assumed a different approach. Though it was not "consciously decided upon or thought out," this new direction "didn't blame the victim" the way, the AVs believed, the CSM did. Describing the new strategy as an "evolving thing," Mulloy claimed that it grew from a "give and take process between us and the people we were working with." "It was 'do gooder' work is what we were doing—fixing up schoolhouses," Mulloy recalled, "it was good, it was needed, but really the system should have provided for that." It was a "band-aid on a cancer approach." While the local people—those at the heads of the "holler"—appreciated the AVs' work, they told the reformers "during the long evening hours sitting around talking" that, "if you really want to help us, we got this bulldozer coming down this mountain, that's what we need some help on right now." Mulloy continued: "I felt that I was radicalized or politicized or whatever by the people that lived in the mountains themselves—the natives. That's what started my consciousness."[3] Like Jones's decision to support Ayer, Mulloy's decision to act on his newfound "consciousness" proved significant for the future of the new Appalachian Volunteers and for the War on Poverty in Appalachia.

Bolstered by this new consciousness, the Appalachian Volunteers held its initial organizational meeting on May 15, 1966. The first order of business that day was a review of the organization's history, culminating with the reasons why it severed its ties with the Council of the Southern Mountains. As Ogle explained, the break was "inevitable" because the Council was "a program agency" while the Volunteers were "definitely an action agency." According to the Volunteer leader, the CSM "did and does not want to become an agency to provide direct services to communities as AVs do in their direct work with the people of the communities." As he also noted: "Competition would and had developed between the CSM and the Action group." Though the Appalachian Volunteers tried to reach an understanding with the Council, they could not arrive at a suitable arrangement. Then, on May 11, 1966, the Board of Directors of the CSM voted to grant the Appalachian Volunteers independence and sent a letter to the OEO requesting that all funds allocated to the Council for their AV program be transferred to the new Appalachian Volunteers, Inc. "We are in the process," Ogle announced, "of receiving these funds at present."[4]

In an attempt to prevent any significant decrease in Appalachian Volunteer activity and progress, Ayer and the Council staff aided the AVs in their move to the new office in Bristol, Tennessee. In addition, the CSM transferred all property purchased for the AV project and funds—which amounted to $728,000—to the new independent organization. Washington granted Ayer's request to fund the Appalachian Volunteers independently of the Council and implemented that funding on May 23, 1966. By the end of June, the Volunteers had collected $883,318 from federal and private sources. Ninety-eight percent of that sum, however, came from the OEO.[5]

While the Council of the Southern Mountains tried to recover from the loss of its most visible and successful program, the board member Harry Caudill found the new Volunteer organization a blessing for the Southern mountains. "The Appalachian Volunteers," he declared, "are young people and understandably should take a more militant stand on public issues than has the Council in past years." According to Caudill, the Volunteers needed to "impress upon the electorate the fact that they are living on a rich land whose inhabitants are poor because of mismanagement of the land base and the almost endless exploitation of soil, minerals, and timber by both local residents and giant absentee corporations." "The Volunteers," he concluded, "can carry this message to the people and, with good fortune, could set in motion a revolutionary change of thought."[6]

The Appalachian Volunteers' first attempt at setting in motion a "revolutionary change of thought" came during the summer program of 1966. Coming so close on the heels of the split, the program reflected both the

influence of earlier CSM-AV school-based projects and the new direction
plotted by the Appalachian Volunteers, Inc. In terms of demographics, the
1966 project closely resembled that of the previous year—half the participants came from outside the Appalachian region. This second summer
endeavor, however, employed over twice the number of volunteers as had
the previous year's, a total of five hundred. According to Milton Ogle, 90
percent of those who entered the AVs' ranks that summer were college students from two hundred institutions across the United States. While some
of these students were returning volunteers, others came to the program
because they had learned about it through media exposure and through the
AVs' own recruiting efforts. Additionally, the Volunteers drew from regional colleges (which did not necessarily guarantee that these students were
from the area) and from among community residents. This latter group
represented a new initiative for the Volunteer program. Through these paid
"community interns," the Volunteers hoped to cultivate local leaders who
would, under the direction of AV supervisors, organize their own communities for the sake of local improvement. Through this program, the Volunteers adopted at least the appearance of allowing local people to help each
other.[7]

VISTA (Volunteers in Service to America) associates participated in the
summer project as well. Just as in the first summer program, they spent
only the summer, not the entire year, in the mountains. The AVs controlled
their recruitment and selection, and the relationship between the AVs and
the federal government seemed inverted. Although the OEO wanted someone representing VISTA to "make the final determination concerning the
selection of Volunteers for service," the AVs wanted only a VISTA liaison
officer—"a person agreeable to the Appalachian Volunteers"—to aid in the
selection process. Reflecting that same self-confidence that characterized
early AV reform efforts and the new militant attitude, the actual projects
undertaken during the summer would be "developed by local community councils, AV's and AV field staff." While the AVs recognized that most
efforts would be centered around the schools and would include renovation and enrichment, their desire to develop programs independent of any
school connection was reflected in their insistence on letting "community
councils" design programs. This was different from what the federal government wanted. The OEO believed that renovation and enrichment were

the best paths toward community development and wanted the entire summer project to be "organized around local school houses."[8]

The AVs anticipated a successful summer. Writing to Manuel Strong, the assistant director of the Middle Kentucky River Development Council in Breathitt County, the Volunteer staff member Mike Kline urged both Strong and the county school superintendent, Marie Turner, to meet with the volunteers assigned to their county, stating: "I think it will be a good, friendly summer." Many accounts indicate that it was just that. At Jones Creek, for example, volunteers swam in the local creek and, reflecting preconceived gender roles, held knitting classes for the girls and hiked with the boys. Verda, in Harlan County, enjoyed a literary program coupled with crafts lessons. The scenario was similar at nearby Evarts. Here, the volunteers conducted a tutoring program and a charm school for the community's girls. Still other communities in eastern Kentucky played host to these same types of projects, such as the tutoring program at Goose Creek and the softball tournament at Bear Creek. In the reports that followed the summer project, every community listed had a school-based project.[9]

While these few reports reflect the activities at only a handful of the counties that the Appalachian Volunteers entered that summer, they clearly illustrate that the AVs' approach remained in line with the Council's earlier methods. Nevertheless, this first independent AV program did institute a number of changes. First, it marked the expansion of the overall Volunteer program into the states of Virginia and West Virginia. Though the majority of Volunteer activity remained in twenty-one eastern Kentucky counties, nine additional counties—Boone, Clay, McDowell, Mercer, Mingo, Raleigh, and Wyoming in West Virginia and Wise and Scott in Virginia—came under the Volunteers' umbrella.[10]

Second, the Appalachian Volunteers placed considerable emphasis on their community interns and community councils. Contrary to the Council of the Southern Mountains' conception of reform, which involved community representatives working in cooperation with existing local authorities, the AVs' community interns and councils operated independently of county officials and community action programs (CAPs). Once they organized their communities, the Volunteers reasoned, they could then influence OEO-funded county programs. "Perhaps the greatest weakness of the typical Community Action Program in the Appalachian area," the AVs contended, "is its failure to involve the poor in the planning, conduct, and review of programs." The CAP director, along with certain members of his board, devised local community action efforts, and the poor were permitted only "to ratify a 'pre-planned' program." The Volunteers claimed that target-group representation on the governing board was "limited to a few 'Toms' selected by the dominant figures": "Even in the best situations the elected representatives of the poor constitute a small, silent minority." This failure to involve the poor stemmed from a number of issues, including the desire of local officials to get federal funds as quickly as possible and a lack of faith in the ability of the poor to make informed decisions. Equally important, as the Appalachian Volunteers argued, the local county governments exhibited an "unwillingness to allow a dilution of centralized political power" in each jurisdiction and a belief in the absence of an organization and leadership among the poor themselves. For the Appalachian Volunteers, the remedy was the intern and community council approach.[11]

In their search for community interns, AV staff looked to hire people from poor local communities who exhibited "leadership potential" and a commitment "to the ideals of the Economic Opportunity Act." They hoped through training to instill in the interns "a sense of identification with the interests and aspirations of the poor and a belief in the right and the ability of the poor people to make their own decisions." Working in conjunction with the community councils, each mountain neighborhood could then determine its own plans and goals for the AV summer project. Utilizing this strategy, the community became the Volunteers' advisory board. Its responsibility was to ensure resident participation in the summer efforts, to administer the funding (each participating community received $300 from the Appalachian Volunteers to help pay for its activities), and to find acceptable room and board for the Volunteers. In short, community organizing at the grassroots level was the AVs' ultimate goal in the summer of 1966.[12]

This desire to organize communities by creating community councils explains, in part, why the summer affair so closely resembled the CSM-sponsored activities. As the Volunteers themselves recognized, schools were the closest most mountain neighborhoods came to a local organization, and the AVs hoped that their new tactics would help them avoid the pitfalls of the previous summer. Interestingly, this new Volunteer outlook rejected the optimism that tinged most AV workers' perceptions of the first summer project. Despite reports to the contrary, the Volunteers now argued that in almost no community that took part in the 1965 effort did the activities "involve the parents and other interested citizens actively": "In many cases the . . . program seemed to belong to the Volunteers rather than the community." In 1966, the AVs decided that the community council would have to run the program. The Appalachian Volunteers would not act unilaterally.[13]

Though the Appalachian Volunteers did conduct a summer school for impoverished mountain residents of any age, the real beneficiary of the summer program was the Appalachian Volunteers as an organization. The summer project ultimately resulted in yet another transformation of the AVs. So many soldiers in the field strained the organization's supervisory resources tremendously. Their activities were fairly simple—renovation, tutoring, and enrichment in most cases—and the Volunteer staff supervised their workers casually, if they did so at all. Quoting AV fieldmen who were responsible for fifty to sixty volunteers each, David Whisnant described the summer project as "'ridiculous,' 'a circus' and 'a disaster.'" By the end of the program, Whisnant concluded, the AV leaders realized "that as a tactic for bringing about change in the region, invasion by battalions of summer volunteers was not very useful." The AV consultant Dr. Robert Coles made a similar observation. In his evaluation of the summer effort, he noted that the AV staff "was not only overworked but simply could not . . . cope with the problem of dealing with five hundred students." Following this program, the Volunteers placed increasing emphasis on the community interns and councils.[14]

In other ways, the summer project was a catalyst for change within the Volunteer organization. Bringing a large number of people into the region and training them with a limited staff resulted in more than one personnel problem. One volunteer from New York City, for example, had trouble adjusting to her new surroundings. In reviewing her performance, the fieldman Flem Messer observed: "She was placed in a community that was extremely conservative socially and very far removed from the type of environment she was used to coping with." Though Messer believed her to be dependable, she "did have considerable problems and conflicts adjusting to the very strict social situation." In his evaluation of the Volunteers, Coles noted a "continual outpouring of all the anxieties, fears, depression, anger, and everything else that goes along with being transplanted from one world into another and having to come to terms with it intellectually and emotionally." Another volunteer caused problems when he failed to pay his "host family" for his room and board. (Each mountain family that housed a volunteer was supposed to receive an allowance of $12.50 per week to help defray expenses.) Over four months after the close of the summer project, this volunteer still owed his hosts over a month's rent. This situation reflected poorly on the entire Volunteer program and exposed the quantitative reasons why some local people, at least in part, accepted the Appalachian Volunteer program.[15]

While the summer program definitely exacted a toll on the Volunteers themselves, those who did come to terms with their situation seemed committed to substantial change in the mountains. A survey of both VISTA volunteers and VISTA associates conducted by the Volunteer staff revealed the typical individual the AV program attracted, the methods he or she hoped to use to initiate change, and weaknesses in the program. When asked whether a conference among AVs and VISTA volunteers would prove beneficial, nineteen of twenty-two VISTA volunteers responded favorably. Of these affirmative responses, many expressed a concern over fragmentation in the overall program. One hoped to decide "how to . . . coordinate our activities toward . . . common goals." Another sought ways to facilitate the integration of the Volunteers' "organization efforts across county and state lines." Still others wanted a conference that focused on Appalachia's problems and how the "cooperative efforts of AV-VISTAs [could] combat them." Finally, Volunteers sought better communication between the field personnel and AV headquarters. Of the nineteen, thirteen commented on how the Appalachian Volunteers needed to improve their organizational structure for their efforts to be fully effective.[16]

Other VISTA volunteers warned about spreading the Volunteers too thinly across the central Appalachian highlands. The Volunteers, believed David Thoenen, should concentrate their "resources within [a] small geographic area to achieve max [sic] effectiveness . . . and results." Cathy Lochner echoed this sentiment by commenting that the Volunteers needed to work on a countywide basis but not let themselves get so diluted that they would cease to be productive. Issues, however, were not limited to geographic distribution and organization. Some AV members wanted to hold a conference that addressed what Carol Wolfenden called the "specific problems that have confronted us" over the past summer. These problems included local CAPs and county judges. The Volunteers needed to either find a way "to work around them, or get them on [our] side." Candy Colin, who spent the summer in Mendota, Virginia, wanted to see the phrase "m[aximum] f[easible] p[articipation]" of the poor included in all CAP bylaws.[17]

Both VISTA volunteers and VISTA associates recognized similar problems during their brief stays. Responses to a questionnaire about their experiences during the summer of 1966 revealed a desire to go beyond the enrichment and renovation exercises of the past and cited the problems that came with such a huge influx of volunteers. While David Altschul of Amherst, Massachusetts, questioned the relevancy of OEO programs for Appalachia's poor, Robin Buckner of Georgetown, Kentucky, and Carol Wolfenden, a VISTA volunteer working in Frakes, Kentucky, expressed a desire for more stringent restrictions on strip-mining practices in the region. "Is there anything we can do to these m[oun]t[ain]s," Wolfenden asked, "that have been ruined by strip mining?"[18]

Other AV workers experienced frustration in dealing with local CAPs and county officials. Though one activist from Indiana asked for "information on all local CAP boards—structure—function, what we should know about them as AVs working with them," Jerry Knoll, stationed in Clospoint, Kentucky, hoped the Volunteers could meet with Edward Breathitt, the governor of Kentucky, "and other official types that can pressure out AVs' from their states." Joining Knoll were Karyn Palmer, who worked in Inez, and Patricia Dicky, who worked in Bethany, Kentucky. Palmer looked for ways to get "thru the 'structure,'" whereas Dicky wanted the AVs to "try to get [congressmen] to represent thier place of office like the people expected them to when they elected them in."[19]

Coupled with this concern over the AVs' ability to operate within the confines of eastern Kentucky's political system were issues that posed serious questions to the Appalachian Volunteers as an organization. Judith Jacobs, a native of Great Neck, New York, for example, complained of the lack of follow-up projects in certain communities where the Volunteers had worked. She also called into question the training, selection, and assignments of those who participated in the AV program. In a question that resonated throughout the entire Volunteer camp, she wondered why the AVs had experienced minimal success in community development. Her fellow Volunteers made similar statements, especially about training. Ed Turner, who came to the mountains from Atlanta, thought that the Volunteers should have had a better understanding of their communities' problems before actually arriving in them. While this might have been a monumental task for the trainers, another AV member from Pennsylvania suggested that each community expressing a desire to host volunteers form a committee that could "determine how to best use the A.V.'s instead of letting them over-run the community." Harvard University's John Zysman added that the Volunteers themselves needed to set goals and priorities—"something left generally undiscussed with Volunteers"—for the program's participants. A forth summer volunteer, also from Pennsylvania, vocalized a sense of frustration that the antipoverty organization had failed so far to get "something done about the problems we went looking for."[20]

This sense of frustration permeated the thoughts of many AV workers after the summer project. Sheila Musselman of Newton, Iowa, resented the fact that the community in which she worked "was expecting cheap laborers!" While it is clear that she did not expect to exert herself physically, Musselman did not explicitly state what she thought she was supposed to do while a volunteer. It is possible, nevertheless, that she was not sure of her role in the mountain community. Another respondent from Hartford, Connecticut, wondered about the Volunteers' conception of the "poor" and "how social change came about." "What I am trying to avoid," she continued, "is the AV's feeling of distress when confronted w[ith] a situation he *cannot verbalize* to himself except to fall back on his middle class understanding of the 'poor.'" John Campbell of Chester, Pennsylvania, agonized over the "power of the poor." "Is it realistic," he pondered, "to think in grass roots terms in the 20th century bureaucratic society?"[21]

As these responses show, the Appalachian Volunteers' summer 1966 project offered more questions about than solutions to the region's problems. More important, however, those taking part in the project exhibited a growing willingness to take an increasingly combative stance, prompting an organizational change in the Appalachian Volunteers. Issues concerning communications between the field and the office and among volunteers themselves, fears of overextending the program, difficulties with local politicians and CAPs, and community obstacles to organizing caused Ogle and

Perley Ayer (in 1963), the director of the Council of the Southern Mountains, 1951–1967. (Courtesy Records of the Council of the Southern Mountains, 1970–1989, Southern Appalachian Archives, Berea College.)

Loyal Jones (in 1972), the assistant director of the Council of the Southern Mountains, 1958–1967, director, 1967–1970. (Courtesy Records of the Council of the Southern Mountains, 1970–1989, Southern Appalachian Archives, Berea College.)

(*Above*) Milton Ogle (in 1964), the director of the Council of the Southern Mountains' Appalachian Volunteer project and then, following the split with the Council, the first director of the Appalachian Volunteers. (Courtesy Records of the Appalachian Volunteers, Southern Appalachian Archives, Berea College.) (*Below*) Phil Conn and Milton Ogle (ca. 1965). (Courtesy Records of the Appalachian Volunteers, Southern Appalachian Archives, Berea College.)

A Council of the Southern Mountains staff group photograph (ca. 1965). (Courtesy Records of the Council of the Southern Mountains, 1912–1970, Southern Appalachian Archives, Berea College.) *First row, left to right:* Milton Ogle, Eleanor Ball, Verdelle Vaughn, Martha Abney, Loyal Jones, Perley Ayer, Ann Pollard, Bill Suters, Dorothy Crandall, Mace Crandall. *Second row:* Isaac Vanderpool, Wanda Farley, Vivian Fish, Thomas Parrish, Jim Templeton, Ann Floyd, Nancy Graham, Judy Trout, Nina Worley. *Third row:* Dave Lollis, Gibbs Kinderman, Sylvia Forte, Tom Rodenbaugh, Jim Blair, Jean Moister, H. J. Homes, Sue Giffin, Maureen Stoy. *Fourth row:* Julian Mosley, J. H. T. Sutherland, McArthur Watts, Roslea Johnson, Dorothy Haddix, Diane Bayne, Pauline Smith, Jane Harold.

Left to right: Unidentified, Milton Ogle, U.S. Senator John Sherman Cooper, Loyal Jones. (Courtesy Records of the Appalachian Volunteers, Southern Appalachian Archives, Berea College.)

Through 1964 and 1965, most Appalachian Volunteer projects focused on the renovation of many of eastern Kentucky's rural one-room schoolhouses. This photograph shows eight male students in front of a schoolhouse. (Courtesy Records of the Appalachian Volunteers, Southern Appalachian Archives, Berea College.)

(*Above*) A typical eastern Kentucky one-room school. (Courtesy Records of the Appalachian Volunteers, Southern Appalachian Archives, Berea College.)
(*Below*) Another eastern Kentucky one-room school. (Courtesy Records of the Appalachian Volunteers, Southern Appalachian Archives, Berea College.)

In their early years (1964–1965), the Volunteers focused on school repairs and renovation projects in schools. In these efforts, men and women shared most of the work equally, although men usually did the repairs while the women did the painting. This photograph shows window repair and painting under way. (Courtesy Records of the Appalachian Volunteers, Southern Appalachian Archives, Berea College.)

Another example of a school repair and renovation project, this one involving exterior painting.

The residences of many mountaineers were as poor as their schools. This, according to the Volunteers, was the "Shells' place," near Lewis Creek, Kentucky (in 1968). (Courtesy Records of the Appalachian Volunteers, Southern Appalachian Archives, Berea College.)

(Above) Shortly after their initial renovation and repair projects, the Appalachian Volunteers included enrichment projects in their program. The Books for Appalachia project collected from across the nation used books that the Volunteers then distributed to the region's rural schools. This image shows books arriving in Kentucky via military aircraft (ca. 1965). (Courtesy Records of the Appalachian Volunteers, Southern Appalachian Archives, Berea College.) *(Below)* Jean Moister, the Council of the Southern Mountains' librarian, meets with an unidentified Louisville and Nashville Railroad agent to take possession of a boxcar full of donated books. (Courtesy Records of the Appalachian Volunteers, Southern Appalachian Archives, Berea College.)

(Above) After the Appalachian Volunteers unloaded the books from the boxcars, they trucked them to various locations throughout the region. (Courtesy Records of the Appalachian Volunteers, Southern Appalachian Archives, Berea College.) *(Below)* In addition to planes and rails, some supplies arrived in large trucks. (Courtesy Records of the Appalachian Volunteers, Southern Appalachian Archives, Berea College.)

This photograph illustrates the poor state of most rural schools. (Courtesy Records of the Appalachian Volunteers, Southern Appalachian Archives, Berea College.)

Here three youngsters read Dr. Seuss's *The Cat in the Hat.* (Courtesy Records of the Appalachian Volunteers, Southern Appalachian Archives, Berea College.)

Berea College education professor Luther Ambrose at the Rosenwald School. At the center of the photograph are the Appalachian Volunteer "book boxes," built in various shop classes in colleges in eastern Kentucky. While most volunteers worked in the local communities, shop class students became "volunteers" by building these boxes. (Courtesy Records of the Appalachian Volunteers, Southern Appalachian Archives, Berea College.)

One volunteer, while working on a renovation project, noticed that the school had absolutely nothing with which to work—no paper, no pencils, no books. This photograph shows what was, the Volunteers claimed, fairly typical of the resources that rural schools had. (Courtesy Records of the Appalachian Volunteers, Southern Appalachian Archives, Berea College.)

(*Above*) This photograph shows a school that underwent an Appalachian Volunteer renovation project. (Courtesy Records of the Appalachian Volunteers, Southern Appalachian Archives, Berea College.) (*Below*) Along with the Books for Appalachia project, the Appalachian Volunteers included "curriculum enrichment projects," which covered nearly everything from science experiments to world cultures demonstrations. Many Appalachian Volunteers believed, especially in the first few years of their organization's existence, that the poor quality of the schools and the depressed state of the environment resulted in a depressed populace and created the "culture of poverty" among the mountaineers. (Courtesy Records of the Appalachian Volunteers, Southern Appalachian Archives, Berea College.)

Curriculum enrichment included anything from remedial reading and spelling to art projects. (Courtesy Records of the Appalachian Volunteers, Southern Appalachian Archives, Berea College.)

A curriculum enrichment art project. (Courtesy Records of the Appalachian Volunteers, Southern Appalachian Archives, Berea College.)

By 1965, many projects combined renovation and enrichment. This photograph shows that this particular effort included fresh paint for the school and a basketball goal for the playground. (Courtesy Records of the Appalachian Volunteers, Southern Appalachian Archives, Berea College.)

Usually, men dominated "outside" work. Here, two Appalachian Volunteers erect a basketball hoop for a rural Kentucky grade school. (Courtesy Records of the Appalachian Volunteers, Southern Appalachian Archives, Berea College.)

Art, recreation, and creativity were quite important to the Volunteers' programs. Here, the Volunteers try to brighten the lives of poor rural school children with a puppet show. (Courtesy Records of the Appalachian Volunteers, Southern Appalachian Archives, Berea College.)

The Appalachian Volunteers tried to get the local community involved in their projects in some way. Here, the teacher at the Davidson school, Gilder Noble, helped prepare a pot-luck lunch for Appalachian Volunteers at her school. (Courtesy Records of the Appalachian Volunteers, Southern Appalachian Archives, Berea College.)

Many weekend projects had a social event, such as this bonfire sing-along. (Courtesy Records of the Appalachian Volunteers, Southern Appalachian Archives, Berea College.)

By the end of the decade, the Appalachian Volunteers focused on issue organizing, with the issues including anti-strip-mining, improved education, and welfare rights. Along with this new focus came new tactics stressing confrontation rather than cooperation with county officials. (Courtesy Records of the Appalachian Volunteers, Southern Appalachian Archives, Berea College.)

In 1966, following their split with the Council of the Southern Mountains, the Appalachian Volunteers began organizing to demand more say in local issues. The sign carried in this photograph reads, "Poor power: We demand fair taxes, good roads, decent schools, qualified teachers, job training, honest officials, jobs!" (Courtesy Records of the Appalachian Volunteers, Southern Appalachian Archives, Berea College.)

The demonstrators in this photograph wore bags on their heads because they feared retribution from those on whom they focused their protest. (Courtesy Records of the Appalachian Volunteers, Southern Appalachian Archives, Berea College.)

Fox to reevaluate their efforts. A more politically aggressive Appalachian Volunteers was the result.

Continued local resistance to AV programs was also a factor prompting the switch to a more politically aggressive stance. According to a *Louisville Courier-Journal* article on June 27, 1966, Clay County prohibited the Volunteers from the use of six schools, and Owsley County denied access to the Indian Creek, Mistletoe, Licking Fork, and Wolf Creek schools. Despite a petition from 135 Owsley residents that requested county support for the program, the superintendent stated that the Volunteers "could pack up and go home, ... the county could take care of itself." Similarly, Neureul Miracle, the superintendent of the Rockcastle County schools, informed the Appalachian Volunteers that the county did not need AV services. Federal funding, she maintained, made it possible for her to improve the county's education system without AV help. "This way," she told the Volunteers, "we will be able to employ people from this area and people who understand our problems and our way of living. People from outside sometimes cause more problems than they help to solve."[22]

In Martin County, the Appalachian Volunteers encountered a recalcitrant welfare department. According to the terms of the summer program, mountain residents who housed summer volunteers received a $50 per month stipend to help cover expenses. When the county welfare office learned of this arrangement, it threatened to reduce welfare payments by the same amount if any of its clients accepted Volunteer funds. On learning of the county's position, the Appalachian Volunteers protested to the state welfare department. This move by the county, the Volunteers argued, violated the spirit and intent of the welfare system by punishing those who sought to learn from the Volunteers. The actions of the Volunteers, the AVs themselves claimed, resulted in the removal of people from the welfare roles, and, thus, those most closely associated with the program had the best opportunity to become fully productive citizens. Ultimately, AV pressure convinced the state office that the county was in error. Because the income gained through the summer project lasted only a few months, the welfare department considered it "non-continuing" income, which did not affect regular benefits.[23]

Though quite a number of summer volunteers questioned the practice of strip mining, at least one discovered the impact that the coal industry alone had on the mountaineers. Working in a former company town, Judy Stewart discovered that a major concern in her assigned community was the water supply. The American Association, a major international corporation, installed a water system, but, "when the mines played out, the American Association absolved [itself of] all responsibility for keeping up the homes" that it still owned. Finally, Stewart continued, "the central pump quit working, [and] the lines rusted out." Despite the fact that this was an important issue, the community residents did little to resolve it because they felt "completely caged in by the power the American Association wields over their lives." These people, she further explained, were "hungry for approval, for encouragement, for some reason to have confidence in themselves against the dead weight of the social and economic pressures which drive them down to self deprecation and sullen resentment."[24]

After considering these developments, the Appalachian Volunteers determined that the roots of poverty lay not in the poor education that the rural mountaineers received but in the political and economic structures of the region. In Appalachia, the Volunteers now realized, "the county [was] the basic unit of local government." Serving as the administrative and judicial head of each county, the county judge also presided over the county's fiscal court. Probably even more powerful was the local superintendent of schools. Because he controlled "the largest budget and the largest patronage in terms of jobs in and around the county schools," he was the most powerful local political figure. "This political structure depends, in mining counties particularly," the Volunteers noted, "on the good will and support of the mining interests." On the other hand, the electorate in eastern Kentucky consisted mostly of a rural population living "at or below subsistence level." The "isolated geographical situation in which these people live" and "their inadequate education or experience in political action" make them "unaware of and unaccustomed to political action as a means of attaining their own interests and needs." This, the AVs strongly asserted, resulted in a "kind of feudalism" or "colonialism . . . throughout the Appalachian region."[25]

According to the Appalachian Volunteers, the county "power structure" coerced the people by manipulating job opportunities. The hiring of, for example, janitors, school bus drivers, and road workers took place at the centers of power. These jobs provided a cash income and were "highly prized among the poor." The AVs argued that their "political disposal" ensured "the perpetuation of the existing political pattern." Through their nearly three years of work in eastern Kentucky, volunteers had witnessed "many examples of how efforts to replace county officials by the election process . . . resulted in the discriminatory hiring and firing as a means of controlling the votes of the poor." These practices "led . . . to still further alienation of the poor from the main stream of American ideas and practices—and of participation." When local elected officials felt threatened, they resorted, the volunteers contended, to the use of "direct bribery in the form of food baskets, 'red liquor' gifts or cash payments" to sway voters to their side.[26]

The AVs were, therefore, determined to make the Appalachian poor more aware of their capacity for "local political participation." The means by which they hoped to do so was the "traditional American way of action: 'town meetings.'" The hope was that, as these meetings became increasingly popular with mountain residents, they would create more formal community organizations: "Local AV representatives [would help] the initial groups . . . develop their own structures and ways of cooperation in single or multi-community areas." In addition, the Appalachian Volunteers would facilitate "the capacity of these groups to cooperate on common ends where . . . these common interests emerged from the discussions in different local communities." Through these community organizations, the AVs asserted, the mountaineers could quickly develop the self-confidence to challenge the existing county power structure.[27]

In order to aid in the creation of these formal community organizations, the Volunteers established, in addition to the intern program, "educational outposts." Set up ostensibly to provide a quality educational experience that was based on the "values and needs" of local children and adults in the region, the outposts soon became a focal point of AV opposition to local county governments and the current trend toward school consolidation then under way in the Southern mountains. The AVs' personal approach in the outpost schools contrasted sharply with the move toward school consolidation, which, according to the AVs, conceived of children as "a product" that could be mass-produced. Another problem with consolidation, they argued, was that it contradicted the whole notion of community action, the alleged goal of the OEO. Consolidation destroyed the centerpiece of the local community—the school—and undermined the mountaineers' belief in the superiority of personal over economic relationships. The outpost schools therefore became an important component in the AV program of individual and community development.[28]

Each outpost operated independently, and the curriculum varied from outpost to outpost "due to the different skills that the local instructor possess[ed]." What the outposts had in common, however, was that they represented a "technical service staff" on which the local community could draw. For example, they developed "expertise . . . in such areas as strip-mining, welfare rights, educational opportunities, and similar problems." Their very existence thus represented a threat to local school superintendents and the other people and institutions seen by the AVs as the cause of poverty in the Southern mountains.[29]

As the Appalachian Volunteers became more and more involved in community organizing, they "gradually phased out the more direct physical and social services which they undertook in the initial stage of their activities." The emergence of grassroots political organizations among the mountain communities also had "repercussions . . . on the structure and functions of the AVs themselves." These repercussions manifested themselves in the "shifting emphasis from summer volunteer activities to year round services." "Physical and social" problems remained, but "the importance of year-round local community organization[s] [had] become more evident."[30]

With this dramatic shift in emphasis, the original Appalachian Volunteer concept rapidly faded. No longer did the AVs send local college students to remote mountain communities to repair schools and houses. In fact, there were very few volunteers from Appalachia in the organization; the majority of participants were VISTA volunteers assigned by the OEO to the Appalachian Volunteers, Inc. The composition of the organization itself consisted of a paid, professional staff utilizing "'outsiders' . . . oriented toward service and educational functions," which had now become "the core of the AV program." Thus, the end of the summer 1966 program marked another change in the meaning of the term *Appalachian Volunteer*. The organization now utilized few pure volunteers, and it no longer relied on Appalachians to perform the work.[31]

The effects of these changes emerged surprisingly quickly. Even before the end of the summer program, some of the volunteers had already embraced the new approach to community action. The minutes of a July 1966 ad hoc meeting of the AV Board of Directors indicate that, while the early renovation and enrichment projects did not "muster much community participation," the current emphasis on community organization did. Now "communities were directly involved in the work of the AVs."[32]

It did not take long for evidence of the success of the AVs' new approach to surface. In October 1966, the communities of Wilkerson, Midspring, Gatliff, and Hanging Rock (the latter hosted an AV outpost), in Whitley County, sent representatives to the county CAP meeting to request road improvements. When they introduced the issue, the agency director ruled them out of order. In response, the towns of Hanging Rock and Wilkerson organized petition drives. Because Hanging Rock received only a "token" response to its petition, the VISTA volunteers and AVs assigned to the county made arrangements for fifty people from not just Hanging Rock but also Wilkerson, Midspring, and Gatliff to visit the county fiscal court. According to a Volunteer report: "For the first time people from several communities stood together. Two of these communities are now directly feeling the effects of their efforts. Wilkerson is actually building their own road with some county support." Even more dramatic: "Midspring is now taking steps that may lead to a suit being filed against the county fiscal court." Things did not stop there, however: "Folks from several areas in Whitley County participated in a multi-county effort to (1) demand more representation of the poor on the [CAP] board and (2) . . . force the board to submit to their demands or at least keep the board honest." Should the county CAP refuse to cooperate, the Volunteers promised to help the poor people of the county form their own CAP and apply directly for OEO funding. Already the new, more confrontational approach of the Appalachian Volunteer program had made one county in Kentucky a political battleground in the War on Poverty.[33]

One consequence of the success in Whitley County was the curtailment of Volunteer work in northeast Kentucky. Following the end of the summer project, the northeast fieldman Bill Wells informed his superiors that the last eighteen months "would not be considered a period of accomplishment." Rather, it was just a period of learning about the region. This "education" had convinced Wells that, while destitution was widespread in northeast Kentucky, there was a "fundamental difference between poverty in an agricultural region and poverty in a coal region." Culturally, he argued, small farmers were more independent and reliant on their own abilities and initiatives to make a living. They did not expect assistance from their neighbors or the government. Community organizing was the solution to poverty in this region as well as in the rest of eastern Kentucky, but the people of the northeast needed to organize themselves around agricultural questions such as crop diversification. These were problems, Wells believed, that the Volunteers were ill equipped to handle or understand. He thus recommended that they try to introduce to the region an organization better equipped to help farmers. "I feel," he concluded, "that in order for the AVs to continue to work in the area would mean a kind of emphasis that we are neither equipped to understand nor prepared to support in light of the opportunities for successful concentration in other areas."[34]

The first expression of this newfound focus on the coalfields was the AV-sponsored Appalachian Community Meeting, held in Washington, DC, at the end of August 1966. Though billed as the product of the "shared experience of poverty [in the coal camps] and a heritage of economic and political exploitation" and as an attempt to establish "a dialogue between Appalachian people and those who control the resources of this country," the Appalachian Community Meeting was, in actuality, an indictment of the CAPs in the Southern mountains. Because the CAP staff developed programs, set priorities, and determined budgets "with virtually no active involvement on the part of the board, poor or otherwise, and least of all by those to be affected by the programs," the AVs asserted, there was only "nominal . . . representation of [one-third] poor" on agency boards. What organizing these CAPs did accomplish was "geographically based" and reflected a limited neighborhood approach to the problem of poverty. Under this approach, the AVs argued, the poor once again were simply recipients, not participants.[35]

Not content just to condemn, the Appalachian Volunteers offered solutions. Most of these struck at the heart of county-run CAPs. First, county CAPs needed, the AVs believed, to provide the poor in their jurisdiction with "the necessary technical assistance" that would enable them to make thoughtful decisions concerning the poverty programs they wanted. Hand in hand with this idea went the demand for increased public accessibility of such information as budget reports, meeting proceedings, and advanced notice of planned meetings and their agendas, which would further facilitate poor people's ability to generate their own antipoverty efforts. Additionally, the AVs contended, too much program money was tied up in staff salaries. Funds from CAP grants should immediately be made available to those local community groups willing to tackle the problem of poverty. This would give the poor the "most powerful kind of local control"—financial control.[36]

The Appalachian Volunteers decided to put their ideas to a test. When a 1966 amendment to the OEO act allowed for 5 percent of Title II funds to be allocated to organizations operating independently of a funded CAP, they provided the residents of Myers Fork, in Menifee County, with information on how to apply for a federal grant. Unfortunately, such an application was replete with potential political difficulties. If Myers Fork was funded, the AV staff member Bill Wells believed, the Licking Valley Community Action Agency's grant would be reduced by the amount that Myers Fork received. He therefore told the head of the Myers Fork organization: "I think you can see the kinds of pressure that you will be up against." Wells intimated that he had contacted the state OEO office, which concurred with his position. He added, however, that the state office advised him to "keep it quiet so that the various politicians . . . in the area don't get wind of [the application]." Though it is not clear whether the Myers Fork group ever received its funding, this exchange indicates the growing antagonism between the poverty warriors and the local establishment.[37]

Much like the new OEO rules, welfare in the Appalachian South, the Appalachian Volunteers believed, actually resulted in the "enforcement of pauperism" because eligibility requirements prohibited welfare recipients from accumulating "more than a very small amount of wealth as a source of economic security": "In Kentucky, for example, a family of six on welfare is permitted a total wealth of only $1100 in addition to a homestead." Employment restrictions, they felt, also "tend to foster dependency upon the welfare system." In many cases, "the rigid determination of welfare payment makes the acceptance of anything but the most lucrative job impractical from the point of view of the individual." A job usually meant no significant change in income because the individual's welfare benefits would be reduced by a comparable amount, if not cut entirely. When faced with this dilemma, "the practical and economic decision is to do nothing."[38]

Welfare payments alone produced distrust and hostility on the part of the recipient. For one thing, they were "shockingly small" and based on "inadequate and antiquated standards which again prevent economic security and independence." In addition, the county welfare office kept secret its criteria for eligibility. Therefore, the AVs concluded, "basic decisions about [the recipient's] way of life—his income, his expenditures, and his food—are made at the welfare office at the county seat without his knowledge or consent." Distrust and hostility were, of course, focused on the welfare caseworker, the actual decisionmaker, who had "the power, in practice . . . , to force the recipient to follow his directives on a wide range of issues."[39]

To remedy the situation, the Appalachian Volunteers proposed certain changes designed to put the poor in control. Caseworkers should concentrate solely on administering such social services as offering advice on budgeting and purchasing. Eligibility for, or any change in, benefits should be determined by an investigator working independently from the caseworker. Recipients should receive "a written notice thirty days prior to any change of payment, giving the nature and cause of the change." Finally, the welfare department should establish an appeals procedure that allows recipients to question benefit changes without "fear of further cuts or discrimination."[40]

Equally important, the AVs felt, was the welfare department's need for an independent source of information, and to that end they proposed a "welfare advisory board." This group should "exist and be active at all levels of welfare administration, yet independent of it." To "reduce the possibility of political domination," it should include a majority of welfare recipients elected by fellow welfare recipients. In addition to providing a source of information, it should also act as a "check on the welfare department" and hear appeals of controversial cases. Those not on the advisory board should, moreover, be organized into "unions of welfare recipients." These unions should keep members informed of their rights and aid in protecting them. Were these changes to be realized, the AVs concluded, they would remedy the present situation in which "governmental agencies . . . maintained to afford economic security and independence to needy people, by their own regulations and administrative procedures, further increase the burden of poverty."[41]

The Appalachian Volunteers had also come to believe that the coal industry dominated the Appalachian South politically. The "political structure depends," they argued, "on the good will and support of the mining interests," the relationship between local politicians and mine operators worked to the disadvantage of the poor, and, in return for political and economic support, county judges gave the coal companies virtual carte blanche. Additionally, technological changes in the mining industry and the impact that these changes had on employment further concentrated economic and political power in Appalachia.[42]

Strip mining, the method of removing coal from the land used increasingly in Appalachia by the late 1960s, began during the Second World War, when the nation needed an economical and faster means of mining. By the 1950s, it was rapidly replacing underground mining. The strip-mining process involved the miner removing the topsoil or "overburden" off the top of a coal seam and pushing it down the mountainside to form a "soil bank." Next, he stripped the layer of shale covering the coal seam and dumped it onto the soil bank. Finally, he dug the coal. In the end, a vertical wall, known as a "highwall," remained where soil and coal once were. Because the shale now formed the top layer of the soil bank, it seriously hindered the growth of new vegetation. What was once a lush, green mountainside now was desolate. Even worse, loose rock and soil frequently washed down the mountainside, causing even more damage to the land and, more important, the mountaineers' homes and property.[43]

So widespread was the destruction from strip mining in the state of West Virginia that, on May 8, 1966, the governor, Hulett Smith, declared: "The rape of West Virginia has occurred." Strip mining, however, did much more than just scar the land. Because one man operating a bulldozer could do the work of many men using picks and shovels, the most obvious human hardship it caused was unemployment. Also, because it severely restricted the number of jobs available, the coal operator (i.e., mine owner) could use those jobs to exercise his own political and economic position, just as school superintendents did with the jobs they controlled.[44]

With Governor Smith taking the lead, West Virginia sought to reform its strip-mining laws, and the Appalachian Volunteers gave their full support to the effort. With the help of the AVs, the people of West Virginia worked diligently to "make their voices heard and their opinions known," and the first step was "to see that further damages do not occur from irresponsible mining operations." Recognizing that Appalachia needed land reclamation on a large scale, the AVs called on the federal government to provide funds to help West Virginia restore its damaged land. These funds should not be provided indiscriminately. Instead, they "should be tied to requirements of state laws and state enforcement of the laws to see that the future cost is born by the stripping company."[45]

Acting as a lobbyist organization, the Appalachian Volunteers formally announced its support of strip-mining-reform laws at their 1967 winter meeting in Huntington, West Virginia. The people who attended the conference, "representing all of Southern Appalachia," deplored "the waste and destruction that has occurred . . . as a result of irresponsible and reckless strip mining operations." This meeting culminated in the endorsement of the bill to reform strip mining introduced in the West Virginia legislature by Governor Smith and the action of the citizens' task force on service mining.[46]

Though not as destructive as strip mining, deep mining, the process of going underground to remove coal, also came under AV attack. The Appalachian Volunteers accused deep-mining operations of causing serious air and water pollution. Water, which naturally accumulated in a deep mine, absorbed large quantities of the iron and acidic chemicals found in coal. After the water was pumped out, or after it drained naturally, it seeped into aquifers, ruining the water supply—sometimes permanently. It also flowed into nearby creeks and streams, killing plant and animal life—destroying potential food sources. As the streams flowed into one another, the contamination traveled with it, and the effect of water pollution was often widespread. Those living farther away from the mine felt the same effects as the people who lived in its immediate vicinity. "Gob piles," the waste removed from the mine to reach the coal and usually containing iron, sulfur compounds, and low-grade coal, also created a serious air pollution problem. Spontaneous combustion resulting from pressure and heat or fires set intentionally by the company as a means of waste control released toxic carbon monoxide gas and caused serious health problems for local residents. These fires, moreover, burned for years once ignited.[47]

The foremost obstacle to solving these problems at the local level was, the AVs felt, the industry's claim that "there is no economically feasible way to treat waste materials so as to prevent pollution." This claim, they insisted, attempted to cover up the industry's "reluctance to seek a way" to clean up pollution. Because local or state governments were not in a strong enough position to "force industry to carry its share of the burdens it creates," the Appalachian Volunteers called on the federal government to step in with money and a research program to solve the pollution problems.[48]

Initially, the results of the Volunteer onslaught were mixed. Judy Ross, a VISTA volunteer assigned to the Perry County CAP, complained: "I found myself in the frustrating position of recognizing effective ways of encouraging change but being powerless to do so." Her relationship to the sponsor "was superficially cordial but honestly antagonistic; they neglected to furnish adequate supervision but restricted independent and potentially subversive activity." Despite its initial enthusiasm for the project, one mountain community failed to push the county to resurface its road "in order to avoid possible political implications." Volunteers in general, Ross asserted, "lacked the power and authority to carry out plans worked out with the people . . . as long as these plans challenged [the] established political structure." "The causes of poverty, at least in Appalachia," she concluded, "are fundamentally political, and that the people of Appalachia need to be encouraged to exert their own political power."[49]

Exerting collective political power was the goal of a letter-writing campaign targeting the teacher of the Abner's Branch school in Leslie County. As with similar AV projects, the letters followed a certain pattern. All began with proper grammar and correct spelling but closed with a rougher pen and noticeably poor grammar, suggesting that the authors received help. All addressed the same general topics—the terrible physical condition of the school and playground and the fact that the teacher, Ruth Lewis, failed to adequately supervise the students. As for the latter charge, a series of serious accidents had, allegedly, occurred during school hours. Two youngsters had broken arms, and one girl had broken her leg in two places. In each case, the teacher was accused of exercising poor judgment, of not properly supervising the children, and of not reacting appropriately after the injuries occurred. All this could have been avoided, one resident wrote, if the school had a responsible, adequate teacher. This same person claimed that the Leslie County superintendent, Hays Lewis, canceled the state-administered achievement tests "to save embarrassment." Another resident wrote that, even though he lived in Leslie County, he sent his children to Harlan County schools because "at the Abner Branch School our children aren't watched." Lewis allowed them to wander up to a half a mile from the building to play. Further, even though most children earned As and Bs, they still were unprepared for high school. When some of the Abner's Branch residents requested a new teacher, the superintendent's response was "that its in the family and thats as far as we got."[50]

Other communities took up the banner of school reform. The people of Buffalo, in Rockcastle County, protested the fact that, as they put it, they had "no actual cooperation from the school board" when they asked for improvements for their school. "Oh yes, we have the seeming cooperation[;] the very syrupy sweet greeting . . . and the perpetual answer 'we will do all we can,' then nothing." Moreover, board meetings were "closed as far as we are concerned." When the protestors finally managed to send a representative to a meeting, the board discussed "things of no interest" to the community and then let the Buffalo delegate know that it was time to leave by refusing to answer his questions.[51]

As these examples illustrate, by the fall of 1966 the Volunteers experienced, at best, eroding relationships with many eastern Kentucky school superintendents. When Julia McKeon, an educator from the Bronx, New York, asked for help finding a teaching position in eastern Kentucky, the AV staff member Thomas Rhodenbaugh admitted that the Appalachian Volunteers "do not have the best working relationship with many school superintendents." In fact, they had troubles with nearly every level of local government. In November, Steve Daugherty became enraged when he learned that the postmaster of Evarts had hired his own wife as postal clerk. "We are attempting to fight a War on Poverty," Daugherty wrote to the regional director of the U.S. Postal Service, "and yet, how successful can we be if even the positions created by the various government agencies are filled only with members of the same family." Still, the AVs felt that they were achieving some level of success. "Three years ago," the antipoverty organization announced, "the primary words used to describe the isolated Appalachian Mountaineer were apathetic, unmotivated, uninspiring, culturally deprived, and in some cases even dull. At the present time we are hearing him described as activist, trouble-maker, organized, impatient, frustrated, and in some cases angry. The reason for this change is attributed to [AV and VISTA] Volunteers." According to the AVs, the catalyst for this change was "*dependable* information which tends to decrease or even eliminate the activity of the *rumor mill* which previously was the primary source of 'information.'" That is, whereas the organs of local government gave local residents disinformation, thereby keeping them in a subservient position, the Volunteers gave them the knowledge they needed to make informed decisions about the issues affecting their lives.[52]

Through the remainder of 1966 and into 1967, the Volunteers worked to liberate mountaineers from poverty and subservience. Impoverished rural mountaineers were not unambitious, strange, or quaint, Milton Ogle informed Robert Kennedy. They were "exploited, underdeveloped, and basically bypassed by the progress of the nation as a whole." Appalachia's problems, Ogle declared, were very similar to those of the "'third world.'" The people of the region were "weary from exploitation," and, because they "provided the backbone of the nation's resources," they "must do whatever it takes to begin to benefit from these resources." This statement became the battle cry of the Appalachian Volunteers for the next year.[53]

In order to help the local people of Wise County, Virginia, help themselves, the fieldman Joe Mulloy proposed the creation of a reference book on the political, economic, and social fabric of the county. "This idea," he explained, "grew out of the lack of information—the lack of [data] that the folks have about what is available and the fact that the . . . service agencies are not doing the job they should." This volume would allow the mountaineers to discover the "who, what and how of welfare, health and sanitation, coal operations, unions, [and] pensions." This information was important because rural people needed to know how the system worked "in order to operate within [this] structure and bring about effective change." It would illustrate the flaws of the existing power structure and make their exploitation more successful. Taking a cue from the civil rights movement and the Highlander Folk School, Mulloy thought that his reference book could become the text for an "Appalachian Freedom School."[54]

Mulloy's tactics apparently achieved some success. In a memorandum to the OEO, Tom Rhodenbaugh indicated that the board of directors of the Wise County CAP fired the agency's director, James Sommerville, who was sympathetic to the AV position. Rhodenbaugh claimed that Sommerville did not wish to see the county's CAP turned into yet another "paternalistic" social program and that he supported, with AV help, a group of African American women in the town of Norton who organized a "domestic services corporation" (a laundry service) and a sewing cooperative headquartered at a CAP-run community center. After the co-op asked the local CAP for additional funding, rumors that the grassroots organization really was an AV-inspired and -led domestic workers' strike circulated throughout the town. In what the Volunteers interpreted as an attempt to keep the people dependent, the majority of the program's board decided that the women then working in the center should be rotated out after only a few months in order to give more people a chance to benefit from the program. Those then working protested the decision, and Sommerville organized their appeal. He claimed that the Volunteers saw the tension between himself and the board as an opportunity to direct the entire county program toward the problems of the poor, and they then approached the board with ideas for additional projects to benefit the impoverished in the county.[55]

At a meeting on September 29, 1966, the Wise County CAP president announced that there "was an internal force seeking to disrupt [the program] and to subvert its expressed purpose." In response, the Volunteers issued a "propaganda piece" called "The Wise Owl" that carried the news of the board's earlier decision to close the county's Program Development Office and then "championed [this decision] as a beginning of the end of Appalachia's problems as the poor shouldered arms to wage their own fight." Following the distribution of this newspaper, the program labeled the AVs "subversives," and, at the suggestion of the AVs, the poor began to form people's committees. As these committees protested the action of the Wise County CAP, the board relieved Sommerville of his duties as director. Until they could get Sommerville returned to his post, the Volunteers added him to their staff so that the work in the county could continue unabated.[56]

To the north, in Raleigh County, West Virginia, the Appalachian Volunteers realized their greatest success to date. Here, more than in any other county in which they worked, they demonstrated that "democracy is real and functioning at the grassroots level." After establishing a people's committee, they succeeded in replacing the local CAP director with Gibbs Kinderman, an AV staff member. Raleigh County, like most of the other counties of southern West Virginia, had a strong union and an organizing tradition, which aided Kinderman in his assent to power in the county CAP. Moreover, the county CAP was inadequately funded and badly run. As a result, official opposition to the Volunteers was weak and poorly organized. In Mingo County, West Virginia, by contrast, after the county CAP director,

Huey Perry, resigned after a losing battle with the local political hierarchy, the Volunteers tried unsuccessfully to "take over" that CAP as well.[57]

In eastern Kentucky, where the majority of Volunteer activity still took place, the results and consequences were not yet so dramatic. Nevertheless, the AVs did make an impression on many county officials. It was "flap time," Ogle informed the AV membership. By this, he meant that the Volunteers had gotten "enough community people together and talking that the hair on the backs of some of the more unresponsive 'public servants' [was] standing on end." As a consequence, those "public servants" mounted a campaign to discredit the Volunteers in the eyes of the OEO. To counteract this, the Volunteers embarked on their own campaign to bolster their position with the federal government. Ogle asked his fieldmen to gather petitions, letters, and testimonials of community action from mountain folk that could be presented to OEO. "Its important," Ogle concluded, "that the CAPS begin to realize that the A.V.s are for real and that community organization is part of their job."[58]

The AVs did continue organizing in eastern Kentucky. "Appalachian Volunteers and VISTA Volunteers are constantly harassed by public blasts from local politicians who see poor people becoming more knowledgeable and more experienced," Ogle declared. There was "as a result," he continued, "a loosening of the grip of the political patronage system on which the poor have been forced to depend. Isolated mountain people are finding that their voices have an important effect on updating and upgrading the social and economic institutions in their localities."[59]

According to the AVs, much of this "upgrading" "has been diagnosed by county leaders as 'agitation' or as a response on the part of isolated poor people to agitation by Vista and Appalachian Volunteers." Tracing the history of the War on Poverty in Breathitt County, for example, the AVs argued that, in the beginning, the men and women who led the antipoverty agencies "operated on the assumption that the 'target population' possessed neither organizational or administrative skills nor the gumption to acquire such skills": "Consequently, involving the poor in the conception, design and implementation of anti-poverty programs has been kept to a minimum." Because the local administration ignored them, the people along the north fork of the Kentucky River began to hold their own meetings. On May 3, 1966, Buck Maggard, a local resident, called a meeting at Lost Creek and formed the Breathitt County Grassroots Citizen Committee. According to the AVs, Maggard's motivation for his new organization was his "antagonism for the Community Action Office in [the county seat of] Jackson which he contended was controlled by the power structure." The AVs themselves argued that the "county has been dominated for forty years by one political family which has virtual control of the county, its resources and its people." As a result, "misuse of funds, graft, and patronage" were "realities" that the Volunteers needed to address in Breathitt County.[60]

Operating independently from the local CAP, Maggard's Grassroots Committee and the AVs worked with the poor of Sandy Ridge in neighboring Wolfe County to form a pine roping and Christmas decoration manufacturing cooperative and established a quilting shop in Malaga, also in Wolfe. With Volunteer help, it created community libraries at Barwick, Haddix, Hayes Branch, and a number of other small communities in Breathitt County. As of November 1966, the committee continued, with absolutely no help from the county CAP and little expectation of getting any, to organize the poor around issues that were important to them. By 1967, the Volunteers aided in the establishment of a local chapter of the Appalachian Group to Save the Land and People (AGSLP). A somewhat militant anti-strip-mining organization, AGSLP grew out of the actions of Knott County's Mrs. Ollie "Widow" Combs and Dan Gibson in 1965. During the next three years, the AVs worked to form AGSLP chapters in Breathitt, Pike, Floyd, and Harlan counties.[61]

In addition to the work with AGSLP in Harlan County, the Volunteers founded an outpost at Evarts. Using that outpost as a headquarters, the AVs conducted programs on welfare rights and established an "independent" Head Start–like program that the county school board effectively shut down because of what the Volunteers labeled simply a "contract violation." Moreover, the AVs sought to develop indigenous local leadership within the county, a project that would make "the future of the A.V.s HELL." The AV HELL—or Headquarters for Education of Local Leadership—program in Harlan County called for the establishment of a center that would be a gathering place for the poor to think creatively about their problems and possible solutions. At this proposed educational institution, a project somewhat similar to Mulloy's textbook on Wise County politics, would be a library of information about local, state, and federal governments. HELL would also, the Volunteers hoped, publish a newspaper meant to assist "in educating people about the political scene." The end result would be a homegrown pressure group that would "make [local] institutions more responsive to the needs of the people."[62]

In the fall of 1966, taking action of a more concrete form, the Volunteers backed a candidate for the Harlan County school board in opposition to the "county dictator," James Cawood. Though their candidate lost, the AVs believed that they issued a "strong challenge to the Cawood political machine" and that they had established an organizational base as a result of the campaign. This was the foundation, they believed, "for the development of new skills in [the] democratic political process, [and for] true economic equality and power for the masses." Having established this base and the HELL program, the Volunteers embarked on an effort to "break the control over the [community action] programs by the county school superintendents; programs which involved several thousand dollars worth of patronage."[63]

In Floyd County, Volunteer efforts resembled both the past and the present orientation of the organization. In addition to conducting school repair, the AVs also helped found the Highway 979 Community Action Council (979 CAC), composed of representatives from twelve small communities along Highway 979. The 979 CAC started a local newspaper, the *Hawkeye*, which sought to break down the barriers of intercommunity communication. In June 1966, a group of citizens from the community of Mud Creek traveled to the state capital to discuss the community's water supply. According to an AV report, the water for Mud Creek came from open wells, at least 75 percent of which were contaminated. As a result of this meeting, Governor Breathitt declared Mud Creek an emergency area and provided OEO funds for the construction of a new water system. Others from the 979 CAC bypassed their local officials and went straight to the state capital. Representatives of Little Mud Creek and the Right Tolar school paid visits to the state highway commissioners' office and the state board of education to ask for better roads, better school buildings, and, most important, better teachers.[64]

Activities in Letcher County centered on the Volunteer outpost center at Carcassonne. High on the priority list was the creation of a welfare rights organization, but the Volunteers suddenly encountered the apathy so commonly ascribed to mountain people—that same attitude the Volunteers were, they claimed, helping mountaineers overcome. "Development of any sort of welfare rights organization here is difficult and slow work," the Volunteers claimed, "largely because very few welfare recipients have any prior experience at working together and because even fewer really expect to see any substantial improvement in welfare programs." Despite the difficulties, the Volunteers continued organizing in Letcher with the support of the local AGSLP chapter. Unlike welfare reform, this issue of strip mining seemed to energize people. Those "who used to believe that nothing could be done to protect their land now realize they can do just that by acting together." By functioning as a unit, the people in Letcher County could now come to grips with water pollution, soil erosion, and their legal rights.[65]

Welfare reform and politics also dominated Appalachian Volunteer activity in Pike County, one of the country's principal coal-producing counties. Responsible for Pike was the Wise County, Virginia, AV fieldman Joe Mulloy, who had moved to Pike County in 1967 and focused his activities on three broad topics—strip mining, welfare rights, and the Marrowbone Folk School. Located on Marrowbone Creek, the folk school was a rallying point for AV activity in the county. Shortly after their arrival in 1966, the Appalachian Volunteers charged the superintendent with "misuse of funds" and with selecting teachers for political reasons rather than on the basis of their qualifications. "Education in these counties," the Volunteers announced, "is in need of total revamping." Repeating a common theme, they accused the local CAP of working to maintain the status quo, as opposed to actually working to end poverty.[66]

While rhetoric dominated, activity did not lag. Edith Easterling, a lifelong resident of Poor Bottom, in Pike County, and an energetic AV intern, led a group of local residents to Frankfort in order to discuss education in the county. Though the group had arranged to meet the state superintendent, Harry Sparks, Sparks did not keep his appointment. Instead, the Poor Bottom contingent discussed among themselves how county politics dominated the school system. "We talked about our schools and how the teachers work under pressure," Easterling reported to the Volunteers. "We also talked about politics and how they are played in our community. I worked for the Board of Education and the principal called me in and said 'you vote like we say or you don't work here.' I did not vote like he said and I was not hired back to work the following year." Other teachers would "change their politics so they could go on working." These complaints were not exclusive to teachers but came "also from local citizens." "Can't we, as Americans get help so we can be free?" Easterling appealed.[67]

In the wake of these accomplishments, the Appalachian Volunteers entered the summer of 1967 feeling most potent. At a June 1967 Board of Directors meeting at Beckley, West Virginia, the antipoverty group made one of its most bold statements: "The board made a resolution that all people involved in community action should write letters to their congressmen and senators against elected officials making up or sitting on advisory boards concerned with poverty." It further asserted that "the people should run their own affairs without some 'joker' in a plush office telling people what they need, and what to do" and that either "more poor people should run for office or people who fairly reflect the feelings of those who elect them."[68]

Strip mining, like politics, was again an important topic of discussion. Six months earlier, at their winter meeting in Huntington, West Virginia, the Volunteers had called for restrictions on strip mining on the grounds that it threatened personal property, "scenic spots," and "recreation areas" and caused "extreme or severe pollution." Calling it their "number 1 problem," they proclaimed: "Stripping in these mountains should be outlawed." Ogle added that everyone interested in central Appalachia "should work to abolish it." Other board members suggested that the Volunteers help local residents establish their own utility districts that, unlike the Tennessee Valley Authority, would not use stripped coal. This, they hoped, would lead to the end of that mining method.[69]

The AVs also indicted the county-administered CAPs in eastern Kentucky. The CAP in Wolfe County, one participant stated, "don't want poor folks to get involved." Someone from Breathitt County exclaimed: "All we get is promises." Nancy Coles proclaimed that, because the Volunteers informed the poor about the Breathitt County CAP, it "won't have anything to do with [the AVs]." Gordon Meade of Floyd County asserted that the county CAP had concealed its activities from the poor: "AVs told us about CAP and that's what makes CAP mad." The result: "They knock us down faster than they pick us up." Summing up the situation, the Volunteers determined that county officials gave jobs to their relatives and that politicians, in general, "by pass the poor and do what the middle class and high class of people want." In the end, the poor resigned themselves to this situation. Don Turner, an AV intern from Breathitt County, declared: "They feel they can't ask the local CAP for help because they won't help them."[70]

Realizing that school-based academic projects failed to address overwhelming problems, whether those problems were immediate or long term, the Appalachian Volunteers concluded that the region's complex political relationships operated to the detriment of those most in need of government services, the poor and the unemployed. While international energy corporations, including the American Association, in part controlled mountain politics, an indigenous political force nevertheless existed. In cooperation with major internationals, local political and economic power brokers emerged in the mountains in the 1950s and 1960s with the expansion of federally funded social service programs, such as social security, Medicaid, and the War on Poverty. Mechanization of the coal-mining industry and the rollback of United Mine Workers of America benefits in the late 1950s provided local elites with further opportunities to solidify their hold on power. As this native power structure attempted to bolster its position through control of the federal largesse provided by the Johnson administration, it faced open opposition from the Appalachian Volunteers. Through issue organizing, direct political campaigns against corrupt officials, and attempts to control local CAPs, the AVs challenged multinational conglomerates and, more important, the local politicos who exerted direct and overt control over the rural mountaineers of eastern Kentucky.

Institutional autonomy was, nevertheless, only the beginning for the Appalachian Volunteers as it prepared for 1967. Rejecting the Council of the Southern Mountains and its cooperative approach to solving problems in the Appalachian coalfields, the AVs transformed themselves from a volunteer service association into a professional political organizing institution. Along with this metamorphosis came changes in personnel and strategy. Still, while their analysis of the region's problems shifted from a "cultural" explanation to one emphasizing the "colonial" relationship the mountains had with the rest of the country and, thus, itself required a quantitative solution to Appalachian problems, the Volunteers still spoke in terms of Appalachian "isolationism." While, on the one hand, they began to understand the nature of the region's poverty, they still—as their descriptions of "isolated" mountaineers and the "peculiar" world with which Volunteers would have to come to terms suggested—held the impoverished to be outside modern America. Somehow, the contradiction of the mountaineers being simultaneously victimized and isolated eluded the Appalachian Volunteers. Their failure to rectify this dichotomy, again, proved detrimental to their reform efforts.

Peace without Victory

Three Strikes and a Red Scare in the Mountains

That some employees of the Appalachian Volunteers and other federally financed anti-poverty programs have collaborated and cooperated with known communist organizers to help them organize and promote the violent overthrow of the constitutional government of Pike County.... That the contract of the A.V.s who are operat[ing] on a Federal Grant of $1,500,000 be immediately canceled.
—Report of the September 1967 Pike County Grand Jury

"Appalachia needed help. I can't say that they needed the War on Poverty," Louie Nunn remembered in 1993, "but I think they got too much help. . . . They got food, they got medicine, they got everything that they needed and they didn't have to work for anything. Consequently they decided that they never would work." Elected in 1967, Louie Nunn was the first Republican governor of Kentucky in twenty-four years. Running a campaign that stressed the social turmoil of the latter half of the decade, Nunn typified the desires of many who were, as the *Hazard Herald* stated, "tired of the beatniks, hippies, and civil righters" whom the "decent, law-abiding, constructive citizens who form the heart and conscience of our nation" saw as the source of that turmoil. Nunn claimed to have coined the term the *silent majority,* a phrase that figured significantly in Richard Nixon's 1968 presidential campaign, and, in many ways, his election foreshadowed the national conservative backlash against the reform efforts of the Johnson administration. Nevertheless, Nunn objected to the War on Poverty for reasons other than his conservative ideology. He believed that government at all levels—local, state, and federal—used the federal programs as a way to buy votes.[1]

According to Nunn: "There was a lot of pork-barrel legislation going on in [the War on Poverty]. And they started doing what I call main-
lining—like a dope addict going into the vein." The Democratic representative Carl Perkins (from the Seventh District, in southeastern Kentucky), in
particular, though "probably well-intended," "did more harm to the mountains of eastern Kentucky than any other single person"—"social and . . .
economic harm"—because he used his seniority to "get programs through
that were patterned primarily for the Appalachian area" and that "show[ed]
how they were focusing in on specific areas." Thus, Perkins got "legislation
that fit [his] congressional district": "Rather than poverty as a whole, they
got down to where they had select areas of poverty and it was a vote getting
process, . . . and everyone found an excuse to be needy, . . . so some of those
programs were being used for political purposes and that's where I drew the
line." After Nunn raised objections to the War on Poverty, somebody from
Perkins's district said: "'Why hell governor, if you take that poverty away
from us we won't have nothing left.' And that was about the attitude."[2]

Because of that "attitude," the "political purposes," and the fact that
the War on Poverty was "detrimental to the 'morality' . . . of the community," and because "the benefit ratio didn't begin to match the expendi-
ture," Nunn "thought the dollars could be better spent." In response, he
started CREATE, or Community Resources for Employment and Training
Effort. Unlike what Nunn considered the handout, entitlement programs
of the Johnson administration, CREATE attempted to prepare people for
employment. Further, Nunn supported a state initiative, the Kentucky Un-
American Activities Committee (KUAC), that, ultimately, questioned the
patriotism of those seeking to end poverty and, in the end, contributed to
the end of the Appalachian Volunteers (AVs). Interestingly, the AVs considered KUAC—created by both Democrats and Republicans—to be a political tool. Ironically, Nunn, for all his protestations against strict political
maneuvering, "didn't see any harm in it": "Hell, [it was] just like the wind
blowing through the trees. It makes some noise today and tomorrow, . . .
and sometimes they'll blow a few things out. . . . The rotten limbs will get
blow off. . . . So let it blow through; if the rotten limbs fall out, well that's
fine. If there aren't any rotten limbs, nothing gonna fall out."[3]

Ironically, both Nunn and the Appalachian Volunteers condemned the
War on Poverty for basically the same reason, Nunn because people like

Perkins, and the AVs because local governments and especially community action programs (CAPs), used it for political purposes. Still, however, internal questions preoccupied the antipoverty warriors in the late spring and early summer of 1967. Just as in early 1966, questions about personal appearance figured prominently in the discussion. While it was acceptable for a volunteer to get dirty in the course of performing his duties, all AVs should strive to be as "neat" as possible. "There was a feeling," the board prophetically declared, "that a large number of people are looking for things to use . . . against the AVs." Training of new Appalachian Volunteers should make the recruits "aware of the types of conduct that the people consider acceptable." In addition, the Volunteers announced, female volunteers could not wear short skirts in mountain communities.[4]

Personal conduct was not the only problem with which the Volunteers had to cope. Dennis Forbes, a visitor to Breathitt County who wanted to join the AV staff, observed during his stay in eastern Kentucky that "the basic problem of the Appalachian Volunteers is getting the cooperation of the people." He encouraged the Volunteers to be flexible and to adapt to many different types of issues and circumstances: "Each county will have different problems to solve so it is doubtful that one program will solve the entire situation." Forbes believed that a number of smaller programs would be necessary to make major improvements in the central Appalachian highlands. Apparently, similar feelings existed within the Volunteer ranks, especially concerning the difficulties of getting rural people to cooperate with and participate in AV efforts. The Volunteers' job was to advise the people and to "let the people do the work themselves." During the 1966 summer project, some complained, "the AV's did everything and when they left almost everything they had done fell apart."[5]

Joining in this self-examination was Richard Boone, who, along with Milton Ogle, originally conceived of the idea of the Appalachian Volunteers. Boone agreed with the AV intern Tom Hamilton that the AVs were "spreading themselves too thin," and he argued that they should go into "one area with sufficient personnel and a definite plan." Moreover, the Volunteers should make common cause with as many "democratically controlled" CAPs as possible. Together, the AVs and their CAP allies could put pressure on those programs that were "unresponsive to the poor" and those that had lost "their democratic function" and bring them back in line.[6]

As the Appalachian Volunteers developed programs to fight the coal companies and county officials, they certainly were overextended. In order to help as many mountain residents as possible, they moved quickly from county to county and from state to state, "responding to whatever things caught their eye." As a consequence: "The development of a field 'turf' was, at best, haphazard." This rapid pace prevented the AVs from following up in many counties where they had performed work. After the program's extension to West Virginia and Virginia, they "suddenly neglected" such Kentucky counties as Jackson, Rockcastle, and Knox. As a result of this "passing commitment," many of the poor became disillusioned with the AVs—which may explain the "apathy" some volunteers claimed they witnessed—and "expressed regret at being left 'high and dry'" by them. Many AVs themselves, fieldmen as well as volunteers, "suffered a feeling of isolation from other field areas and ideas—and from the Bristol Office." Communications between the office and the field were hazy and confusing. Should the organization continue in this "'thither and yon' kind of style," the AVs reasoned, "the errors will persist and . . . we [will be] sitting ducks for the well organized forces which oppose us. . . . Implications of this hard fact are that the AV effort can only be described in terms of isolated individuals—like the interns who, so far have been unable to co-ordinate any kind of group action—and not in terms of a movement or a regional attitude about problems." The most significant problem was that those places that the Volunteers believed most needed their attention were too far away.[7]

Because "no one person knew enough about the whole AV operation to make any intelligent speculation about what should be done," the Appalachian Volunteers formed an evaluation team called the "E-Squad." Consisting of two people from the central office and two from the field, the E-Squad traveled throughout the entire AV operating area and looked for ways to make improvements. In particular, it sought a way to focus the AV effort into a more limited, defined area. Though its members thought in terms of contiguous counties with common features, the E-Squad was not confined by state boundaries. "Too much of our energy," the team decided, "is spent thinking about state structures and boundaries and . . . we ought to be thinking much more in terms of poor Appalachians as a class of people and Appalachia as a region." Working from this basic idea, the E-Squad reasoned that, with "a lump of Kentucky and a neighboring lump of West

Virginia" and the central office relocated in that newly defined region, the Volunteers could stimulate teamwork and mutual support.[8]

After surveying the expanse of AV territory, the E-Squad recommended creating four districts, roughly equal in population and size, with at least two fieldmen in each. From west to east, these counties were Breathitt, Wolfe, Floyd, Pike, and, ultimately, Harlan, in Kentucky, and Raleigh, Wyoming, Mingo, and Logan in West Virginia. These counties, explained the E-Squad, "would receive the full attention of the AV outfit," which would "go for broke" in them. To better serve the proposed area, the E-Squad advocated once again relocating the central office, this time to Pikeville, in Pike County, Kentucky. Pikeville was "the most central point of [the] new arrangement . . . [and the] most suitable setting" for their headquarters. Because of its distance from the majority of Volunteer activity, Bristol was in "another world," too far from the new area of concentration to be an effective headquarters. The move to Pikeville would ensure a more effective AV program.[9]

Probably to finalize the recommendations of the E-Squad, the Appalachian Volunteers held a meeting in Pikeville in May 1967. Not only was the proposed new location in the center of the recently redefined Volunteer "turf," but the E-Squad believed Pikeville to be in the "most populous (and perhaps most progressive) county in eastern Kentucky." Also, the city was close to those areas, most notably Whitley County, Kentucky, and Wise County, Virginia, from which the AVs had retreated but still hoped to influence. Despite the advantages of the location, the recommendation of the E-Squad to limit the scope of AV activity and to make Pike one of those counties to see a concentrated Volunteer effort proved to be a monumental error—one that, ultimately, proved fatal to the organization.[10]

Many people in those counties "dropped" by the Volunteers did feel a sense of abandonment. After a Volunteer meeting, AV Joel Hasslen had dinner with a few of the AV interns who lived in counties scheduled for termination. "They talked about their work," Hasslen wrote to Ogle, "and their feelings about being dropped, [and] as they talked I begin to see the AV's in a different light. They begin to look a lot like county politicians or established CAPs. I thought it was only my Fieldman that had begun to identify with the enemy, (wants a pine paneled office and digs Cadilacs) but the AV program is beginning to look like a East Kentucky election promise. . . . In one area scheduled to be rubbed out of AV land the folks seem to take a resentful, 'hell with them attitude.'" Hasslen argued that he "could see too clearly that arguments brought forth . . . to drop certain areas [were] not necessarily going to convince the folks that the AV's [were] acting in their best interests." Rather, he concluded, this action instilled in the poor mountaineers a sense of "distrust and contempt" for the Appalachian Volunteers.[11]

Ironically, distrust and contempt long characterized the history of the Appalachian Volunteers in Pike County. On October 21, 1965, in the initial stages of their reform efforts, the Volunteers first strained relations with Pikeville's business community when, in an early step that went beyond the cooperative approach favored by the Council of the Southern Mountains (CSM), Flem Messer traveled to Pikeville College to explain the Volunteer program and to recruit participants from among the student body. During his presentation, Messer discussed the "hopelessness of the situation because of the lack of jobs and the shortcomings of the various welfare programs" and argued that "the politicians and the banks . . . concentrated . . . all the money and power" of the county in their hands and reinvested nothing in the community. Rather, the wealth of the county flowed out and left the people impoverished. If used to establish new enterprises locally, Messer explained, this money could help develop jobs in the region. "The War On Poverty," he concluded, was an "opportunity . . . to see that turn around."[12]

These statements angered John Yost, then a vice president of the Citizens Bank of Pikeville, who interpreted them as an indictment of his institution's business practices. Denying that he singled out Yost's bank or implied any sort of irregularities on the part of the establishment, Messer attempted to resolve the conflict with Yost. Though Messer phoned Yost to assure him that he meant no harm, his efforts exacerbated the already tense situation. The bank executive notified Messer that the conversation was being recorded and "spent approximately one hour on the phone talking a great deal . . . and seemingly heard very little." Yost then informed Messer that he did not know much about the AV program and that, given his experiences thus far, he did not wish to learn anything more. Ending the exchange with a threat, Yost warned Messer that "the people at the heads of the hollows . . . are happy and that [the AVs] would do damn well to leave them alone."[13]

Yost's reaction to Messer involved more than a defense of his bank.

His desire to see the Volunteers out of Pike County indicated that he knew something about the program and that he viewed it as a potential threat. Moreover, the Persimmon Fork organization in Leslie County, among others, provided Yost with examples of AV activity. Coupled with the roving picket movement of that same period, these developments surely placed those individuals such as Yost who benefited significantly from the established system on the defensive.[14]

Yost's recording of the phone conversation also revealed that his concerns went beyond his business. On the surface, this could simply be a bluff designed to intimidate Messer and the AVs. Taking this incident a bit further, however, it appears that Yost hoped to gather some sort of evidence either to help him defend his position or to inflict damage on the Appalachian Volunteers.

School renovation projects that began in 1965 also gave Yost an opportunity to hear and learn about AV activity in the area. Interestingly, it was in Pike County that an early AV school renovation project yielded disastrous results. According to the AV fieldman Messer, not only did the local community fail to take part, but the project proved to be "a waste of materials, and more importantly a great waste of enthusiasm for . . . the Appalachian Volunteers program." Unknown individuals almost immediately vandalized the newly refurbished building.[15]

Failed projects were not the only source of trouble for the volunteers in the county. Following up on the E-Squad's desire to provide more direction to the AV program, the organization hired the professional organizer Alan McSurely, who had worked in antipoverty programs in Washington, DC. By the time he arrived in the AV offices, David Whisnant has written, McSurely "was convinced of the need for a fundamental transformation of the nation's political and economic system, pertinent models for which he located in aspects of both socialism and communism." McSurely spelled out his ideas on this subject in a paper called "A New Political Union," which he subsequently distributed among the Volunteers. McSurely wrote the essay, which was replete with leftist overtones, "with the aim of producing ordered discussion and decisions which will lead to the organization of a national new political union." Because of the "irrelevancy of the ideas and the ineffectiveness of the programs" of the existing national parties and the "inability and unwillingness of the capitalist ruling class to make good on any of the promises it has made," the only alternative was "taking national power."[16]

With the goal of organizing the "decision-making and accountability process," and in order to "get the job of the revolution over with," the paper outlined the foundations of a national party with a central committee and a national program. McSurely called for strong commitment. "One must set his goal," he contended, "determine the theory he is going to operate on, and then *never, never veer* from this path . . . because when the struggle heats up, we must live and die with those ideas and theories we have finally chosen.[17]

Many of the Appalachian Volunteer staff rejected McSurely's dogmatic ideas. Milton Ogle described them as a "totally simple, almost naive plan for the rigid domination of a people by a small group." On April 16, 1967, "the full staff, with one dissenting vote, agreed that Mr. McSurely was not to act as a member of the Appalachian Volunteer staff."[18]

McSurely's ideas, nevertheless, seemingly resonated throughout the Volunteer ranks. After all, the AVs were organizing in opposition to the established political system in the mountains. The key to unlocking the political puzzle, the Volunteers had begun to realize, was undermining the power of the coal operators, and the best way to do that was to halt the destructive practice of strip mining. Symbolic of the power of the coal companies was the "broad form deed." This legal construction originated in the late nineteenth century when mineral agents bought only the coal, not the land under which it lay. As interpreted by Kentucky courts, these transactions "transferred to the [coal operator] all of the mineral wealth and the right to remove it by whatever means necessary, while leaving the farmer and his descendants with the semblance of land ownership." With the advent of stripping for coal, later generations felt the ultimate impact of the broad form deed. In addition to the loss of rights to the minerals, the deed also forced those living above the coal to relinquish "such other rights to the surface of the land as to limit its use for residential or agricultural purposes." Because of the destruction strip mining caused, the Volunteers recruited and employed law students to work on ways to halt the practice and called on state governments to abolish it if slopes were too steep or the threat of pollution and erosion was too great.[19]

In 1966, when it amended the state mining code, Kentucky had some

of the toughest restrictions in the Appalachian coalfields. Because enforcement was so lacking, however, local groups such as the Appalachian
Group to Save the Land and People (AGSLP) began to form in the 1960s.
For the Volunteers' part, their concern over the issue focused on AGSLP
and Pike County. The Volunteers had already made headway in their
battle against strip mining by joining with Hulett Smith, the governor
of West Virginia, and they continued to press the issue with that state's
general assembly. In Kentucky, progress was slower but no less dramatic.
In Harlan County, the Volunteer staff member Steve Daugherty used the
issue as a focal point around which he sought to organize the poor, and, in
Letcher County, the AV-VISTA Mike Shields helped a local farmer resist a
local strip-mine operator.[20]

These accomplishments, nevertheless, proved to be minor in comparison to what happened in Pike County during the summer of 1967. More
than in any other county, coal was king in Pike. Bill Peterson of the *Louisville
Courier-Journal* identified over fifty coal millionaires in Pikeville's population of less than five thousand, while one of the city's demographers found
a supporting cast of forty lawyers. Even Edith Easterling commented that
people were "so frightened of county authorities that they hadn't been out
of the hollows in twenty years." It was in this county that the Volunteers
made their stand against King Coal.[21]

Heading the fight was Joe Mulloy, on whom McSurely probably had
his greatest influence. Originally from Louisville, Kentucky, Mulloy became
interested in eastern Kentucky because his family on his mother's side had
come from the mountains. While residing in Pike County, he apparently
stayed in contact with McSurely, who also lived there as a staff member of
the Southern Conference Educational Fund (SCEF). Led by the well-known
social activists Carl and Anne Braden, this association helped shape Mulloy
and his actions in the county.[22]

After the first few school renovation projects, the Appalachian Volunteers began to invest considerable effort in Pike County's Marrowbone Folk
School. Mulloy initially organized the school—founded at Poor Bottom,
a tributary of Marrowbone Creek, in early 1967—as a community center
meant to house a library and quilting sessions for the Poor Bottom Quil-
ters. By the summer of that year, however, Mulloy started to push for road
improvements, and he began working with the anti-strip-mining AGSLP.

From this start, Mulloy and the Volunteers moved quickly to end strip mining and to attain better roads.[23]

On June 3, to help plan the new issue-organizing campaign, AVs from Floyd, Harlan, and Pike counties met at the Highlander Center (formerly the Highlander Folk School) in Knoxville. The language employed at this meeting revealed the direction that Mulloy, his fellow AV staff, and his supporters had taken in recent years. Participants in this meeting reaffirmed the decision to organize around issues such as road improvements, stopping strip mining, and welfare reform. All present resolved to work, and, reflecting the new reorganization scheme, the "idea of state and county lines was thrown out the window."[24]

The Pike County representatives announced that their area of concentration would be Marrowbone Creek. "On July 7, five [branch] creeks on Marrowbone will strike for roads," announced the AVs, but other "ideas like picketing, sit-ins on the roads, and blowing up bridges were all discussed." After his return from Highlander, Mulloy continued his work with the local AGSLP chapter. Believing that to "solve poverty, you [must] change some of the structures that cause that poverty," Mulloy sympathized with AGSLP's goal. A few weeks after the Highlander meeting, on June 29, 1967, Jink Ray, a farmer in the Island Creek section of Pike County, set the stage for a confrontation when he blocked a Puritan Coal Company bulldozer from strip mining on land he had farmed for over forty years. Mulloy and AGSLP members supported Ray at the scene. Despite a court order in favor of the stripper, this demonstration continued every day until Edward Breathitt, the governor of Kentucky, suspended the mining permit on July 18, 1967. Two weeks later, the state revoked the permit altogether because the land was too steep to meet mining regulations. AGSLP and the Volunteers had defeated the powerful coal-mining interests, but this victory proved to be short-lived.[25]

The local coal operators believed that they "had to put a stop to this." They portrayed Mulloy as a subversive outsider and the key organizer and moved to destroy the anti-strip-mining movement. Just ten days after Breathitt rescinded Puritan Coal's permit, the Pike County sheriff, Perry Justice, arrested Mulloy and Alan and Margaret McSurely—both of whom worked for the SCEF in Pike County—for sedition against the county government. Mulloy's arrest was the culmination of attempts—including the disconnecting of his telephone and the canceling of his automobile insurance—to pressure Mulloy into ceasing his activities. More important, the Volunteers believed, Robert Holcomb, the president of both the Pikeville Chamber of Commerce and the powerful Independent Coal Operators Association, engineered Mulloy's arrest.[26]

Immediately following the arrest, the sheriff's department searched Mulloy's home and claimed to have found a "communist library out of this world" that included *The Communist Manifesto* and a collection of Russian short stories—conveniently ignoring copies of Barry Goldwater's *Conscience of a Conservative* and the Bible. On September 11, 1967, on the basis of such "communist" evidence, a Pike County grand jury indicted Mulloy, the McSurelys, and Carl and Anne Braden of the SCEF for sedition under Kentucky Revised Statute 432.040, which prohibited teaching or advocating criminal syndicalism against the state. Specifically, the grand jury declared that "a well organized and well financed effort is being made to promote and spread the communistic theory of the violent and forceful overthrow of the government of Pike County" and that the Appalachian Volunteers cooperated in this subversive endeavor. Three days later, however, a federal court in Lexington declared the state law unconstitutional.[27]

Prosecutors could not have been surprised by the federal court's ruling. In 1954, a Louisville court had indicted and convicted Carl Braden of sedition against the state using the same law. Two years later, in June 1956, the Kentucky Court of Appeals in Louisville overturned Braden's conviction. Citing a similar decision in Pennsylvania in 1956 that the U.S. Supreme Court affirmed on April 2, 1956, the appeals court ruled that acts of sedition could be directed against the nation only, not a state. Quoting the federal opinion, the state court echoed: "The federal statues 'touch on a field in which the federal interest is so dominant that the federal system (must) be assumed to preclude enforcement of state laws on the same subject.'" Unfortunately for Mulloy and the SCEF members, this decision was binding only in the Louisville district and merely set aside the conviction without removing the laws from the statute books, leaving them available to the Pikeville court. Because of Braden's first case, the prosecutors certainly knew that a conviction would not stand and that the statute employed against those arrested would be declared unconstitutional.[28]

The language of the report of the Pike County grand jury, however, revealed an understanding of these legal precedents and a desire to challenge them. In charging the activists with sedition against the county, the grand jury recommended "that in the event our present laws on sedition are declared unconstitutional by the federal courts . . . the next session of the Kentucky Legislature pass new laws which will control such activities in the future." This case was not about enforcement of the law or anticommunism. Rather, county officials were positioning themselves to attack the mountain reformers.[29]

In the wake of the arrests, the Appalachian Volunteers tried to place themselves on the side of the common folk. They proclaimed: "[By] helping the very many eastern Kentuckians who are threatened by strip-mining, we have found ourselves opposed to the very few eastern Kentuckians who profit from it." As a result, they continued, those who benefited from the coal industry "have chosen to attack us as radicals and as seditionists and to attempt to drive us out of the area." Although, in legal terms, the AVs were cleared of the charges, for all practical purposes their position was very tenuous. Regardless of the validity of the charge, the stigma of being associated with communism seriously damaged their credibility, and, early in September, Governor Breathitt announced that all AV funding would be cut immediately.[30]

This declaration brought a flurry of responses to the governor's office. A Whitley County resident wrote about the AVs: "They have taught people their human rights; they have brought the very best libraries into the hollows and backwoods; and one of the greatest things they have brought was the truth." Others were not so positive. An editorial in the *Jackson Times* entitled "Do We Really Need These 'Helpers'?" supported the "Pike County officials who acted . . . to put a scotch under the wheels of the volunteers who are allowed to [foment] trouble wherever and whenever they will." Even more damning, Al Whitehouse, the director of the Kentucky Office of Economic Opportunity (OEO), issued a statement endorsing the governor's action withdrawing support from the AVs. "We believe," Whitehouse announced, "that the community action programs developed at the local level are the *prime offensive weapon in the War on Poverty.*" The two funded agencies—the CAPs and the Volunteers—Whitehouse continued, "working in the same . . . areas in the field of community organization is not only very confusing to the groups we are trying to reach but has also *proven unwork-*

able in most instances. Volunteers working at the grassroots level . . . *must be under the umbrella of the [CAPs] if we are to unite the community in an all out effort that can win the War on Poverty.*" While the AVs accused White-house of "making an effort to gain control of the A.V. program," Ogle, who certainly understood that the Appalachian Volunteers relied on OEO fund-ing for their survival, believed that the Mulloy incident "pointed out some areas of work" for the Volunteers, including "improving the relations with state offices . . . [and] local officials." When the dust finally settled, the AVs kept their OEO funds, but the grants were due to expire the following year, and Ogle probably knew that renewing them would be difficult.[31]

Throughout the remainder of 1967, the Volunteers tried to maintain a lower profile because, as one staff memorandum warned, the organization "cannot afford another Pikeville."[32] A low profile, however, was far more difficult to maintain than anyone ever imagined. A new issue arose within the ranks of the Volunteers—that of military conscription for the war in Vietnam—that proved to be more divisive than any other with which the Appalachian Volunteers had had to deal.

Though Mulloy did register with the Kentucky draft board, many of his compatriots enjoyed certain types of deferments. The staff members Bill Wells, Joel Hasslen, Jack Rivel, Thomas Rhodenbaugh, Steve Kramer, and Douglas Yarrow all had either occupation deferments or conscientious objector classifications. In addition, conscientious objectors so filled the ranks of AVs and VISTA volunteers in the Southern mountains that one Volunteer, Linda Cooper, wished the AV staff "Happy Draft Deferments" on the back of one of the surveys she returned to the main office. Mulloy, too, had an occupational deferment—until the state revoked it following his arrest in Pikeville. In an effort to stay in Appalachian Kentucky and out of the war, he then attempted to get classified as a conscientious objector after his local draft board ordered him to report for induction on August 18, 1967. Unfortunately for Mulloy and the Appalachian Volunteers, the board refused his appeal.[33]

In response to the draft board's action, Mulloy announced that he would refuse induction into the army: "My position is that there are far too many problems, injustices, and inequalities in these United States for us to play policeman of the World. . . . But our President and others would have us fight and die in the rice fields of Asia before they would guarantee a truly free society at home. . . . Poverty in Eastern Kentucky and the war in Vietnam are the same issue. The advocates of war and the businesses that prosper from it are the same absentee landlords that have robbed Eastern Kentucky blind for years." Mulloy, then, believed that he must resist induction into the army in order "to bear witness to the hypocrisy of our government's posture and the crimes being committed by this government in Vietnam."[34]

After Mulloy announced his intention to refuse induction, Milton Ogle and another Volunteer staff member, David Walls, urged him to resign his AV position. Ogle and Walls felt that Mulloy's action was a personal matter and that a majority of mountain residents would not agree with his position. Ogle maintained that, in light of the recent sedition trial, the AV organization should not take a stand on the war issue. After conferring with Edith Easterling, Walls reported that she was apprehensive about the newly formed Marrowbone Folk School. In addition to the personal threats "sparked by the sedition charges[,] [s]he received one threat that the newly constructed [Marrowbone Folk School] would be dynamited." According to Walls, Easterling "was worried about the consequences for the local people working with her as AV's of Joe's planned refusal to report for induction": "Edith was afraid that most of the people in the Marrowbone area, including many of the local AV workers, would have nothing more to do with the AV's or the Marrowbone Folk School if the AV's or the [school] became identified with Joe's stand on the draft." In addition, Walls maintained, Mulloy had a "moral obligation" to leave the Appalachian Volunteers "when 14 out of the 17 of the east Kentuckians present at the Jenny Wiley staff meeting indicated they did not want to defend Joe's refusal to be inducted." Among those who asked that Mulloy be relieved of his Volunteer responsibilities was a miner "who lost his job in a Pike County coal mine for defending Joe from the sedition charges." In the end, Walls contended, Mulloy's unwillingness to resign from the staff left many eastern Kentuckians who supported the Volunteers "in the position of being forced to support Joe's stand, against their wishes."[35]

Mulloy, however, refused to resign. Then, on December 2, 1967, because his "declared position on the draft and the Vietnam War and the likelihood of it being identified as a stand of the AV program . . . [had] render[ed] him ineffective to work with the people of the Appalachian mountains," the Kentucky AV staff fired him by a vote of 20–19. According to David Whisnant, the vote to fire Mulloy took place "amid charges of procedural irregularities" and "rumors" that local interns and some members of the AV staff would lose their jobs if they supported Mulloy (since the organization would lose its funding) and that Ogle had "set up [the vote] to back [his] pre-formed decision." In addition, Whisnant described the AV executive office as using "home style Appalachian politics." Ogle and Walls defended the AV staff action by asserting that the local people involved in the AV program had the right to choose the issues for which they would fight and that, although Mulloy had made a courageous moral stand, he had no right to force others to embrace his position. While Ogle referred to Mulloy's decision as a "rather selfish stand" that jeopardized those "infrequent instances in which we have been moderately successful" in organizing local people, Walls defended his position, declaring: "The local people, the ones on the battle line, decided the fate of the organization and themselves, rather than having the outsiders impose their decisions on the people of the mountains in the traditional pattern."[36]

The decision split the Appalachian Volunteers. A significant number of those who voted against the firing resigned and accused the organization of "doing the politically expedient thing rather than facing a problem frankly and honestly." Just as important, the volunteer Michael Clark argued, "firing Joe will not stop people from associating him with the AVs. He is and will remain an AV in the minds of most people and no purge or inquisition will change that fact." Clark called on the Volunteers to support Mulloy because the draft notice was a direct response to the failure of the sedition case to rid eastern Kentucky of the Volunteers. The fieldman Steve Daugherty referred to Mulloy's firing as "a gutless, unprincipled decision made on the basis of expediency rather than justice." The AV organization, he claimed, was "shot through with hypocrisy": "It is an organization which self-righteously advocates the promotion of civil liberties in Eastern Kentucky and yet smothers and destroys unpopular opinions by members of its own staff." Daugherty charged: "The administrative staff had already made the decision and was merely seeking rubber stamp approval." In his letter of resignation, Tom Bethell claimed that the decision to terminate Mulloy as an Appalachian Volunteer showed "how miserably the Appalachian Volunteers organization fails to practice what it so insistently preaches": "We talk endlessly about educating people to make their own decisions about the issues that affect their lives. We do not stipulate that their decisions be popular or noncontroversial. To deny to a staff member the same thing that we ask him to teach is to make the entire Appalachian Volunteer's program meaningless—a sorry testimonial to hypocrisy."[37]

Many Appalachian Volunteers supported Mulloy in his stance against the Vietnam War and believed that the organization as a whole should have adopted his particular position. Fourteen members of the Volunteer staff then working in West Virginia who did not attend the meeting at which Ogle fired Mulloy petitioned the AV administrative staff to reinstate Mulloy and threatened to sever their ties with the AVs and form their own independent version of the organization. A common theme running through all the opposition to the firing concerned the need of the Volunteers to be a "moral force" in the Kentucky mountains. Those who resigned maintained that these issues should be discussed with eastern Kentuckians as a whole and that the Volunteers were responsible for making mountaineers aware of the adverse impact on them of the war. "There may come a day," Tom Bethell predicted, "when local people alone can govern Appalachia, or, before that, correct its endless ills. But that day isn't here yet."[38]

Interestingly, these statements came *after* Walls had informed the Volunteers of how the people at Poor Bottom and Marrowbone Creek felt about Mulloy's decision. Edith Easterling herself, the most active and outspoken Appalachian Volunteer supporter in Pike County, answered most of the charges leveled by those who resigned. "Are we the A.V. thinking of ourselves or are we thinking of the community and people we are working with?" she asked. "As [for] myself, I feel like Joe has helped me a lot and as myself I am for Joe but I am not thinking of myself, I am thinking and speaking for the community people. I have talked to lots of people and they don't believe in the war but they think if you are called you should go." Moreover, she claimed: "The people need the help that we get from the A.V.s and we could not work in Pike County if Joe stayed on here."[39]

Easterling went on to detail what she thought the consequences would be if Mulloy attempted to continue working in the area: "I feel it would all go down if Joe stays. The day that the news came out about Joe not going into the army in Pike County, the Marrowbone Folk School in which Joe has helped get started had what looked like a shot put through the front window. I don't want to spend my time trying to defend myself or the A.V., I want to work with the people. . . . *I noticed that the ones that wanted Joe to stay on was not local people.*" For an organization that professed to respect the wishes of the people, the Volunteers had been placed on shaky ground by those of its employees who chose to support Mulloy on the draft issue. This desire of some to "make Vietnam an issue" in eastern Kentucky flew in the face of what, as Easterling explained, many mountaineers believed about patriotism and duty. Even more significant, it exposed the attitudes of many staff members toward the people they professed to serve.[40]

The Appalachian Volunteers faced yet another challenge when, on March 27, 1968, the Pike County grand jury got its wish for a replacement of the state's sedition law. Three months after the controversy over the draft, Concurrent Resolution HR 84 passed the Kentucky General Assembly, and, with the support of Louie Nunn, the Republican governor, it established KUAC. Set up ostensibly to combat the "grave public dangers from enemies both within and without [the state's] boundaries" who operated "under the color of protection afforded by the Bill of Rights," KUAC filled the void left by the ruling on Kentucky's sedition law. Section 1 of the resolution echoed the state's former sedition statutes: "Said committee shall study, investigate, and analyze all facts relating directly or indirectly to the subject expressed in the recitals of this resolution; to the activities of groups and organizations which have as their objectives or as part of their objectives the overthrow of the Commonwealth of Kentucky." Though the state first used this piece of legislation to quell civil rights demonstrations in Louisville, Pike County officials believed that the Appalachian Volunteers unquestionably fit the description of an "enemy."[41]

At the request of unspecified residents (the AVs believed it was Tom Ratliff, the sedition law prosecutor), KUAC announced that it would hold hearings in Pikeville in October 1968. According to the transcript of those hearings, some county residents accused the AVs of attempting to undermine a proposed public utility, the Marrowbone Creek Water District, because they argued that the tap-on fee was too expensive for the poor.[42] In their efforts to secure cheaper water rates for the Marrowbone Creek residents, the Volunteers again engaged in behavior considered dangerous to the public good.

Though KUAC "invited" the Volunteers to appear, David Walls, who became acting director following Ogle's resignation in September 1968, declined to make an appearance. Walls believed that the dispute over the tap-on fee should be "a matter for a Public Utilities Commission hearing, not a legislative investigation." He continued: "We think nothing is more Un-American than labeling your opposition Communist in order to deny them the Constitutional rights of freedom of speech, freedom of association and assembly, as well as the right to petition government for redress of grievances." No matter how accurately Walls portrayed this violation of civil liberties, he unwittingly played into the hands of his adversaries. The legislature had, after all, directed KUAC to weed out those individuals "hiding" behind the Bill of Rights. The Appalachian Volunteers fell into a trap that dated at least to the McCarthy era—they were guilty by denial.[43]

Despite AV protests labeling the effort a "red-baiting, witch hunting campaign," the committee forged ahead with the scheduled hearings. Though KUAC asserted that it held "no preconceived views on the facts in Appalachia at the time" and that the members simply wanted to look into "certain problems in the Appalachian region of the state," it spent much time scrutinizing Volunteer activities.[44] KUAC discussed the water district controversy and also reexamined the sedition trial of the previous year. Throughout the investigation, KUAC accused the Volunteers of such relatively minor offenses as "aggravat[ing] political situations" and "caus[ing] a great deal of conflict, a great deal of confusion," as well as leveling more serious charges, such as striving "to gain power and . . . control their government." A committee witness insisted that an AV employee informed him that the AVs had Communists in the "Congress and Senate" and "would overthrow the government anyway in the next three years; that we would all be communist anyhow."[45]

Others testified that the AVs sought the redistribution of wealth: "They believe that money ought to be taken from the rich and given to the poor." Further, the nation's money supply would be undermined. One witness testified that "[an AV] said they was going to get rid of the money," that "if they establish new money, everybody would be equal." When rehashing the sedition arrests and the confiscation of material from the McSurely residence, the KUAC investigators asked witnesses such questions as, "Are you aware of the fact that in the material there was a plan to overtake the mountains in Kentucky?" and, "Did they make any statements to you as to how they were going to overthrow the government?" Responding to this line of questioning, one witness affirmed: "There were just grounds for the action by the law enforcement officers of Pike County and . . . efforts [were] being made to subvert our government."[46]

During the course of the hearing, KUAC portrayed the AVs as manipulating the poor, threatening the real interests of the mountaineers, and conspiring against the government.[47] Perhaps the most damaging characteristic attributed to the Appalachian Volunteers by KUAC and its carefully chosen witnesses, however, was that they were outsiders espousing a foreign ideology. One witness who claimed to have happened to walk in on an AV meeting at the Marrowbone Folk School described the situation in these terms: "Well, I got up there, there were cars . . . from different states . . . one from Virginia and one from North Carolina and one from Washington . . . and . . . over there is a car from California and one from Chicago." After she entered the building, she heard one man state: "Now this is what you comrades have to teach your children and you are asked to start teaching your children at the age of two." At this point, the witness claimed, the group leader noticed a stranger in the room, and he stopped speaking while other AVs removed her from the meeting.[48]

Testimony of this sort helped KUAC exploit the AVs' ties to that "Communist training school," the Highlander Folk School, where the Volunteers had held a number of meetings and retreats. Founded in 1932 as a training center for social activists, and located in Blount County, Tennessee, Highlander had had, virtually since its conception, to defend itself against charges of communism. Because the most recent attacks occurred between 1965 and 1968, Highlander experienced essentially the same problems that the AVs did and at essentially the same time. Though the school was geographically distant from the AVs, it was, for those mobilized against the mountain activists, ideologically much too close. With a long history of supposed Communist tendencies, Highlander, where "they . . . teach you to try to get people to understand [a different] way," was also far from "patriotic" America. This association between the two organizations provided KUAC with additional "evidence" that, like Highlander, the AVs were Communist subversives.[49]

Additional witnesses supported the contention that the poverty workers were little more than troublesome outsiders. Regarding the people he saw coming and going from the former McSurely residence in Pike County, the home's owner testified that the newcomers "explained to us that they were from different states. They [were] from Oregon . . . Florida, California, Maine." Further, he attested: "They didn't clean up as we did, they didn't shave, they needed haircuts." Most important, when he visited, the house was full of literature "on the Communist line"—"lots of books on Russia and some on China, . . . a picture of Khrushchev"—and pictures of "a white woman and colored children." One witness even criticized the FBI for not running a security check on the people involved in the poverty programs. Accepting as fact that the AVs were positively seditious, he opined: "Such people as that working in these type programs is a liability to our nation . . . county and . . . state." A third expressed his concern that the reformers' cause "was in sympathy with the communist way of life." According to those activists with whom he had spoken, "They were going to educate the people and teach them to take . . . their part in politics and political life, [they] wanted them to stand up for their rights." If the poverty programs were to work, he surmised, "they should work in cooperation with the Judge of the county and the officials."[50]

Summing up the effects of the Appalachian Volunteers in the Kentucky mountains, those testifying before KUAC reached a consensus: the AVs created a situation so bad, not just in Pike County but in all of eastern Kentucky, that virtually nothing of any value could be accomplished. "When the AVs first came into the area," one testified, "they got into some bad trouble . . . with some people that they brought in that wasn't local people. They were outsiders that they brought in from all over the nation . . . [and] the local people . . . resent[ed] them." Another claimed that, in his efforts to form a community organization in Van Lear, in Johnson County, the volatile situation precipitated by the Volunteers forced him to assure the mountain residents that he had no connection with the Appalachian Volunteers. "I was asked specifically," he told KUAC, "if the AVs would have anything to do with the organization of the club, . . . and they said if they did, we could forget about organizing it right then and there." Another witness insisted that the AVs were "a liability to our nation and to our county and to our state, and unless laws are passed to prevent people of this caliber entering into these programs, then we are going to have trouble, more trouble."[51]

After listening to testimony for two days, KUAC adjourned. Just over a month later, the committee issued an interim report to Governor Louie Nunn in which it asserted that the AV program in Pike County "has served as a tremendous detriment to the deserving people of this region." The committee contended that the Volunteers had no clear purpose or program and actually worked at "cross purposes" to the county officials and the local CAPs, which were trying to help the poor mountaineers. Moreover, they created "strife" rather than improving the situation of the people. "After hearing all the evidence," the report concluded, "the committee recommends in the strongest terms that the Governor take whatever steps necessary to make certain that the AV program is permanently discontinued."[52]

Ultimately, the influence exerted by those prosecuting the AVs spread beyond the boundaries of Kentucky and into the neighboring state of West Virginia, where the AVs also worked. On October 3, 1967, Robert Byrd took the Senate floor and read a letter from Governor Hulett Smith to Sargent Shriver. Smith claimed that many in his state regarded AV-VISTAs as "'trouble-makers' who offer only negative solutions to community problems." These same people also asserted that the activists taught the poor "'ideas that are Communistic.'" Byrd exploited this attack on the Volunteers and took the opportunity to discredit the OEO as well. He claimed that the OEO's vindication of the AVs in the sedition case was merely a "defensive report" that indicated "the agency actually [had] little control at the local level over a number of activities carried on in its name." While he understood that the Appalachian Volunteers "were not directly employed by the OEO," he asserted that "they were identified in the public eye with its activities" and dependent on public funds. "So the damage," the senator argued, "is done. The poverty program, by the very nature of the way in which it is set up, is given another nationwide black eye." More important than the OEO's incompetence, Byrd continued, was the fact that "outside agitators in the guise of seeking to help poor natives have, instead, brought deep dissension and set neighbor against neighbor." In his final evaluation, the antipoverty warriors in Kentucky and West Virginia were "revolutionaries bent on destroying the present order of society instead of trying to improve conditions within the framework that exists."[53]

Following this period of turmoil, the Appalachian Volunteers struggled to survive. In the aftermath of the original sedition arrest, the organization rejected the proposed move to Pikeville in favor of relocating to Prestonsburg, in Floyd County, Kentucky. However, Volunteer activities after January 1968 again landed the Volunteers in a position precariously close, in the eyes of local officials, to Moscow. In addition to their anti-strip-mining activities, the Volunteers' protests against the Economic Opportunity Act's Title V programs further alienated the powers that be. By providing the unemployed with "work, experience, and training," Title V hoped "to expand the opportunities for constructive work experience and other needed training available to persons who are unable to support or care for themselves or their families." Administered at the local level through the social security system, this program trained unemployed fathers so that they could find jobs and end their dependency on welfare.[54]

Although they were in favor of job training for unemployed mountaineers, the Appalachian Volunteers believed the Title V programs were not the answer. In a 1965 article in *The Nation,* Richard Cloward had made some observations that the AVs apparently took to heart: "The chief concern of the federal anti-poverty program is the victim of poverty, not the source of his disability." Men who previously had no job were, indeed, working, Cloward conceded: "And to that extent the work and training programs of the Office of Economic Opportunity have been a success. But the work which they perform is quite different from that anticipated by the framers of Title V."[55]

Cloward's analysis rang true in Appalachia. Rather than performing meaningful tasks or learning a marketable trade, the newly employed could, the AVs proclaimed, "cut weeds or clean out old cemeteries." Not only were the jobs, in terms of training, meaningless, "but they [had] very little educational significance": "Men . . . learned long ago how to cut weeds or pound rock into a road." While the Volunteers found fault with this antipoverty program throughout Appalachia, the CAP in Floyd County, the agency that administered Title V programs in that county, complained loudly to Governor Nunn in April 1968: "The AV's have knowingly associated with communists and subversive elements in this and other states." Interestingly, the AVs had a hand in forming the local Floyd County AGSLP chapter. Seemingly, wherever they tried to establish a presence following the first troubles in Pike County, the Volunteers found themselves unwelcome.[56]

Before the summer of 1968, the Appalachian Volunteers felt the effects of this turmoil. Reporting from West Virginia, David Biesmeyer informed the Volunteer staff that he witnessed a great amount of "demoralization and disorganization" among those operating in the Mountain State. As evidence of this depressed condition, Biesmeyer cited a "lack of knowledge and concern on the part of the staff as to what the other members of the staff are doing and the usual lack of agreement on goals and techniques": "At least several members of the staff are talking of the demise of the AVs in West Virginia by the end of the summer and I believe this is a common assumption." Many volunteers made "no plans for what they will be doing the next several weeks or months from now." The following October, Biesmeyer informed the central office that, because the West Virginia AV project "was not approved for continued use of . . . funds after October 1," "nearly all the staff had new jobs with other agencies." Moreover: "The most viable CAPs in West Virginia—Raleigh and Mingo–will be taken over by the county courts, and . . . many of the really fine [local] organizers and leaders we have identified will be putting themselves and their work on the line as never before."[57]

Biesmeyer was one of those who found refuge in other agencies. By May 1969, he was the president of Designs for Rural Action. This West Virginia–based organization, through its "Knowledge Power" project, proposed to "demonstrate the utility of providing leaders of the poor with the skills in researching . . . and . . . dealing with their problems." So poisonous was the atmosphere surrounding the War on Poverty by this time, however, that Biesmeyer's new efforts met with the condemnation of at least one member of the state senate. Writing to the new Republican president, Richard Nixon, State Senator Neal Kingsolving called Designs for Rural Action a "dummy corporation" that operated "over the objections of our duly elected governor." "To permit public funds to pass into private hands for such questionable purposes," he continued, "without the approval and supervision of duly elected representatives of the people, is highly disruptive of good government and flies in the face of American tradition."[58]

In Kentucky, the situation was no different. By the end of 1968, the AV board of directors admitted that "active participation in its activities suffered severe blows by the sedition arrests in 1967 and the KUAC hearings in 1968." The established rhetoric of the Appalachian Volunteers, however, remained. The AVs' "primary role," it was declared, was "the building of Appalachian poor people's organizations for economic and political change."

These organizations would wreck "the political bases of southern dema-
gogues locally and nationally" and "confront the colonial institutions of the
region."[59]

Four years had now passed since the Appalachian Volunteers completed their first school renovation project in Harlan County, Kentucky. The
energy, enthusiasm, and optimism characteristic of those early projects
had long since dissipated; the organization now fought for survival. By the
end of 1968, it had alienated every group—from its parent organization,
the Council of the Southern Mountains, to its benefactor, the OEO—with
which it had worked. A future that in 1964 looked so bright and promising
was now dark and uncertain. "Where hundreds of volunteers had worked in
the area in the past," the Volunteers reported, "during the summer of 1968
the AVs carefully used the skills of only fifteen subsistence workers."[60]

Other than attempts to continue issue organizing, most AV activity reverted back to the service projects that were the hallmark of the organization's early years. At this point, the AVs entered their forth and final phase,
during which those most active in the overall AV program, people such
as Edith Easterling and the community interns, were again Appalachians,
not outsiders. They were not, however, necessarily volunteers. Instead, they
were Volunteer employees. This last manifestation of the AVs was illustrated through the organization's tenuous relationship with the Pike County
Citizens Association (PCCA). Founded just prior to the sedition arrests in
1967, the PCCA was an attempt by the Volunteers to create a countywide
base of support. By 1969, however, only residents of Marrowbone Creek
participated in the group. The fact that the AVs hired the staff but required
local people to accept full responsibility for the group was indicative of this
new version of the Appalachian Volunteers. One exception to this shift was
a legal services effort headed by the Yale-educated lawyer Howard Thorkelson. Focusing on issues such as black lung disease and welfare rights, even
this program represented a change from the AVs' issue-organizing days.
While these questions remained crucial to both the Volunteers and local
mountaineers, legal services, though adversarial, operated through the
courts rather than through open confrontation. More significantly, the
legal services effort represented a philosophical shift within the Volunteer
organization. Instead of attacking the "corrupt system," the AVs worked to
remedy the plight of the poor through legal action *within* the system.[61]

Included among the activities of the new local Appalachian Volunteers was the registration of indigent mountaineers on the county welfare roles so that they could receive such benefits as food stamps. Despite this effort, however, one AV mountaineer implied in his report that many people still had a difficult time receiving the benefits to which they were entitled. Other volunteers conducted projects reminiscent of the group's early years. In Letcher County, the Volunteers sponsored two programs, a woodworking cooperative in Carcassonne and a low-cost housing project in Blackey, but they canceled a third slated for Kingdom Come because the people there had "heard so much talk about the AV's" that the group found it "difficult to work there." An AV economic consultant, Ben Poage, advised the Volunteers to select certain communities for demonstration greenhouse projects and woodworking cooperatives that specialized in the construction of stringed instruments and custom rifle stocks. Other volunteers undertook similar efforts. With AV help, the poor of Logan County, West Virginia, established a "very small" Aid to Dependent Children welfare-rights group, and other AV workers set up boys' and girls' basketball teams and held "socials" for local children on weekends. After the tremendous pressure brought to bear on them by the sedition affair, the antiwar episode, and the KUAC hearings, the Appalachian Volunteers returned to those programs that would generate the favorable publicity and exposure that they had enjoyed in 1964.[62]

Money was also very scarce as the last OEO grants, "originally made in 1967, were due to expire at the end of April 1968." Because of extremely conservative spending measures on the part of the AVs, "substantial funds remained unused, [and] the program year was extended by three and six month periods through March, 1969." Grants from private foundations such as the Field Foundation, the New World Foundation, and the Aaron Norman Fund helped the AVs operate at a reduced level after the OEO grant expired.[63]

In August 1968, the Appalachian Volunteers submitted an application for refunding to the OEO for the calendar year 1969. After the OEO approved the application in December 1968, it sent it to Louie Nunn for his approval. Asking for only $116,116, an amount considerably smaller than previous grants, the AVs stated that they "voluntarily limited the application to this amount because they wanted to restrict their activities to the

Cumberland Valley of Kentucky." This restriction, however, did not seem to be voluntary. Douglas G. Robinson, the lawyer hired by the AVs to help them obtain money from the OEO, reported that he had doubts whether the OEO would accept this argument "since West Virginia Governor Smith told the OEO director unequivocally that he would no longer give his approval to AV programs in his state."[64]

Following Governor Smith's lead, Governor Nunn rejected the application because it did not "clearly spell out the AVs' objectives," and the board and staff members were not listed. The Appalachian Volunteers filed an amended application in early March. Before the application ever reached his desk, however, Nunn informed the state OEO office that he would not approve the second AV grant proposal. Because of this, the Kentucky OEO office never sent the AV application to him. As a result, the money set aside by the OEO to cover the grant never reached the Appalachian Volunteers. By June 1969, the Volunteers' executive director, David Walls, announced that, while the Volunteers would help with travel funds and act as a liaison with the various foundations from which they hoped to gain financial support, individual volunteers would need to raise the funds for their own specific projects themselves. Walls also informed the Volunteer staff that he had earmarked most of the remaining funds for administrative overhead until the antipoverty organization closed its books in the Prestonsburg office.[65]

With their backs against the wall and money due to run out by October 1, 1970, the Appalachian Volunteers played their last card. Claiming that the failure to send the second AV grant application to the governor and the denial of "reasonable notice and opportunity to be heard on the refusal to refund" violated the Economic Opportunity Act, they sued the OEO for funding early in January 1970. This action did little to help the Volunteers, and Walls himself resigned from the organization in May. The Appalachian Volunteers did not outlast the summer of 1970.[66]

Ironically, as the Appalachian Volunteers, Inc., withered away, many former staff members found their way back to the Council of the Southern Mountains. In a second irony, the Council, which was now a coalition of various "Commissions" such as the Community Action Commission and the Black Appalachian Commission, had reverted back to the loose, voluntary organizational structure that had characterized it in the 1910s and

1920s. This transformation was the result of the Council's 1969 annual conference, held at Fontana Dam Village, North Carolina. About a thousand people from all over the United States attended, and many of the issues that had caused havoc within the ranks of the Volunteers came to the fore. After the Council—in part under the influence of those returning AVs, but also as a result of what seemed to be a more politically motivated local populace—passed a resolution that allowed everyone attending, whether they were paid Council members or not, to vote, "conference participants established new commissions on Black Appalachians, Poor People's Self-Help, Aging, and Natural Resources." The newly expanded membership also passed several resolutions of a highly political nature, including calls for a guaranteed annual income and the immediate withdrawal of American troops from Southeast Asia. Even the leadership of the CSM had changed. By the summer of 1970, David Walls, the former AV director, had become a commanding presence within the Council of the Southern Mountains.[67]

At the next annual conference in 1970, held at Lake Junaluska, North Carolina, the CSM further felt the influence of this activism. Indicative of the prevailing attitude at the Junaluska conference was a resolution made by the Youth Commission stating that the "defined operational goal of the Council of the Southern Mountains should be the democratic public control of Appalachia's natural resources, basic energy development and transportation, emphasizing decentralization, democratic community and workers' control." As some members of the Board of Directors embraced this statement and others emphasized "the need for social change" and "social action," Loyal Jones, who had replaced Ayer as the executive director of the more moderate Council in late 1966, resigned on June 1, 1970. He was not the only member to leave as a result of what some referred to as the "socialistic, if not . . . communist stand" taken by the CSM.[68]

Although the Council expressed regret over Jones's resignation, it continued to move toward a more radical stance. "New blood," the *Berea College Pinnacle* announced in May 1970, "is beginning to flow in the veins of social revolution in Appalachia." There were hopes, the article continued, that this new "era" would be the "most . . . radical in the Council's history." This loosely organized coalition of diverse interests actually accomplished much without the money and support it had under Ayer and Jones. Operating out of Clintwood, Virginia, the CSM found, however, that its highly politicized agenda severely restricted its base of support, and it never enjoyed the status it had had in the 1960s. Finally, in 1989, after working for change in the Appalachian South for seventy-six years, the Council of the Southern Mountains officially disbanded.[69]

Conclusion

Live to Fight Another Day

> In truth, controversy—from the grassroots level of mountain
> communities to the remote marble canyons of a giant federal
> bureaucracy—has been as much a hallmark of the AV's as the
> programs the organization says it conducts in the Appalachian
> mountains.
>
> —Richard Boyd, "Appy Volunteers
> Are Accustomed to Controversy"

This attempt to integrate the Appalachian South into urban, mainstream America, in many ways an "unfinished revolution," as Eric Foner described the situation in the South after 1877, was decidedly problematic. Nevertheless, this episode in Appalachian history provides insights into the nature of liberal reform, of change, of change agents, and of those in the coalfields who opposed them during the 1960s. These lessons would also apply to the struggles that characterized the War on Poverty in other regions of the United States. Ever since Appalachia's first attempted "reconstruction," which came at the hands of the local color writers, the settlement school workers, and the Northern industrial conquest of the region in the late nineteenth century and the early twentieth, government agencies, local elites, and outside interest groups have dominated "legitimate" change in Appalachia—that is, change interpreted as beneficial. From settlement school teachers to antipoverty warriors, those who came to "save" the mountaineers viewed their subjects as quaint, yet helpless and ignorant at best, and violent and resistant to improvement at worst. Rooted in the perceptions of rural mountaineers held by most Americans, the ideas and conceptions that reformers brought with them to their job betrayed the fact that these outsiders in Appalachia saw the Appalachians themselves as outsiders. While most histories, either popular or scholarly, of the region portray the mountaineers as the ones to perpetuate the insider/outsider dichotomy, a closer look reveals that, in many cases, including the War on Poverty, it was the activists who saw the mountaineers as outsiders because they did not represent what the outside world considered normative. Reporting in the *New York Times* on the Harlan County mine war of the early 1930s, for example, Malcolm Ross perpetuated that disparaging image when he noted that Appalachians were inherently unfit for industrial work: "The coal diggers of the Appalachian mine fields are mountaineers by birth and miners by accident. . . . Whether they escape into the scrubby back district or whether they remain miners, the mountain character of this unadapted people is the most important thing about them. It will not do well to catalogue them as 'mine labor.'" "The mountaineer-miner is a salty individual," he continued, "prejudiced, ignorant, and usually owning a personal charm matched only by his irresponsibility."[1]

About thirty years later, the operative assumptions of the Council of the Southern Mountains (CSM) and the Appalachian Volunteers (AVs), especially during their first few years, professed a cultural explanation of the mountaineers' inadequacies that essentially mirrored Ross's. While the educational enhancement programs certainly held some benefit for mountain children, those efforts, and the generalizations the Volunteers made about rural Appalachians, especially in the training sessions held in Berea, revealed the AVs' preconceived ideas about mountaineers and the sources and causes of poverty. First, the reformers' generalizations about mountain schools and teachers transcended physical conditions and implied that virtually all rural mountaineers, adults as well as children, were insufficiently educated, unimaginative, unable to express themselves, and socially inadequate. The solution to these problems, the Council leadership and a significant number of volunteers believed, was an AV curriculum enhancement and school repair project that would bring the region to, and entice these seemingly deprived children to enter, the Volunteers' world. This perspective prevented the Volunteers themselves from delving beyond surface appearances or discovering their own class biases. In fact, this perspective precluded any sort of class or economic analysis. While they did understand that there was a connection between education and poverty, the Volunteers failed, at least through early 1966, to look beyond their own cultural limitations and consider why the education system was inadequate to the needs of the poor. They did not consider what purpose the mountain education system did serve or what type of education rural mountaineers, in fact, did have. The Council and the Volunteers accepted the prevailing liberal notion of education (which still exists today) as the key to vanquishing want and blamed the victims for their own condition. The mountaineers were poor because they had no education, and, if they failed to get an education, it was their own fault that they remained poor. Questions concerning the economic or political environment do not enter into this simplified analysis, which confirmed the initial position taken by these latter-day mountain reformers. Because it focused on the poor rather than on poverty, this point of view revealed more about the reformers and their vision of the United States than it did about those whom modern society had left behind, and, until they unearthed deeper causes of poverty, renovation and enrichment efforts monopolized the Volunteers' activity in Kentucky's eastern coalfields.[2]

The federal government's War on Poverty merely perpetuated this misconception. As the centerpiece of the Economic Opportunity Act, the community action programs (CAPs), at least two-thirds of the boards of which were populated by representatives of public and private local interests, guided as they were by the vague notion of the "maximum feasible participation of the poor," guaranteed yet another top-down reform effort in the coalfields. By mandating the participation of local private and public concerns, both dominated by the coal industry in Appalachian Kentucky, the federal government ensured that local CAP boards would at least uphold, if not resolidify, the status quo. In short, the federal program's approach to ending poverty played into the hands of those who controlled eastern Kentucky's natural and political resources and, in essence, asked the poor to participate in their own exploitation.[3]

By May 1966, however, the AVs did find a new explanation—colonialism—for the dire conditions that they witnessed in the Southern mountains. This new interpretation demanded new tactics, and, for the Appalachian Volunteers, the solution was open confrontation with the colonizers and their local allies. In essence, the AVs finally realized that rooting the region's problems in a simple construction such as *education* did not take into consideration the social, political, and economic context in which that education took place. Many volunteers, moreover, began to question the validity of American democracy in the region and, instead of working within existing political structures, decided to step outside the established system and engage it in battle. Of course, on one level this called for the creation of new institutions—and new hierarchies—to administer those battles.

As the Volunteers prepared for their confrontation with the powers of the coalfields, they unfortunately retained the paternalistic notions that had driven them since their organization's inception more than two years earlier. After May 1966, rather than exhibiting themselves as models of "proper living," the AVs became–especially in the case of the Vietnam War—"Appalachian spokesmen" for the poor. Impoverished mountaineers, they believed, needed Volunteer assistance if they were to succeed in the war against colonial oppression. The AV "recruiter" and participant Harold Kwalwasser wrote from Swarthmore, Pennsylvania, warning about those poor with whom the AVs worked who aspired to attain "middle class" status in American society. In reference to one mountaineer in particular Kwalwasser noted:

> Carl and the other really bright people we have working *for us* and hope to have working with us are upwardly mobile socially. They have good heads on their shoulders and they know it. Moreover, as they move into positions of trust and status, their feelings are confirmed. That means to them that they are on their way up, toward the middle class and *the ideal way of American life.* Obviously it is a great thing and one of their most longed for goals is to be middle class Americans. They therefore want to act like middle class Americans and will internalize all the values of the middle class. And not only will they internalize them, but they will hold on to them with greater strength than a normal middle class person because it is important that they act middle class-like since their economic position does not totally justify their claim to belonging. In other words in so far as the middle class is identified with laissez faire economic doctrine then these people, like Carl, will come to believe in it. That means that things like welfare . . . are viewed with distaste.

According to Kwalwasser, this new "Appalachian attitude" had dire implications for the Volunteers should these middle-class aspirants "ever accede to power in the hills." "They obviously need government help," Kwalwasser contended, "and I hope they know it." Unfortunately, he warned, this middle-class attitude would force them to reject the help they so desperately need: "And if you disagree about calling [the rejection of aid] all the cause of middle classism, then call it mountain independence and you get the same answer."[4] Thus, even as the Volunteers rejected a cultural explanation of mountain poverty, notions of superiority remained within the organization.

Yet another example of the Appalachian Volunteers' rejection of an antipoverty program that truly called for the establishment of a bottom-up approach to solving the region's ills was the ready abandonment of the basic tenet on which the organization was founded—local people helping each other. When, after VISTA volunteers and non-Appalachians entered their ranks and openly confronted the established system, the antipoverty group was left vulnerable to charges of outside domination or of being outside agitators. While, as an organization, the AVs never were Communists or actually radical, a significant number were not Appalachian either. The fantastic charges of subversion notwithstanding, when witnesses testified before the Kentucky Un-American Activities Committee (KUAC) that outsiders were present in the hollows, their charges were plausible. In the hands of savvy Pikeville politicians, who then used the insider/outsider dichotomy in the more familiar fashion, the leap from outside origin to outside ideology was easy.

As the split within the ranks over the decision to fire Mulloy revealed, a significant number of AVs ultimately rejected any input from those they sought to help. Their desire to make the war a Volunteer and Appalachian issue—even after "14 out of the 17 of the east Kentuckians present at [an AV] staff meeting indicated they did not want to defend Joe's refusal to be inducted"—revealed (once again) the belief that Appalachians could not recognize those issues that were most important to them and that local people needed—as Kwalwasser, among others, declared—the Volunteers' leadership. Though many AVs sought to keep the Vietnam War out of the antipoverty dialogue, in Appalachian Kentucky this incident had a profound effect on the War on Poverty. First, the issue split the Appalachian Volunteers, an organization that was already weakened by the sedition charges pressed earlier that year and that would soon face KUAC. Second, Mulloy's and his supporters' stance discredited the Appalachian Volunteers, as a whole, with many mountain residents. As John Dittmer persuasively argues, the willing and active participation of local people was absolutely critical to the success of any social movement.[5]

Nevertheless, the fact that the most serious attacks on the AVs happened in Pike County, one of the state's leading coal-producing counties, points to the accuracy of the Volunteers' final analysis of eastern Kentucky's problems and the fundamental flaw in the three-legged structure of the CAPs. Coal operators, with the willing support of the local authorities, dominated the lives of the region's poor for their own gain. Equally important, however, the fatal attacks on the antipoverty group in that county demonstrated how far dominant groups will go to prevent or influence change and just how unbalanced—socially, politically, and economically—the antagonistic forces of reform and regime maintenance are in Appalachia and the United States as a whole. Such willingness to exploit postwar fears of communism, to manipulate the judicial system, and to use the force of the state in order to further a private agenda should cause us to reevaluate just who the radicals were in the 1960s.

As the president of the Independent Coal Operators Association and the Pikeville Chamber of Commerce and a resident of one of Kentucky's largest coal-producing counties, Robert Holcomb had the most to lose had the AVs succeeded. On this level, the Pike County experience was unique. Nevertheless, that the Volunteers threatened the local political machines was not unique to Pike County or even the eastern Kentucky coalfields generally. In December 1966, an AV tried to organize a parent-teacher association for the Blue Springs school in Rockcastle County. One of the goals of the nascent PTA was to wrap and distribute Christmas gifts donated by a New York woman to Blue Springs through the AV organization. The county Board of Education, however, denied the AVs access to the school, and "A Tax Paying Citizen" sent a derisive letter to the Blue Springs benefactor. The author of that letter claimed that the AVs were "trying hard to tear down what many of the great people of this community have worked hard for years to build" and that "most of our people are solid, hard working, God fearing, and are not ready for Socialism and/or Dictatorship."[6]

Furthermore, the mountain reformers most definitely failed to recognize the strength and resiliency of the local county power structures. In their confrontations with local government, the AVs became embroiled in the struggle "over who are going to be the generals and who will be the privates" in the War on Poverty. Again, the top-down nature of the War on Poverty prevailed. This contest for leadership was, ultimately, between the Appalachian Volunteers and the county governments. Ironically, the poor, who were supposed to be equal participants, instead became the targets of the war. In most American towns and cities, Daniel Moynihan stated as early as 1969 in *Maximum Feasible Misunderstanding*, "to a pronounced degree events . . . are influenced by a fairly small number of men in banks and law firms." These people "outwait [an antagonist] anytime if that individual is dependent on the House of Representatives and the General Accounting Office to stay in business." Thus, right or wrong, the poverty programs were of secondary importance to the wishes of the "tough power brokers" of any locale. Add coal operators to Moynihan's list of bankers and lawyers, and the result is the situation faced by the Volunteers.[7]

In their dealings with the state Office of Economic Opportunity (OEO), county CAPs, controlled by the special interests in the region, again exhibited and exerted the type of power that guaranteed their dominance. With the passage of the Green Amendment, in October 1967, which essentially gave local governments control over CAPs, this scenario became even more pronounced. The Office of Economic Opportunity, in essence, became subservient to county-administered CAPs. As the AV approach to ending poverty became increasingly confrontational, eighteen of twenty-four eastern Kentucky CAP directors had already, by September 1967 (even before the passage of the Green Amendment), exerted enough influence, utilizing their ready access to government organs, to prompt Al Whitehouse, the director of the Kentucky Office of Economic Opportunity, to proclaim that the CAPs were the "prime offensive weapon in the War on Poverty" and that cooperation with the AVs "prove[d] unworkable." If the War on Poverty was to be won, he continued, the Volunteers must be "under the umbrella of [the CAPs]." Those refusing to work in harmony with the CAPs, Whitehouse concluded, "just gotta go."[8]

Further, by relying on charges of sedition and accusing the AVs of un-American activities, the Pike County officials exercised agenda control using techniques that have a prominent place in Appalachian as well as American history. As John Gaventa shows in *Power and Powerlessness,* charges of communism seriously thwarted miners' attempts to organize in the 1930s. Under the direction of local elites, the portrait of a Communist painted in the 1930s bears a striking resemblance to the image used by Ratliff and KUAC in the 1960s. During the union struggles, Gaventa showed that these elites identified six characteristics of Communists: they hated God, favored the destruction of property, encouraged racial and social equality, distributed revolutionary propaganda, sought to destroy representative government, and preached the overthrow of capitalism.[9]

KUAC raised all these specters at the October hearings in Pikeville. Witnesses reported seeing pictures of blacks and whites together as well as the Volunteers' desire to destroy the government and the money supply and to redistribute the wealth. Further, during both the sedition trial and the KUAC hearing, testimonies spoke of the vast amounts of "communist" literature found at the McSurely and Mulloy residences—the "communist library out of this world."[10]

A short example, again from the October KUAC hearing, illustrates that the county elite also used Gaventa's first point: hatred of God. After being told that the committee would be interested in what a certain AV had to say about religion, one witness related the following: "[The AV] asked me a few questions, and well, I got the impression that he didn't think there was any God and so I asked him if he thought there [was] and he said, 'Yes [there has] been a creator at one time . . .' well I got the impression that he thought there wasn't any God anymore."[11]

In a manner similar to that of those attempting to stop the unions, KUAC and its cohorts tried to demonstrate that foreign, AV outsiders threatened the mountaineers' way of life. Accepting the Volunteer point of view spelled certain doom for the Appalachian, and American, way of life.

By coupling the sedition arrests with the KUAC hearing and utilizing the tried-and-true six-point Communist profile, the Pike County elite significantly augmented its position as the local power brokers by becoming "information brokers." These information brokers, through a technique Gaventa calls the "mobilization of bias," kept the issue of communism in front of the mountaineers for nearly eighteen months. Throughout this entire period, county officials forced the people to choose between the "Communists" and those individuals "fairly" and "legally" elected in a "democratic" system. Such phraseology effectively removed the choice from the people, presenting them with only one real alternative—to reject the AVs. While not resorting to overt force to subdue the activists, using monikers such as "communism," Gaventa states, offers yet "more subtle means of discrediting discontent."[12]

Byrd's declarations in the Senate, moreover, placed the AVs and their benefactor, the OEO, alongside the race riots, urban violence, student protests, and marches on the nation's capital that, Allen Matusow argues, led to the "massive defection" of many Americans "from the liberalism that had guided the country since 1960." Add to this list the AVs' troubles in the latter part of the decade. First local officials labeled the Volunteers Communists. Then state officials questioned their loyalty. Finally, the Volunteers themselves—at least one of their number—refused to combat the Red menace. These events in the mountains had much the same impact locally as the marches and protests in the nation's capital did nationally.[13]

In the end the defeat of the Appalachian Volunteers resulted not from their faults alone—myriad though these may have been—but from the political and social resources mobilized against them by a local county power structure seeking to solidify and maintain the status quo. Because their focus shifted from a self-help to a confrontational, issue-organizing approach, the AVs, on one level, had no one to blame but themselves for antagonizing the local county governments. However, they truly believed that they acted in accordance with the terms of the Economic Opportunity Act, especially the "maximum feasible participation" clause. Though able to gain support among some of the mountaineers, they alienated others and, thus, were unsuccessful in overcoming those individuals who, through manipulation, coercion, and control of political resources, held the region firmly in their grasp.

Of course, the hold that the local power/information brokers had was not as tight as they believed, and some of that power certainly slipped through their fingers. These were perhaps the same people that Kwalwasser thought rejected the Volunteers' aid. Though, by 1970, the Appalachian Volunteers were gone and the official War on Poverty was all but over, the Council of the Southern Mountains attempted, at its Fontana and Junaluska conferences, to reestablish itself. Rejecting the old Council "because of its role in the sixties as facilitator of other people's programs . . . especially the government's antipoverty programs," the new CSM also cast off the "outside young activists" who came along with those programs. From this point, the organization declared, the Council would be administered by "real mountain community leaders."[14]

Notes

The following abbreviations are used throughout the notes:

AV Papers   Appalachian Volunteers Papers
AV Papers, Part II   Appalachian Volunteers Papers, Part II
CSM Papers   Council of the Southern Mountains Papers, 1913–1970
FFGF   Ford Foundation Grants Files
OEO Papers   Office of Economic Opportunity Papers
WOP Oral History Project   War on Poverty in Appalachian Kentucky Oral History Project

Introduction

1. Oral History Interview with Joe Mulloy, November 10, 1990, Huntington, WV, War on Poverty in Appalachian Kentucky Oral History Project (hereafter WOP Oral History Project), Margaret I. King Library, University of Kentucky, Lexington.

2. On Kennedy's primary campaign promise, see *The Speeches of Senator John F. Kennedy*, 376. On the origins of the Appalachian Volunteers, see Kiffmeyer, "From Self-Help to Sedition"; Whisnant, *Modernizing the Mountaineer*, esp. chap. 7; Glen, "The War on Poverty in Appalachia"; and Horton, "The Appalachian Volunteers."

3. Patterson, *Grand Expectations*, 451–52, 535.

4. Harrington, *The Other America*; Anderson, *The Movement and the Sixties*, 43–44; Carson, *In Struggle*.

5. Carson, *In Struggle*, 1. On SDS, see esp. Sale, *SDS*; and Zinn, *SNCC*. See also Boyer, *Promises to Keep*, 254–74; and Anderson, *The Movement and the Sixties*.

6. Glen, "The War on Poverty in Appalachia"; Kiffmeyer, "From Self-Help to Sedition," 65–74.

7. Carson, *In Struggle*, 3 (quotes). On Freedom Summer, see also McAdam, *Freedom Summer*.

8. See Anderson, *The Movement and the Sixties*, esp. the introduction and chap. 1.

9. National Security Act quoted in Patterson, *Grand Expectations*, 133. NSC-68 quoted in Powaski, *The Cold War*, 85. On containment policy during the postwar era, see Gaddis, *Strategies of Containment*, 94; and Patterson, *Grand Expectations*, 176–78.

10. Powaski, *The Cold War*, 85 (first quote); Anderson, *The Movement and the Sixties*, 9 (other quotes). See also Patterson, *Grand Expectations*, 240 (McCarran Act).

11. For an in-depth examination of anticommunism and the academy, see Schrecker, *No Ivory Tower*. See also Anderson, *The Movement and the Sixties*, 11–12.

12. On the local color movement in Appalachia, see Shapiro, *Appalachia on Our Mind*. For the selectivity of these early reformers, see Whisnant, *All That Is Native and Fine;* and Forderhase, "Eve Returns to the Garden."

13. While the term *culture of poverty* was not used until the mid-twentieth century, its implications were present in the literature of the time.

14. Frost, "Our Contemporary Ancestors in the Southern Mountains," 311 (quote). On the concept of Appalachian "otherness" and how it affected America's responses to the region, see Shapiro, *Appalachia on Our Mind*. On how the country used these images, see Batteau, *The Invention of Appalachia*. For the early reformers in the mountains, see esp. Whisnant, *Modernizing the Mountaineer* and *All That Is Native and Fine;* Forderhase, "Eve Returns to the Garden"; Campbell, *The Southern Highlander and His Homeland;* and Weller, *Yesterday's People*. On Weller's book as a training manual, see Oral History Interview with Thomas Parrish, April 1, 1991, Berea, KY, WOP Oral History Project.

15. Caudill, *Night Comes to the Cumberlands*.

16. Eller, *Miners, Millhands, and Mountaineers*, 197–98.

17. Hevener, *Which Side Are You On?* 14.

18. Shifflett, *Coal Towns*, 12, 191, 54.

19. Whisnant, *Modernizing the Mountaineer*.

20. On the conflicts precipitated by divisions among contenders for control of community action programs, see Matusow, *The Unraveling of America*, 243–71.

21. O'Connor, *Poverty Knowledge*, 15.

For another biting critique of American social policy, albeit one that takes an entirely different tack, see Murray, *Losing Ground*. Murray contended that social policy in the United States, especially in the 1960s, actually *increased* poverty by fostering dependency on entitlement programs. That is, programs that provide entitlements create an environment in which the poor, rather than taking advantage of the opportunities that society offers, instead choose unemployment, illegitimacy, and welfare over marriage and jobs. In the end, according to Murray, America "lost ground" since those decisions, though "rational" in the short term, created more significant, long-term problems, including an increased number of individuals on welfare and, more important (sounding very close to the 1960s idea of a culture of poverty), a pattern of self-perpetuating, pathological behavior.

Though critics, including O'Connor, countered Murray's data, they were hard-pressed to counter his popular appeal, which reflected the Reagan era's focus on individual responsibility and conservative American values. For critiques of Murray, see O'Connor, *Poverty Knowledge,* 247–50; Greenstein, "Losing Faith in Losing Ground"; Jencks, "How Poor Are the Poor?" and Schram, *Words of Welfare.*

22. Dittmer, *Local People.*

23. Scholars of Appalachia, like their counterparts studying the civil rights movement, are beginning to develop a greater appreciation for the importance of local people in effecting change. See, e.g., Fisher, ed., *Fighting Back in Appalachia.*

24. Pope, "Introduction," 3.

25. Interestingly, American historiography focuses on radicalism on the left of the political spectrum and hardly ever on the right. See, e.g., Young, *The American Revolution;* Wood, *The Radicalism of the American Revolution;* Foner, *Tom Paine and Revolutionary America;* Banner, *Elizabeth Cady Stanton;* Fink, *Workingman's Democracy;* Cameron, *Radicals of the Worst Sort;* Woodward, *Tom Watson;* Goodwyn, *Democratic Promise;* Montgomery, *Beyond Equality* and *The Fall of the House of Labor;* Miller, *Democracy Is in the Streets;* and Rossinow, *The Politics of Authenticity.* For an interesting but dated look at American radicalism, see Lasch, *The New American Radicalism.*

26. O'Connor, *Poverty Knowledge,* 136 (first two quotes), 134 (last quote). For a discussion of some of the dilemmas that activists from the Left (who usually gain the term *radical*) face, see Pope, "Introduction," 4–7.

27. For a discussion of this philosophy throughout the twentieth century, see O'Connor, *Poverty Knowledge.*

1. On the Brink of War

1. Oral History Interview with George Brosi, November 3, 1990, Berea, KY, WOP Oral History Project. For an analysis of Southerners involved in social activism, including civil rights, in the 1960s, see esp. Michel, *Struggle for a Better South.*

2. Oral History Interview with George Brosi, November 3, 1990, Berea, KY, WOP Oral History Project.

3. Ibid.

4. Ibid. For an examination of the "great migration" and its effects on Northern metropolises, see Brown and Hillery, "The Great Migration." In addition to mountain whites, a significant number of African Americans also migrated to the nation's industrial centers during the war and immediate postwar years.

5. Adelbert Z. Bodnar to Council of the Southern Mountains, March 10, 1964 (quotes), Council of the Southern Mountains Papers, 1913–1970 (hereafter CSM Papers), box 102, Special Collections, Hutchins Library, Berea College, Berea, KY. For a discussion of Southern industrialization strategies, see Cobb,

The Selling of the South. On Appalachian migration to Northern industrial centers, see Berry, *Southern Migrants, Northern Exiles.*

6. For a concise yet critical assessment of the Council of the Southern Mountains, see Whisnant, *Modernizing the Mountaineer,* 3–39.

7. Whisnant, "Workers in God's Grand Division," 8. Whisnant's *Modernizing the Mountaineer* provides an excellent, comprehensive view of various reform efforts in central Appalachia. Chapter 1 covers the Council of the Southern Mountains. On the Ayer years, see pp. 18–25. Though Ayer did revive a dying CSM, the decade of the 1950s was still uncertain financially. Whisnant reports that, as late as 1958, Ayer had to borrow $5,000 from Berea College to meet costs. See Whisnant, *Modernizing the Mountaineer,* 19.

8. Galbraith, *The Affluent Society;* Harrington, *The Other America,* 23–24; Coles, *Children of Crisis,* xi–xii.

9. Vance, "The Region," 7.

10. On pluralism, see Dahl, *A Preface to Democratic Theory, Polyarchy,* and *Dilemmas of Pluralist Democracy.* Given that theorists equated pluralism with democracy, it is not surprising that the theory gained popular support during the Cold War.

11. Created in 1943 following the Detroit race riot of that same year, the Mayor's Friendly Relations Committee initially worked to prevent racial tensions precipitated by the influx of African Americans to Cincinnati during World War II. See Burnham, "The Mayor's Friendly Relations Committee."

12. Tucker, "Imagining Appalachians," 105 (first quote); "Hands-across-the-Ohio" Program newsletter, no. 4, September 10, 1962, grant no. PA 61–62, sec. 4 (second quote), reel R-0255, Ford Foundation Grants Files (hereafter FFGF), Ford Foundation Archives, Ford Foundation, New York; Pamphlet [on Characteristics of Southern Appalachian Migrants] prepared by Roscoe Giffin, [ca. 1958], grant no. PA 58–42, sec. 5 (last quote), reel R-0170, FFGF. See also Roscoe Giffin, "Some Aspects of the Migration from the Southern Appalachians," 1957, and James Gladden, "How the Church May Increase the Resources of the Community," both in grant no. PA 58–42, reel R-0170, FFGF. The records of the urban workshops are located in the CSM Papers, boxes 280–84.

Appalachia's critics did have a point when they discussed the Southern mountains' position in the political arena—an interpretation that, unfortunately, fed into their view of the region being without community structures. Because the mountains run in what is essentially a north-south direction, they are perpendicular to state boundaries. This, in critics' analysis, made the Appalachians the "backyards" of states dominated by lowland interests—e.g., the Bluegrass region in Kentucky or the Tidewater-Piedmont region of Virginia. Thus, the mountain regions were minority regions inhabited by a disjointed population. Should reformers succeed in creating a greater sense of community there, mountaineers would then have the organizational force to effect positive change. See Docket Excerpt—Board of Trustees Meeting, Public Affairs: Council of the Southern Mountains, 9/26–27/63, grant no. PA 61–62, reel R-0255, FFGF. This document also recognized a "'mountain culture' which is extremely resistant to change of any kind" and claimed that many Appalachians "will and *should* leave" (emphasis added).

13. Bigart, "Kentucky Miners."

14. Perley Ayer to Jess Wilson, October 5, 1962 (first quote), CSM Papers, box 98; Perley Ayer to D. M. Aldridge, October 9, 1962, CSM Papers, box 70; Perley Ayer to Wilson Wyatt, March 7, 1961 (second quote), CSM Papers, box 68; Perley Ayer to CSM Board, September 13, 1963, CSM Papers, box 70.

15. The 1925 "Program for the Mountains" called for "God fearing homes," improved health and sanitation, agriculture fitted to the mountains, better roads, schools and recreation opportunities, and stronger churches. See "Program for the Mountains," *Mountain Life and Work* 1 (April 1925): 20–22.

Mountain Life and Work was the official journal of the Council of the Southern Mountains. Complete runs of the periodical are in both the Margaret I. King Library at the University of Kentucky and the Hutchins Library at Berea College.

16. Eller, *Miners, Millhands, and Mountaineers*, 7 (quote). On the traditional community in central Appalachia, see ibid., chap. 1. See also Thelen, *Paths of Resistance*, chap. 1; and, for a short discussion of this traditional community in action, Sellers, *The Market Revolution*, 8–16. Waller's *Feud* shows how this traditional community broke down under the weight of late-nineteenth-century industrialization in central Appalachia.

17. Perley Ayer to George Bidstrup, January 26, 1961, and Perley Ayer to John Bischoff, January 26, 1961, CSM Papers, box 40; "Better Life for People Is Council's Aim," *West Virginia Hillbilly* (Richmond), March 7, 1960, 1, 3.

18. Lawson quoted in Carson, *In Struggle*, 23–24 (emphasis added).

19. The general correspondence files of the Council are replete with requests to governors, U.S. senators and representatives, and cabinet members to attend these annual conferences. "Community Resources: Theme of the 48th Annual Conference of the Council of the Southern Mountains," *Berea Alumnus*, April 1960 (quote); Loyal Jones to Charles Hansell, Eastern Kentucky State College, April 14, 1960, CSM Papers, box 51.

20. Bert T. Combs to President John F. Kennedy, November 9, 1961, CSM Papers, box 42; Memorandum, Perley Ayer to D. M. Aldridge, September 27, 1961, CSM Papers, box 39; Perley Ayer to Phillip Aylesworth, U.S. Department of Agriculture, December 18, 1961, CSM Papers, box 70; Senator John Sherman Cooper to Perley Ayer, June 16, 1960, CSM Papers, box 42; D. M. Aldridge to Perley Ayer, October 2, 1961, CSM Papers, box 39. On the ARA, see Matusow, *The Unraveling of America*, 100–101. For a critical assessment of the ARA in Appalachia, see Whisnant, *Modernizing the Mountaineer*, chap. 3. The ARA will be discussed in greater detail in the next chapter.

21. Perley Ayer to Brooks Hays, December 5, 1962 (first quote), CSM Papers, box 81; Milton Ogle to George Hubley Jr., Maryland Department of Economic Development, January 11, 1961 (second quote), CSM Papers, box 171; Perley Ayer to Otto Klineberg, January 31, 1961 (third quote), CSM Papers, box 54.

22. "President's Appalachian Regional Commission Report," October 30, 1963, CSM Papers, box 70; P. F. Ayer to Louis Smith, Dean of Berea College, March 9, 1964 (first quote), CSM Papers, box 117; Perley Ayer to Island Creek Coal Company, March 29, 1962, CSM Papers, box 82; Perley Ayer to W. Ross "Pop" Baley, March 8, 1960, CSM Papers, box 40; B. F. Reed to Milton Ogle, January 6, 1961, CSM Papers, box 171; Perley Ayer to Donald Cook, President, American Electric Power, February 27, 1964 (second quote), CSM Papers, box 100. On the anti-strip-mining movement, see Montrie, *To Save the Land and People.*

23. Loyal Jones to Philip Young, October 10, 1963, CSM Papers, box 99. See also Phil Young to George Chumbley Jr., Battery Park Hotel, October 17, 1963, CSM Papers, box 99.

24. Perley Ayer to the CSM Board, September 13, 1963, CSM Papers, box 70.

25. Perley Ayer to Brooks Hays, January 20, 1962, CSM Papers, box 81; Brooks Hays to Perley Ayer, April 6, 1961, CSM Papers, box 51.

26. Perley Ayer to John Sherman Cooper, January 24, 1961, CSM Papers, box 42; Perley Ayer to John Whisman, January 2, 1961, CSM Papers, box 68; Milton Ogle to John Sherman Cooper, June 2, 1961, CSM Papers, box 236; Perley Ayer to Carl Perkins, July 19, 1961, CSM Papers, box 61; Perley Ayer to John Whisman, February 16, 1961, CSM Papers, box 68. See also Perley Ayer to Wilson Wyatt, February 1, 1961, CSM Papers, box 68; and "Berea Sociologist Raps Welfare 'for Free.'"

27. Loyal Jones to Charles Drake, December 17, 1960 (quote), CSM Papers, box 45; "A Demonstration Project Utilizing a Broad Welfare Concept," n.d., CSM Papers, box 243. See also Oral History Interview with Loyal Jones, November 19, 1990, Berea, KY, WOP Oral History Project.

28. Loyal Jones to Frederick Kirsch, December 1, 1960, CSM Papers, box 54; W. Ross "Pop" Baley to Loyal Jones, April 6, 1961, Loyal Jones to Joe Barker, September 27, 1960, and Loyal Jones to Hattie Bates, December 19, 1961, CSM Papers, box 40. See also Alice Slone to Loyal Jones, June 27, 1961, CSM Papers, box 65.

29. Perley Ayer to Loyal Jones, July 26, 1960, CSM Papers, box 53; Perley Ayer to D. M. Aldridge, June 30, 1960, CSM Papers, box 39; Minutes of the Kentucky Rural Development Executive Committee Meeting, April 7, 1961, CSM Papers, box 45.

30. Milton Ogle to A. Lee Coleman, August 18, 1960, CSM Papers, box 236; "Projects of Progress in Laurel County," November 1962, and "Projects of

Progress in Perry County," November 1962, CSM Papers, box 237. It should be noted that, while these were projects with which CSM members worked, the Council was not solely responsible for them.

31. (Mrs. Ray) Judy Drukker to Perley Ayer, November 8, 1961, and Perley Ayer to D. M. Aldridge, January 12, 1961, CSM Papers, box 39. On the Chicago project, see Whisnant, *Modernizing the Mountaineer,* 22–23 (*Tribune* quote, 22). For further information on the Appalachian Fund, see Parrish, *To Make a Difference.* See also Gitlin and Hollander, *Uptown.* On the Great Cities–Gray Areas program, see O'Connor, "The Fight against Poverty."

32. "Mountain Life and Work . . . Its Scope and Purpose," *Mountain Life and Work* 35 (Spring 1960): 18–19. In the next issue of *Mountain Life and Work,* the Council member Joe Mobley commented that, until 1950, the coal industry actually was a positive force in Appalachia. See Mobley, "A Hard Look at Tomorrow." For more on the importance of the coal industry in the central Appalachians prior to mechanization, see Shifflett, *Coal Towns.*

33. Quentin Allen to Loyal Jones, October 2, 1963, and Quentin Allen to Perley Ayer, October 24, 1963, CSM Papers, box 70.

34. Press Release, Eli Cohen, Executive Secretary of the National Committee on Employment of Youth, [on his Address before the Forty-ninth Annual Conference of the CSM], February 10, 1961, CSM Papers, box 42. See also Eli Cohen to Loyal Jones, January 3, 1961, CSM Papers, box 42. Cohen's theme was echoed by the economist Robert Theobald at the 1964 annual conference when he spoke of the cybernetic revolution that was then sweeping the world. Again, in terms of the implication for impoverished mountaineers, the significance of the speech was the need for improved education.

35. For an overview of Appalachian "otherness," see Harney, "A Strange Land and Peculiar People"; Frost, "Our Contemporary Ancestors in the Southern Mountains"; Fox, *The Little Shepherd of Kingdom Come, Trail of the Lonesome Pine,* and "The Southern Mountaineer"; Semple, "The Anglo-Saxons of the Kentucky Mountains"; Wilson, "Elizabethan America"; and Weller, *Yesterday's People.* For an examination of how literature in the late twentieth century still created an "other" Appalachia, see Duke, *Writers and Miners.*

36. Max Miller, Professor of Education, Pikeville College, to Perley Ayer, January 19, 1963, CSM Papers, box 86; Loyal Jones to Harriette Arnow, September 5, 1961, CSM Papers, box 39; Loyal Jones to Allen Trout, *Louisville Courier-Journal,* June 12, 1963, CSM Papers, box 96.

37. "Council Newsletter" no. 2, 1962, CSM Papers, box 172; Grazia Combs to Perley Ayer, May 7, 1963, CSM Papers, box 74.

38. Charles Drake to Loyal Jones, [ca. November 1960], CSM Papers, box 45. See also Loyal Jones to Charles Drake, November 9, 1960, CSM Papers, box 45.

39. Jones, Parrish, and Perrin, "Problems in Revisionism," 176.

40. Minutes, Board of Directors Meeting, September 16, 1961, CSM Papers, box 17; Perley Ayer to CSM Board, September 13, 1963, CSM Papers, box 70.

41. On the Peace Corps, see Anderson, *The Movement and the Sixties*, 59–60; and Matusow, *The Unraveling of America*, 31, 243–44. For the book project, see Charles Drake to Loyal Jones, February 1961, CSM Papers, box 45; Minutes, Board of Directors Meeting, February 7–11, 1961, Gatlinburg, TN, CSM Papers, box 17; and Charles Drake to W. R. "Pop" Baley, February 24, 1961, CSM Papers, box 45.

42. Loyal Jones to Charles Drake, March 9, 1961, and April 6, 1961, and Charles Drake to Harry Ernst, April 15, 1961, CSM Papers, box 45.

43. Loyal Jones to D. M. Aldridge, April 21, 1961, and Loyal Jones to Louis Armstrong, April 4, 1961, CSM Papers, box 39 (first quote); "University of Kentucky Appalachian Resource Development Project," November 12, 1960, CSM Papers, box 236 (other quotes); Paul Ylvisaker, Ford Foundation, to Perley Ayer, July 2, 1962, and Perley Ayer to Paul Ylvisaker, August 1, 1962, CSM Papers, box 100. See also Septima Clark to Perley Ayer, April 4, 1961, CSM Papers, box 39.

44. Remember that the Peace Corps was supposed to aid *underdeveloped* countries. Thus, by asking for Peace Corps volunteers to come to Appalachia, the Council of the Southern Mountains reinforced the conception, in its own mind and that of the nation, that Appalachians were "contemporary ancestors." Windmiller (*The Peace Corps and Pax Americana*) criticizes the colonial implications of the Peace Corps. On the Kennedys and Operation Bookstrap, see Charles Drake to Mrs. Kendall Bryan, April 15, 1961, CSM Papers, box 45. For the Peace Corps in the Southern mountains, see Warren Wiggins, Acting Director of the Peace Corps, to Loyal Jones, May 11, 1961, CSM Papers, box 88. See also Perley Ayer to Robert F. Kennedy, December 21, 1962 (CSM request of NSC volunteers), CSM Papers, box 85; and Matusow, *The Unraveling of America*, 117 (quotes on the NSC).

45. Matusow, *The Unraveling of America*, 118 (first quote); Richard Boone to Perley Ayer, January 31, 1963 (other quotes), CSM Papers, box 88.

46. Caudill, *Night Comes to the Cumberlands;* Bigart, "Kentucky Miners." On Bigart's influence on the president, see Whisnant, *Modernizing the Mountaineer*, 94.

47. Bigart, "Kentucky Miners."

48. Ibid.

49. Ibid. Bigart also noted that nearby Pike County curtailed a school lunch program at Hellier owing to a shortage of funds.

50. Appalachian Volunteers First Report, March 30, 1964, Appalachian Volunteers Papers (hereafter AV Papers), box 3, Southern Appalachian Archives, Hutchins Library, Berea College, Berea, KY; Untitled Report, n.d., AV Papers, box 8.

51. Matusow, *The Unraveling of America*, 15 (quote). Perhaps the best account of the West Virginia primary is in White, *The Making of the President,*

1960, 96–114. Anderson (*The Movement and the Sixties,* 59) discusses Kennedy's "fix-it social agenda"—which would "spread 1950s affluence and middle class status to all" and which he used during the campaign of 1960.

52. Appalachian Volunteers First Report, March 30, 1964, AV Papers, box 3; Untitled Report, n.d., AV Papers, box 8.

53. Whisnant, *Modernizing the Mountaineer,* 127–31 (on PARC), 128 (quote [from *Whitesburg, KY, Mountain Eagle,* March 12, 1964]). Sundquist, *Politics and Policy,* 102. On the CSM and its relation to PARC's programs, see A Volunteer Component for the Eastern Kentucky Program, [1963], AV Papers, box 20; Policy Statement of the Council of the Southern Mountains, Inc., in Relation to the So-Called "Crash Program" of Emergency Relief of Federal, Regional and State Interests, December 20, 1963, CSM Papers, box 70; Appalachian Volunteers: First Year Working Draft, [1964], AV Papers, box 1.

54. Policy Statement of the Council of the Southern Mountains, Inc., to the So-Called "Crash Program" of Emergency Relief of Federal, Regional, and State Interests, December 20, 1963, CSM Papers, box 70.

55. Appalachian Volunteers First Report, March 30, 1964, AV Papers, box 3; Untitled Report, n.d., AV Papers, box 8.

56. Untitled Report, n.d., AV Papers, box 8; A Volunteer Component for the Eastern Kentucky Program, [1963], sec. 1, Rationale for a Volunteer Program, AV Papers, box 20.

57. A Volunteer Component for the Eastern Kentucky Program, [1963], sec. 1, Rationale for a Volunteer Program, AV Papers, box 20.

58. These colleges included Asbury College, Wilmore; Asbury Theological Seminary, Wilmore; Alice Lloyd College, Pippa Passes; Berea College, Berea; Clearcreek Baptist School, Pineville; College of the Bible, Lexington; Cumberland College, Williamsburg; Eastern Kentucky State College, Richmond; Georgetown College, Georgetown; Lees Junior College, Jackson; Lindsey Wilson College, Columbia; Midway Junior College, Midway; Morehead State College, Morehead; Pikeville College, Pikeville; Southeast Christian College, Winchester; Sue Bennett College, London; Transylvania College, Lexington; Union College, Barbourville; and University of Kentucky, Lexington. A Volunteer Component for the Eastern Kentucky Program, [1963] (quote), AV Papers, box 20; Appalachian Volunteers First Report, March 30, 1964, AV Papers, box 3.

59. Policy Statement of the Council of the Southern Mountains, Inc., to the So-Called "Crash Program" of Emergency Relief of Federal, Regional, and State Interests, December 20, 1963 (first quote), CSM Papers, box 70; A Volunteer Component for the Eastern Kentucky Program, [1963] (other quotes), AV Papers, box 20.

60. A Volunteer Component for the Eastern Kentucky Program, [1963], AV Papers, box 20; Appalachian Volunteers First Report, March 30, 1964 (quote), AV Papers, box 3; Untitled Report, n.d., AV Papers, box 20.

61. Appalachian Volunteers First Report, March 30, 1964, AV Papers, box 3.

62. Ibid.

63. Ibid. See also Oral History Interview with Jack Rivel, February 12, 1991, Berea, KY, WOP Oral History Project.

64. Appalachian Volunteers First Report, March 30, 1964, AV Papers, box 3.

65. Perley Ayer to [the Nineteen Presidents of Eastern Kentucky Colleges and Universities], January 15, 1964, AV Papers, box 1.

66. The idea of using local people not simply as a means of obtaining labor but as a way of involving them in efforts on their own behalf and, ultimately, providing them a way of controlling their own lives, was not exclusive to the Council of the Southern Mountains. Students of the civil rights movement are now seeing that this idea was put into practice by other reform organizations of the era. In *Bearing the Cross*, e.g., Garrow successfully expands the movement beyond its most visible leaders. As such notables as Martin Luther King Jr. are woven into the overall fabric of the movement, local leaders like E. L. Doyle of Selma, Alabama, come into significance. More recently, Dittmer argued in *Local People* that, in Mississippi, indigenous people not only were most important but actually gave the movement shape and direction.

67. See Harrington, *The Other America;* and Galbraith, *The Affluent Society.* For a critique of these works, see MacDonald, "Our Invisible Poor."

2. The Shot Heard Round the World

1. Oral History Interview with Milton Ogle, April 5, 1991, Charleston, WV, WOP Oral History Project.

2. Perhaps the best summation of these models is in Lewis, "Fatalism or the Coal Industry?" See also Lewis, Johnson, and Askins, eds., *Colonialism in Modern America.* Demonstrating the longevity and the attraction of the culture of poverty model in the 1960s is Weller's *Yesterday's People.*

3. Lewis, "Fatalism or the Coal Industry?" Glen, "The War on Poverty in Appalachia," 41 (quote).

4. Johnson, *The Vantage Point,* 79, 70. Two of the better works on the liberalism of the 1960s are Matusow's *The Unraveling of America* and Hodgson's *America in Our Time.* Heath's *Decade of Disillusionment* also provides a critical assessment of the liberalism of these two presidents. While Johnson was a latter-day New Dealer, Kennedy was, according to Heath, "trained in the tradition of noblesse oblige" (11). See also Anderson, *The Movement and the Sixties;* and Hamby, *Liberalism and Its Challengers.*

5. For a legislative history of the Area Redevelopment Act of 1961, see Sundquist, *Politics and Policy,* 57–85 (quote, 62).

6. Ibid., 84 (quotes). See also Levitan, *Federal Aid to Depressed Areas;* and Parmet, *JFK,* 77.

7. Lyndon Johnson began his public career in 1935 as the Texas administrator of the National Youth Administration (NYA), which operated under the umbrella of the Works Progress Administration. His experiences with the NYA exposed him to the problems of the young, the poor, and the unemployed. He then entered national politics, winning the 1937 congressional election in Texas's Tenth District after having run as a fervent supporter of the New Deal. His first attempt at the Senate came in 1941, when the Texas senator Morris Sheppard died and a special election was held to fill the vacant seat. With the firm support of President Roosevelt, Johnson announced his candidacy. While he lost the election by a narrow margin, he had made his political position clear.

Johnson again ran for the Senate in 1948, and this time the results were in his favor. Although he had to placate Texas conservatives, including those in the energy industry, to win the election, his ties with Roosevelt's recovery programs were not that easily severed. Later in his Senate career, as majority leader, Johnson worked on his own party's reform programs, such as Truman's "Fair Deal" measures, and as vice president he supported Kennedy's domestic reform policies. Thus, Johnson entered the White House with a long personal history of support for domestic reform. In fact, the period that his political career had spanned to date (1935–1963, from the New Deal to the Kennedy administration) had witnessed perhaps the greatest effort to solve the problems of poverty, by government and private citizens alike, ever to be attempted. Nevertheless, these concerns were limited and defined by that brand of American liberalism that dominated most reform thinkers in the Cold War era.

8. Johnson, *The Vantage Point*, 71 (first quote), and *A Time for Action*, 168, 170 (other quotes). On the Council of Economic Advisers under Heller, see esp. Matusow, *The Unraveling of America*, 120–23; and Johnson, *The Vantage Point*, 69–71.

9. On "anomie and estrangement," see Milkis and Mileur, eds., *The Great Society and the High Tide of Liberalism*, xiii. For the University of Michigan speech, see *Public Papers of . . . Lyndon Baines Johnson, 1963–64*, 1:704. For the other quotes, see *Public Papers of . . . Lyndon Baines Johnson, 1966*, 1:3–7. For a recent critical assessment of the Great Society and its impact on late-twentieth- and early-twenty-first-century liberalism, see Milkis and Mileur, eds., *The Great Society and the High Tide of Liberalism*.

10. Economic Opportunity Act of 1964, Public Law 88-452, 78 Stat. 508.

11. AV Board of Directors Meeting, 1965, University of Kentucky, Lexington, AV Papers, box 2.

12. Wofford, "The Politics of Local Responsibility," 79 (first quote); Yarmolinsky, "The Beginnings of OEO," 49 (second quote); Kravitz, "The Community Action Program." See also Glen, "The War on Poverty in Appalachia," 42; and Matusow, *The Unraveling of America*, 243–45.

13. Kravitz, "The Community Action Program," 60 (second quote); Wof-

ford, "The Politics of Local Responsibility," 81 (first quote), 79 (third quote). For a discussion of how conflict aids pluralist societies, see Hirschman, "Social Conflicts as Pillars of Democratic Market Society."

14. Perley Ayer to Jack Ciaccio, May 28, 1966 (first quote), CSM Papers, box 129 (copy in AV Papers, box 5); *Mountain Life and Work,* 39 (Winter 1963): 58–59 (second quote). See also Glen, "The War on Poverty in Appalachia," 44; and Whisnant, *Modernizing the Mountaineer,* 19.

15. A Volunteer Component for the Eastern Kentucky Program, [1963], AV Papers, box 20.

16. Roslea Johnson, President, CAMP, to Dr. Kenneth H. Thompson, Associate Dean, Berea College, May 15, 1963, AV Papers, box 20.

17. Ibid.; Memorandum, Perley Ayer to Youth Committee of the CSM, October 11, 1963, CSM Papers, box 100.

18. Appalachian Volunteers By-Laws, [March 1964], AV Papers, box 1; Horton, "The Appalachian Volunteers," 48 (Ogle quote).

19. Telegram, Lyndon Johnson to Milton Ogle, January 25, 1964 (quotes), AV Papers, box 32; Telegram, Eugene P. Foley, Small Business Administration, to Milton Ogle, January 25, 1964, AV Papers, box 32.

20. CSM and ARA Contract for Grant Allocation, 1964, AV Papers, box 3; A Summary of "Special Projects" Aided by the Council of the Southern Mountains' Ford Foundation Grant, 1964, AV Papers, box 20.

21. A Summary of "Special Projects" Aided by the Council of the Southern Mountains' Ford Foundation Grant, 1964, AV Papers, box 20.

22. Ibid.

23. Ibid.; Proposal to the Council of the Southern Mountains Educational Committee, Project Area, Mill Creek, Clay County, Kentucky, [ca. June 1964], AV Papers, box 28.

24. Proposal to the Council of the Southern Mountains Educational Committee, Project Area, Mill Creek, Clay County, Kentucky, [ca. June 1964], AV Papers, box 28; Polly P. Gorman, Appointment Secretary for Governor Breathitt, to Flem Messer, June 8, 1964, AV Papers, box 28. See also "News of State Government," State Office of Public Information, and Press Outlines 1, 2, 3, 4, June 1964, AV Papers, box 28.

25. Flem Messer to Jack Ciaccio, Department of Health, Education and Welfare, July 28, 1964, AV Papers, box 28.

26. Volunteer quoted in Hampton, "Volunteers Pioneer Classes at Mill Creek," 4 (emphasis added).

27. Ibid., 4.

28. Mr. and Mrs. Lester Smith to [Flem] Messer, September 1, 1964, Gilbert Messer to Flem [Messer], September 2, 1964, Crit Gambrel to [Flem] Messer, September 4, 1964, Mr. and Mrs. Mitchell Messer to Flem [Messer], September 4, 1964, and Dave Hubbard to [Flem] Messer, September 5, 1964, AV Papers, box 28.

29. Robert Lee Sigmon to Milton Ogle, December 3, 1964, AV Papers, box 25; Quarterly Report, U.S. VISA Volunteer, Carol Irons, Mill Creek, Kentucky, October 9, 1964–December 21, 1964, AV Papers, box 25. See also Robert Lee Sigmon to Milton Ogle, December 3, 1964, CSM Papers, box 117.

30. Robert Lee Sigmon to Milton Ogle, January 5, 1965, AV Papers, box 25. On the kindergarten program, see Carol Irons to Milton Ogle, July 30, 1965, and Quarterly Report—Terminal for Mill Creek Assignment, July 7, 1965, AV Papers, box 25.

31. Carol Irons to Milton Ogle, February 1, 1965, Robert Lee Sigmon to Milton Ogle, February 2, 1965, Quarterly Report, U.S. VISA Volunteer, Carol Irons, Mill Creek, Kentucky, October 9, 1964–December 21, 1964 (quotes), and Carol Irons to Milton Ogle, May 31, 1965, AV Papers, box 25.

32. Carol Irons to Milton Ogle, May 31, 1965, AV Papers, box 25.

33. Loyal Jones to Robert Lee Sigmon, October 19, 1964 (first quote), CSM Papers, box 117; Quarterly Report, U.S. VISA Volunteer, Carol Irons, Mill Creek, Kentucky, October 9, 1964–December 21, 1964 (other quotes), AV Papers, box 25. To his credit, Messer admitted that he was a Clay County activist at the time of the Mill Creek project. See Oral History Interview with Flem Messer, September 26, 1990, Danville, KY, WOP Oral History Project.

34. Carol Irons to Milton Ogle, February 1, 1965, AV Papers, box 25.

35. Robert Lee Sigmon to Milton Ogle, February 2, 1965, Milton Ogle to Bob Sigmon, February 9, 1965, and Carol Irons to Milton Ogle, February 14, 1965, AV Papers, box 25.

36. Carol Irons to Milton Ogle, February 21, 1965, and Carol Irons to Milton Ogle, March 6, 1965, AV Papers, box 25.

37. Bob Sigmon to Milton Ogle, March 11, 1965, AV Papers, box 25.

38. Ibid.

39. Carol Irons to Milton Ogle, February 21, 1965, Carol Irons to Milton Ogle, March 6, 1965 (first quote), Carol Irons to Milton Ogle, March 21, 1965, and Carol Irons to Milton Ogle, February 27, 1965 (second quote), AV Papers, box 25.

40. Carol Irons to Milton Ogle, April 18, 1965, Carol Irons to Milton Ogle, April 26, 1965, Carol Irons to Milton Ogle, May 2, 1965, and Carol Irons to Milton Ogle, May 8, 1965, AV Papers, box 25.

41. Carol Irons to Milton Ogle, July 30, 1965, and Quarterly Report—Terminal for Mill Creek Assignment, July 7, 1965, AV Papers, box 25.

42. Carol Irons to Milton Ogle, May 31, 1965, AV Papers, box 25.

43. Carol Irons to Milton Ogle, May 31, 1965, Carol Irons to Milton Ogle, June 5, 1965, and Quarterly Report—Terminal for Mill Creek Assignment, July 7, 1965, AV Papers, box 25.

44. Quarterly Report—Terminal for Mill Creek Assignment, July 7, 1965, AV Papers, box 25.

45. Hampton, "Volunteers Pioneer Classes at Mill Creek," 4.

46. Robert Lee Sigmon to Loyal Jones, March 10, 1965, AV Papers, box 25.

47. Loyal Jones to Joe Powles, September 26, 1965, AV Papers, box 25.

48. Loyal Jones to Robert Lee Sigmon, October 19, 1964, CSM Papers, box 117.

3. A Splendid Little War

1. Oral History Interview with Roslea Johnson, June 24, 1991, Des Moines, IA, WOP Oral History Project. (CSM records identify her as "Roselea," but letters that she composed herself are signed "Roslea," and the Berea College alumni directory lists her as "Roslea." Hence, I use the latter throughout.) On Appalachian migration north in the 1940s, see esp. Berry, *Southern Migrants, Northern Exiles*.

2. Oral History Interview with Roslea Johnson, June 24, 1991, Des Moines, IA, WOP Oral History Project.

3. Ibid.

4. Appalachian Volunteers: College Students Wage War on Poverty in Eastern Kentucky, [ca. 1964], AV Papers, box 39. The AVs claimed that Pike County had eighty-two one- and two-room schools, Perry fifty-eight, Knott forty-four, and Leslie fifty-six. Whisnant (*Modernizing the Mountaineer,* 187) specifies that Pike County had seventy-five dilapidated schools, Floyd sixty-four, Perry fifty-one, Clay forty-nine, and Leslie forty-eight. Appalachian Volunteers By-Laws, [March 1964] (quotes), AV Papers, box 1. Figures on the renovation projects and volunteers recruited are in Appalachian Volunteers: First Year Working Draft, [1964], AV Papers, box 1.

5. Final Report on Contract No. CC 6120 between the U.S.A. and the Council of the Southern Mountains, Inc., [ca. March 1965] (all quotes), AV Papers, box 3. The twelve campuses on which AV chapters operated at the time of this report were Alice Lloyd College, Ashland Community College, Berea College, Cumberland College, Eastern Kentucky State College, Georgetown College, Pikeville College, Southeast Christian College, Transylvania University, the University of Kentucky, the University of Kentucky–Prestonsburg, and the the University of Kentucky–Southeast Center. Two other campus units formed immediately after the first meeting. They were located at Union College and Morehead State College. See Appalachian Volunteers First Report, March 30, 1964, AV Papers, box 3.

6. On community organizing as the AVs' ultimate goal, see Final Report on Contract No. CC 6120 between the U.S.A. and the Council of the Southern Mountains, Inc., [ca. March 1965], AV Papers, box 3. [Form Letter to Those] "Expressing Interest in the Work of the Council of the Southern Mountains," [ca. 1965] (quote), AV Papers, box 23.

7. Appalachian Volunteers Curriculum Enrichment, [1965], AV Papers, box 23.

8. Ibid.

9. Ibid. (emphasis added). As with other aspects of the AV program, what was considered "desirable" behavior was not specified. For a discussion of the "proper habits" that industrialists imposed on workers and their children in the early twentieth century, see Hennen, *The Americanization of West Virginia.*

10. Appalachian Volunteers First Report, March 30, 1964, AV Papers, box 3.

11. [Letter], To Those Undergraduates and Others Who Responded to the Appeal of the [CSM] for Volunteer Help in Meeting Current Crises of Need in Mountain Counties, December 28, 1963, AV Papers, box 1.

12. Philip W. Conn to Harold Bennet, April 17, 1964, AV Papers, box 29.

13. Perley Ayer to John Whisman, December 20, 1963, AV Papers, box 70.

14. [Memorandum], Talk to Mark [Furstenburg]—[Milton] Ogle, n.d., AV Papers, box 1. Because this document appeared in the AV Papers, not the CSM Papers, it must have been generated just after the AV program—or at least the idea for the program—began. This would date it to late 1963 or, more likely, early 1964. According to one local newspaper, Whisman tried, as early as 1965, to "collect to himself the tight reins of control on all federal programs within Kentucky." This included the state Office of Economic Opportunity programs, the Appalachian Regional Commission, and the ARA. See *Whitesburg, KY, Mountain Eagle,* November 11, 1965, 1. See also Whisnant, *Modernizing the Mountaineer,* 144.

15. Memorandum, John D. Whisman to Robert Kennedy, Attorney General of the United States and Chairman of the President's Study Group for a National Voluntary Service Program, [1963], John D. Whisman Papers, Area Program Office Series, Programs Subseries, Margaret I. King Library, University of Kentucky, Lexington. At the time of writing the Whisman Papers were not yet processed. I would like to thank Glen Taul for allowing me access to the collection while he organized it.

16. Ibid. (quote); Summary of Active Projects in Special Winter Program for Eastern Kentucky, John D. Whisman Papers, Area Program Office Series, Programs Subseries.

17. Appalachian Volunteers First Progress Report, March 31, 1964, AV Papers, box 21; Contract between the United States of America and Council of the Southern Mountains, Contract No. CC-6120, March 2, 1964, AV Papers, box 3; Department of Commerce, Area Redevelopment Administration Press Release, February 3, 1964, AV Papers, box 20; Standard Operating Procedures—Field Operations, [ca. 1964], AV Papers, box 20; Appalachian Volunteers Third Progress Report, May 1964 (first quote), AV Papers, box 3; [AV] Program Background, [ca. 1964] (second quote), AV Papers, box 1.

18. Appalachian Volunteers: College Students Wage War on Poverty in East-

ern Kentucky, [ca. 1964], AV Papers, box 39; Contract between the United States of America and Council of the Southern Mountains, Contract No. CC-6120, March 2, 1964, AV Papers, box 3; Department of Commerce, Area Redevelopment Administration Press Release, February 3, 1964, AV Papers, box 20. See also Appalachian Volunteers First Report, March 30, 1964, AV Papers, box 3.

19. Perley Ayer to W. H. Ferry, Fund for the Republic, March 10, 1964, CSM Papers, box 106.

20. [Appalachian Volunteers] Second Progress Report, April 1964, on Contract between Area Redevelopment Administration of the U.S. Department of Commerce and the Council of the Southern Mountains, AV Papers, box 20.

21. Ibid. According to this report, school repair remained the dominant AV activity. In April 1964, the Volunteers renovated twelve additional schools in five counties: one in Wolfe, two in Perry, one in Knott, three in Leslie, and five in Clay. Ironically, these projects foreshadowed later AV efforts—efforts that the CSM would oppose.

22. [The Council of the Southern Mountains has been an educational institution since its inception . . .], [ca. 1964], AV Papers, box 27.

23. Jack Ciaccio to Perley Ayer, July 29, 1964, CSM Papers, box 108.

24. Fetterman, "Young Samaritans in Appalachia," 4, and "Volunteers Are a Bargain," 12.

25. Appalachian Volunteers Third Progress Report, May 1964, AV Papers, box 3. In the month of May, the Appalachian Volunteers continued school renovation in five counties and held "organizational" meetings in four—Clay, Perry, Knott, and Leslie—of those five. Of the six communities in which they held meetings, the AVs listed five as desiring school-based projects. According to the report, the sixth, Urban, in Clay County, simply discussed local problems.

26. Ibid.; Appalachian Volunteers: College Students Wage War on Poverty in Eastern Kentucky, [ca. 1964], AV Papers, box 39; Milton Ogle to Grace Dammron, April 21, 1964, AV Papers, box 32; Jack Rivel to Marilyn Haddock, August 28, 1964, AV Papers, box 32.

27. [Appalachian Volunteers] Fourth Progress Report—June 1964, on the Contract between Area Redevelopment Administration of the U.S. Department of Commerce and the Council of the Southern Mountains (second quote), AV Papers, box 3; Appalachian Volunteers By-Laws, [March 1964] (first quote), AV Papers, box 1; Flem Messer to Pauline Winnick, U.S. Department of Health, Education, and Welfare, July 28, 1964 (last quote), AV Papers, box 28. See also [Attachments to] Agenda: Meeting of College Presidents concerning Appalachian Volunteers, July 30, 1964, AV Papers, box 28.

28. [Appalachian Volunteers] Fourth Progress Report—June 1964, on the Contract between Area Redevelopment Administration of the U.S. Department of Commerce and the Council of the Southern Mountains, and [Appalachian Volunteers] Fifth Progress Report, July 1964, AV Papers, box 3.

29. Ibid.; Mary E. Birenbaum, Wilderness Road Girl Scouts, to Jack [Flem] Messer, June 2, 1964, Flem Messer to Mary Birenbaum, June 3, 1964, and [Report on Wilderness Road Girl Scouts' Project, Leslie County, KY], [ca. August–September 1964], AV Papers, box 24. On the Mill Creek Project, see chapter 2 above.

30. [Report on Wilderness Road Girl Scouts' Project, Leslie County, KY], [ca. August–September 1964], AV Papers, box 24.

31. [Plan Outline, "The demands of week-to-week planning will be great"], [ca. 1964] (quote), AV Papers, box 1. On the sense of satisfaction, see Oral History Interview with Roslea Johnson, June 24, 1991, Des Moines, IA, WOP Oral History Project. Johnson was the Berea College representative to the first AV meeting in 1964.

32. [Open Letter about the Appalachian Volunteers], [ca. 1964], AV Papers, box 3.

33. Appalachian Volunteers, Minutes of the Board Meeting, August 25, 1964, Berea, KY, AV Papers, box 2.

34. [Appalachian Volunteers] Sixth Progress Report, August 1964, AV Papers, box 3; AV Board of Directors Meeting, August 25, 1964, Berea, KY, AV Papers, box 2; [Attachments to] Agenda: Meeting of College Presidents concerning Appalachian Volunteers, July 30, 1964, AV Papers, box 28; Oral History Interview with Roslea Johnson, June 24, 1991, Des Moines, IA, WOP Oral History Project.

On the Books for Appalachia project, see School Library Project (Working Draft), [ca. July 1964], AV Papers, box 2; Oral History Interviews with Roslea Johnson, June 24, 1991, Des Moines, IA, and Jack Rivel, February 12, 1991, Berea, KY, WOP Oral History Project; and Books for Appalachia, [ca. 1966], AV Papers, box 8. F. E. Compton donated fifty sets of encyclopedias. See Milton Ogle to F. E. Compton & Co., January 3, 1966, AV Papers, box 21. See also Books for Appalachia, Procedure for Fieldmen, [March 1, 1965], AV Papers, box 28; and [Attachments to] Agenda: Meeting of College Presidents concerning Appalachian Volunteers, July 30, 1964, AV Papers, box 28.

35. Books for Appalachia, [ca. 1966], AV Papers, box 8; School Library Project (Working Draft), [ca. July 1964], AV Papers, box 2; Oral History Interview with Jack Rivel, February 12, 1991, Berea, KY, WOP Oral History Project; News of Importance to the Appalachian South [CSM Press Release], [ca. November 1964], AV Papers, box 3.

36. Appalachian Volunteers Meeting of the Special Advisory Committee, August 20, 1964, Berea, KY, AV Papers, box 2.

37. School Renovation Project (Working Draft), [ca. July 1964], and School Library Project (Working Draft), [ca. July 1964], AV Papers, box 2; [Open Letter about the Appalachian Volunteers], [ca. 1964] (first quote), AV Papers, box 3; Appalachian Volunteers Minutes of the Board Meeting, August 25, 1964, Berea, KY (second quote), AV Papers, box 2.

38. News of Importance to the Appalachian South [CSM Press Release], November 25, 1964 (quote), AV Papers, box 29. On the OEO grant, see Whisnant, *Modernizing the Mountaineer*, 189. On the Mill Creek Project, see chapter 2 above.

39. Dave Craft, Superintendent of Letcher County Schools, to Milton Ogle, September 22, 1964, William O. Gilreath, Superintendent of McCreary County Schools, to Milton Ogle, September 18, 1964, and Miss George Alice Motley, Superintendent of Menifee County Schools, to Milton Ogle, September 27, 1964, AV Papers, box 70.

40. [Appalachian Volunteers] Seventh Progress Report, September 1964, AV Papers, box 3.

41. On the roving pickets, see Whisnant, *Modernizing the Mountaineer*, 188–89. Robin Buckner to Tom [Rhodenbaugh], February 24, 1965 (first quote), AV Papers, box 24; CSM newsletter, no. 2, September 1964, 7 (second quote), AV Papers, box 29. See also Horton, "The Appalachian Volunteers," 55. The SDS volunteers were participants in that organization's Economic Research and Action Project. This was also an effort to help the poor in Appalachia, but through a more confrontational approach. See Sale, *SDS*, esp. 95–150. Though health care could be a qualitative issue, because these benefits depended on the number of union miners, employment was the critical factor.

42. [Appalachian Volunteers] Eighth Progress Report, October 1964 on Contract between Area Redevelopment Administration of the U.S. Department of Commerce and the Council of the Southern Mountains, Inc., AV Papers, box 20; Memorandum, Jack Rivel to Council Staff, October 16, 1964, AV Papers, box 29 (copy also in AV Papers, box 25); Jack Rivel to R. L. Polk & Co., October 15, 1964 (quote), AV Papers, box 29.

43. Milton Ogle to James Dixon, President of Antioch College, October 28, 1964, AV Papers, box 22.

44. [Appalachian Volunteers] Ninth Progress Report, November 1964, on Contract between Area Redevelopment Administration of the U.S. Department of Commerce and the Council of the Southern Mountains, AV Papers, box 20; Elliott County Projects, November 19–20[, 1964], and Attached Report, November 21, 1964, AV Papers, box 30; Ida Brown, Supervisor of Jackson County Schools, to Milton Ogle, November 10, 1964, AV Papers, box 70; Memorandum, Tom Davis to Gibbs Kinderman, November 29, 1964 (quote), AV Papers, box 70.

45. [Report for] Saturday, November 28, 1964, Leslie County, AV Papers, box 29; Report—November 1964, [by] Flem Messer, AV Papers, box 29; [Report for] Leslie County, Saturday November 21, 1964, AV Papers, box 30. Many counties were subject to these types of AV projects. For example, Rockcastle County's Owen Allen, Cove Ridge, and Blue Springs schools all got enrichment projects, which included the provision of basketball equipment, making Christ-

mas decorations, organizing sing-alongs, and presenting a ventriloquist act. In Knox County, the Mills and Erose schoolchildren participated in "games and crafts" as well as chemistry demonstrations. See Report—Rockcastle County, Kentucky, November 28, 1964, Thomas Rhodenbaugh, AV Papers, box 30; November 1964 Report [by] Jack Rivel, AV Papers, box 30; and Report—Rockcastle County, Kentucky and Jackson County, Kentucky, University of Kentucky Volunteers, Saturday, November 21, 1964, AV Papers, box 30.

46. Sargent Shriver to Milton Ogle, December 15, 1964, AV Papers, box 25; Statement of CAP Grant, [Attachment, p. 4], December 10, 1964, AV Papers, box 21.

47. Whisnant, *Modernizing the Mountaineer,* 189; William Wells to Vernon G. Wills, Wilmington College, Ohio, December 4, 1964, AV Papers, box 22; [AV Fieldmen and Counties], n.d., AV Papers, box 39.

48. [Appalachian Volunteers] Tenth Progress Report, December 1964, AV Papers, box 3; Report: Jackson County, Appalachian Volunteers, University of Kentucky, December 5, 1964, AV Papers, box 70; Project Report, Saturday, December 12, 1964, Berea College—Jackson County, AV Papers, box 20; Appalachian Volunteers Activities, Week of December 14–20, 1964, AV Papers, boxes 20 and 30. See also Jack Rivel, [Report for] December 7–12, 1964, AV Papers, box 30.

49. [Handwritten Notes from the AV Fall Conference], [ca. December 5, 1964], Berea College, AV Papers, box 2.

50. University of Kentucky Appalachian Volunteers newsletter, December 7, 1964, AV Papers, box 70.

51. The objectives of the project are contained in News of Importance to the Appalachian South, [CSM Press Release], December 30, 1964, CSM Papers, box 103.

52. Minutes, AV Board of Directors Meeting, August 25, 1964, Berea, KY, AV Papers, box 2.

4. The War to End All Wars

1. Oral History Interviews with Jack Rivel, February 12, 1991, and March 16, 1993, Berea, KY, and Flem Messer, September 26, 1990, Danville, KY, WOP Oral History Project.

2. Oral History Interview with Flem Messer, September 26, 1990, Danville, KY, WOP Oral History Project. Messer and the Mill Creek project are the focus of chapter 2.

3. Oral History Interview with Jack Rivel, March 16, 1993, Berea, KY, WOP Oral History Project.

4. [Suggested Copy for Fund-Raising Brochure], [ca. 1965], AV Papers, box 25. The Appalachian Volunteers was not the first organization to adopt such a vision of the mountain region. See Batteau, *The Invention of Appalachia.*

5. Appalachian Volunteers, Recent Activities, February 1, 1965, AV Papers, box 20; Appalachian Volunteers, Recent Activities, February 9, 1965, AV Papers, box 20; Milton Ogle to Michael Harrington, March 16, 1965, AV Papers, box 27. By exposing the extent of poverty that existed in the United States in the early 1960s, Harrington's *The Other America* also contributed, it can be argued, to the start of the War on Poverty.

6. Milton Ogle to Henry Ford II, November 13, 1964, AV Papers, box 23. Actually, this was a form letter sent to representatives of a number of large corporations. See AV Papers, box 23.

7. Memorandum, Thomas Rhodenbaugh to P. F. Ayer, January 5, 1965, AV Papers, box 29.

8. Report on Appalachian Volunteers Work Camp, Lick Branch School, Ary, Kentucky, January 4–9, 1965, [by Joe Mulloy], AV Papers, box 8; Evaluation of the Appalachian Volunteers Christmas Project, by Marshall Smith, January 11, 1965, AV Papers, box 8.

9. Report on Appalachian Volunteers Work Camp, Lick Branch School, Ary, Kentucky, January 4–9, 1965, [by Joe Mulloy], AV Papers, box 8; Evaluation of the Appalachian Volunteers Christmas Project, by Marshall Smith, January 11, 1965, AV Papers, box 8. Twelve Volunteers originally planned to help at Lick Branch.

10. Activities: January 1–February 23, 1965, under Contract between Community Action Programs, Office of Economic Opportunity and Council of the Southern Mountains, Inc., AV Papers, box 3; Project Report [by] Tom Rhodenbaugh, January 23, 1965, AV Papers, box 70; Report Form 1 Hunting Fork, Wolfe County, February 13, 1965, AV Papers, box 70; Report Form 1 Vortex, Wolfe County, February 13, 1965, AV Papers, box 70; Report Form 1, Dry Fork–South Fork, Jackson County, February 1965, AV Papers, box 70.

11. Project Report, Tom Rhodenbaugh, January 23, 1965, AV Papers, box 70; Appalachian Volunteers Project Evaluation, January 9, 1965, Blue Springs School, Rockcastle County (first quote), AV Papers, box 24; William Wells to Steve Allen, March 19, 1965 (second quote), AV Papers, box 32.

12. Council Staff—March 5, 1965, AV Papers, box 23. Jones quoted and AV personnel discussed in Whisnant, *Modernizing the Mountaineer,* 190.

13. The University of Kentucky project is reported in Zeh, "University Students Protest." Reports on the activities of the Volunteers during the first quarter of 1965 (most activity was during the month of February) can be found in AV Papers, box 70.

14. Appalachian Volunteers, Council of the Southern Mountains, Evaluation Comments, by J. Hoge T. Sutherland, May 15, 1965, AV Papers, box 12. See also Oral History Interview with Roslea Johnson, June 24, 1991, Des Moines, IA, WOP Oral History Project.

15. Appalachian Volunteers, Council of the Southern Mountains, Evalua-

tion Comments, by J. Hoge T. Sutherland, May 15, 1965, AV Papers, box 12. See also Oral History Interview with Roslea Johnson, June 24, 1991, Des Moines, IA, WOP Oral History Project.

16. Appalachian Volunteers, Council of the Southern Mountains, Evaluation Comments, by J. Hoge T. Sutherland, May 15, 1965, AV Papers, box 12.

17. Ibid. While Sutherland believed that improving schools meant consolidating schools, fixing existing structures meant improvement to the AVs and, thus, had the same effect.

18. Ibid. Unfortunately, the actual questions Sutherland asked are not in neither the AV nor the CSM papers.

19. *Christmas in Appalachia*, CBS News Special Report, December 22, 1964; Batteau, *The Invention of Appalachia*, 13 (see also 7, 10, 147, 161, 162–63, 166, 167).

20. Depressed Area USA, Suggested Story Line, [ca. 1964], CSM Papers, box 74.

21. Perley Ayer to Richard Boone, January 28, 1965, AV Papers, box 4. The argument that only the Council was capable of leading Appalachian reform efforts is also articulated in Project Request from the Council of the Southern Mountains, Inc., to the Office of Economic Opportunity, January 26, 1965, AV Papers, box 25. In this document, it is argued that the War on Poverty was failing because local communities lacked the knowledge to fight poverty effectively. The Council was the only agency "that cuts across all governmental lines in the area" and that can provide "the help local communities need."

22. On the three outside colleges, see Activities: January 1–February 23, 1965, under Contract between Community Action Programs, Office of Economic Opportunity and Council of the Southern Mountains, Inc., AV Papers, box 3.

23. Memorandum, Perley Ayer to Dorothy Crandall, November 27, 1964 (first quote), CSM Papers, box 103; Gibbs Kinderman to Chuck Peters, February 4, 1965 (second quote), AV Papers, box 22.

24. Loyal Jones to Donald Crane, University of Pittsburgh, November 18, 1964 (first quote), CSM Papers, box 104; Serge Hummon, United Church Board for Homeland Missions, to Loyal Jones, January 22, 1965 (second quote), AV Papers, box 25; Flem Messer to Rev. Donald E. Van Voorhis, February 19, 1965, AV Papers, box 26; Gibbs Kinderman to Hugh Allen, Beliot College, July 20, 1965, AV Papers, box 20; Milton Ogle to David Madden, University of Louisville, April 21, 1964, AV Papers, box 1; Thomas Rhodenbaugh to M. Eugene Mockabee, Pennsylvania State University, November 16, 1965, AV Papers, box 26; Daniel Fox to James M. Perrin, April 18, 1966, AV Papers, box 25. The general correspondence files of the Appalachian Volunteers Papers are filled with letters to volunteers from all over the United States. See esp. box 26, file 5, Kinderman, Gibbs, Field Coordinator.

25. The Bard College Field Period, [October 1965], AV Papers, box 25; Richard Blass to Lionel Duff, March 23, 1964, CSM Papers, box 101. See also Richard Blass to [CSM], March 17, 1964, and Loyal Jones to Richard Blass, March 19, 1964, CSM Papers, box 101.

26. Clarke Moses to Appalachian Volunteers, October 8, 1966, and Tom Rhodenbaugh to Clarke Moses, November 2, 1966, AV Papers, box 26.

27. Loyal Jones to L. M. Baker, Purdue University, March 11, 1964, CSM Papers, box 101; [Handwritten Notes from the Appalachian Volunteers Fall Conference], [December 5, 1964] (first quote), AV Papers, box 2; Perley Ayer to Paul Cunningham, NBC-TV, September 27, 1964 (last quote), CSM Papers, box 120.

28. Gibbs Kinderman to Tim Sword, Wilmington College Appalachian Project, January 20, 1965, AV Papers, box 22. The article Kinderman was referring to is "Collegians to Fix Jackson School," *Louisville Courier-Journal,* January 20, 1965, sec. 2, p. 1.

29. William Wells to Vernon G. Wills, Wilmington College, December 4, 1964, AV Papers, box 22; [Appalachian Volunteers] Eleventh Progress Report, January 1965, AV Papers, box 3; Otis Johnson to Tom Rhodenbaugh, April 2, 1965 (quote), AV Papers, box 70.

30. Weekly Report for Week of March 19 to March 29, [1965] (first quote), AV Papers, box 30; Appalachian Volunteers Information Sheet for Programs in County School, Bill Marshak, Earlham College [Project], Decoy, Knott Co., March 15–29, 1965 (second quote), AV Papers, box 70. See also Wiley Smith, Earlham College, to Bill Wells, February 21, 1965, AV Papers, box 30; and Bill Wells to Wiley Smith, February 24, 1965 (for the Decoy project), AV Papers, box 30.

31. Queens College Appalachian Summer Program, [ca. 1965], AV Papers, box 22.

32. Ibid.

33. Thomas Rhodenbaugh to Larry Qualls, March 9, 1965, AV Papers, box 28; Thomas Rhodenbaugh to [University of Kentucky AV Spring Break Project Participants], March 6, 1965, AV Papers, box 28.

34. Appalachian Volunteer Information Sheet for Programs in County Schools: Larry Qualls, Spruce School, Knox County, March 15–20, 1965, Appalachian Volunteers Information Sheet . . . Benjamin Kutnicki, Spruce Pine School, Knox County, March 15–20, 1965, Appalachian Volunteers Information Sheet . . . Carol J. Powell, Spruce School, Knox County, March 15–20, 1965, Appalachian Volunteers Information Sheet . . . Frank McCough, Ligon School, Floyd County, March 15–20, 1965, Appalachian Volunteer Information Sheet . . . Lainy Grosscup, Bruin School, Elliott County, March 15–20, 1965, Appalachian Volunteer Information Sheet, Dave Keller, Bruin [School], Elliott County, March 15–20, 1965, and Appalachian Volunteers Information Sheet . . . Joseph

A. Blazie, Wellhope School, Rockcastle County, March 15–20, 1965 (quote), AV Papers, box 28.

35. Appalachian Volunteer Information Sheet . . . , Tongam H. Loebis, March 15–20, 1965 (first quote), and Appalachian Volunteer Information Sheet . . . , George Dritsas, March 16, 1965 (second quote), AV Papers, box 28. Both these individuals visited four schools. For information on mountaineer attitudes toward education, see chapter 3.

36. Appalachian Volunteer Information Sheet . . . , Lainy Grosscup, . . . March 15–20, 1965 (first quote), Appalachian Volunteer Information Sheet . . . Frank McCough, . . . March 15–20, 1965 (second quote), and Appalachian Volunteer Information Sheet . . . , Dave Kelleher . . . , March 15–20, 1965, AV Papers, box 28.

37. The biographical data sheets are in AV Papers, box 28.

38. [Appalachian Volunteer Biographical Information Form], [ca. March 1965], respondents G, B, and Y, respectively, AV Papers, box 28 (all emphasis added). Because federal law protects the privacy of those who worked in publicly funded programs, the individuals in question cannot be identified by name. The letters correspond with the order in which the forms are filed in the AV Papers.

39. Ibid., respondents T, C, S, and J, respectively.

40. The twelve counties, and the communities in which VISTA volunteerss operated, are listed in Appalachian Volunteers VISTA Schools, [1965], AV Papers, box 12. See also Appalachian Volunteers Progress Report, January 1–March 31, [1965], AV Papers, box 3.

41. For the number of summer volunteers and their states of origin, see High-Lights of Appalachian Volunteer Program, [ca. 1965], and Memorandum, Milton Ogle to William Lawrence, OEO, July 16, 1965, AV Papers, box 20. Loyal Jones to Burton Rogers, October 18, 1965 (first quote), AV Papers, box 25; AV Distribution of VISTA Application, Sister Eileen to Milton Ogle, September 9, 1966, AV Papers, box 31; Bill Wells to Forrest E. Simomeau, September 10, 1966 (second quote), AV Papers, box 31; Thomas Rhodenbaugh to Miss Jean Schnall, May 12, 1967 (third quote), AV Papers, box 31; [Memorandum], To the Members of the A.V. Board from Mark Cheren, n.d. (last quote), AV Papers, box 7; and Kim [Hashizumi] to [Appalachian Volunteers], February 3, 1967, AV Papers, box 24. See also Bill Wells to Cleveland Sellers, April 14, 1967, AV Papers, box 31.

42. Memorandum, To All Appalachian Volunteers Staff from D.M.F. [D. M. Fox], [ca. 1965], AV Papers, box 25. See also Perley Ayer to Wiley R. Smith Jr., July 1, 1965, AV Papers, box 4. The Library of Community Action Styles is in AV Papers, boxes 123–25. The "library" presented certain situations to the trainees without offering resolutions. It was the potential volunteer's job to determine how to resolve the problem contained in each particular case study.

See also Oral History Interviews with Jack Rivel, February 12, 1991, and March 15, 1993, Berea, KY, and Loyal Jones, November 19, 1990, and March 15, 1991, Berea, KY, WOP Oral History Project.

43. The responses of the Earlham students are in Appalachian Volunteer Information Sheet for Programs in County Schools, [1965], AV Papers, box 22. See esp. the forms completed by Christine DeCou, Wiley Smith, and Philip Scott. Yet another Earlham student, James Read, stated that he had "had no orientation."

44. John W. Hogarty, Antioch College, to Milton Ogle, March 15, 1965, AV Papers, box 22.

45. Handwritten Memorandum, M[innie] M[aude] Macaulay [to Perley Ayer], [ca. June 1965], AV Papers, box 4; Florence Brooks to Perley Ayer, [ca. June 1965], AV Papers, box 4.

46. Bob [Coles] to Dan [Fox], July 13, 1965, AV Papers, box 12; Harry Caudill to Mrs. [Ann] Pollard, March 6, 1965, AV Papers, box 21; James W. Haas, OEO, to Dan Fox, December 22, 1965, AV Papers, box 35.

47. Annual Report—VISTA, [ca. 1967], AV Papers, box 28 (first quote); Council of the Southern Mountains, Inc., Report of Appalachian Volunteer Activities, 1965 (subsequent quotes), AV Papers, box 8.

48. Council of the Southern Mountains, Inc., Report of Appalachian Volunteer Activities, 1965, AV Papers, box 8.

49. Appalachian Volunteers Community Case Studies: Joshua: The Trumpet of Hope (Addendum to OEO Demonstration Grant Proposal), 1965, AV Papers, box 3.

50. William Wells to Mr. Lacey, John F. Kennedy Memorial Library, November 29, 1966, AV Papers, box 26; "This refers to community work that I did in Northeast Kentucky . . . ," by Bill Wells, [1966], AV Papers, box 21; Memorandum, Flem Messer to the Executive Staff of the Council of the Southern Mountains, [1966], AV Papers, box 34.

51. Weekly Report from Area IV Period: 30 January–7 February, 1965, [by Bill Wells] (first quote), and Weekly Report for Week of March 19 to March 29, [1965], [by Bill Wells] (second quote), AV Papers, box 30.

52. Activities Report—Monday, May 24–May 28, [1965], Flem Messer, AV Papers, box 29; Ivy L. Reese, Some of My Work, [ca. 1966], AV Papers, box 29; James E. Kendrick to Appalachian Volunteers, September 23, 1965, AV Papers, box 25.

53. Sue Leek to Milton [Ogle] and Dan [Fox], n.d., AV Papers, box 34.

54. Loren Kramer to Milton Ogle, December 16, 1965, AV Papers, box 25; Kim [Hashizumi] to [Appalachian Volunteers], February 3, 1967, AV Papers, box 24. For a discussion of the attitudes and desires of "change agents" in the southern Appalachians, see Whisnant, All That Is Native and Fine.

55. Merrill, "Strategy in the War on Poverty." Merrill came to the mountains as an AV-VISTA.

56. Ibid.

57. P[aul] D. Merrill to Dan [Fox], January 29, 1966, AV Papers, box 34.

58. See Matusow, *The Unraveling of America,* 254–65.

59. Thomas Rhodenbaugh to Walter Dillon, Assistant Editor, *Kiwanas Magazine,* November 16, 1965, AV Papers, box 22.

60. Flem Messer to Marvin C. Swanson, Cushing Academy, Ashburnham, MA, February 18, 1965, AV Papers, box 31.

61. Hoskins, "Appalachian Volunteers Evaluate Project."

62. William Wells to Larry Kelly, University of Kentucky AV Chapter President, April 9, 1965, AV Papers, box 30; Activities Report, April 26–April 30, [1965], Flem Messer (first quote), AV Papers, box 29; Activities Report for March 29–April 10, [1965], Flem Messer (second quote), AV Papers, box 29.

63. Grisham, "A Hollow Place."

64. Jack Rivel to Judy Grisham, *Kentucky Kernel,* April 25, 1966, AV Papers, box 35.

65. Judy Thomas to Dan Fox, March 24, 1966, AV Papers, box 25.

66. Judy Thomas and Julia McKeon to Eleanor Constable, VISTA, Washington, DC, May 31, 1966, AV Papers, box 35. The Bell County Economic Opportunity Council was the county CAP.

67. See, e.g., the discussion of the Mill Creek Project in chapter 2.

5. The New Model Army

1. Oral History Interview with Loyal Jones, November 19, 1990, Berea, KY, WOP Oral History Project.

2. Ibid. See also Lilienthal, *TVA.*

3. Milton Ogle to Governor Edward T. Breathitt, April 20, 1965 (quote), AV Papers, box 20.

4. Statement on the AV-VISTA Program, [ca. 1965], AV Papers, box 35. On the issue of local acceptance of the Volunteers, see Oral History Interviews with Jack Rivel, February 12, 1991, Berea, KY, and Flem Messer, September 26, 1990, Danville, KY, WOP Oral History Project.

5. Report for the Week of April 26 through May 8, [1965], [by Bill Wells] (quote), AV Papers, box 30.

6. Reflections on Trace Fork, n.d., AV Papers, box 3.

7. Impressions of Thousandsticks, by Judith Allcock, n.d., AV Papers, box 3 (emphasis added in last quote). Records indicate that Allcock hailed from New Jersey.

8. Ibid.; Reflection on Trace Fork, n.d., AV Papers, box 3.

9. Flem Messer to Dr. B. H. Jarman, President, Pikeville College, April 2, 1965, AV Papers, box 26.

10. Gish's statements are contained in "Eastern Kentucky: Where Did Hope

Go?" (speech delivered at the Urban Affairs Workshop of the Council of the Southern Mountains, Berea, KY, July 14, 1964), AV Papers, box 31.

11. Report of the Area Director to the NE. KY. Council, September 21, 1965, AV Papers, box 26.

12. Ibid.

13. Ibid.

14. Lee W. Taylor, Area Program Director, Northeast Kentucky Area Development Council, to Alan Zuckerman, CSM, September 23, 1965, AV Papers, box 26.

15. Memorandum, Eastern Kentucky Report, Frank Prial to Bill Haddad, OEO, June 7, 1965, attached to Memorandum, Bill Haddad to Ted Berry, June 11, 1965, AV Papers, box 27. Prial's report is also in Office of Economic Opportunity Papers (hereafter OEO Papers), "Appalachia," National Archives II, College Park, Maryland.

16. Ibid.

17. Ibid.

18. Ibid.

19. Memorandum, Jack Ciaccio to Sidney Woolner, June 21, 1965, AV Papers, box 27. The same letter is also preserved in OEO Papers, National Archives II, College Park, MD.

20. Memorandum, Jack Ciaccio to Sidney Woolner, June 21, 1965 (quotes), OEO Papers/AV Papers, box 27; Glen, "The War on Poverty in Appalachia," 42–43.

21. Jack Ciaccio to Sidney Woolner, June 21, 1965, OEO Papers/AV Papers, box 27.

22. Appalachian Volunteer Community Case Studies, Verda—Learning to Live and Work Together (Part of the OEO Demonstration Grant Proposal), AV Papers, box 3; Jack Ciaccio to Sidney Woolner, June 21, 1965 (quotes), OEO Papers/AV Papers, box 27.

23. [The Fonde Volunteer] to Perley Ayer, August 13, 1966, AV Papers, box 31 (first quote); Appalachian Volunteer–Vista Associate End-of-Service Questionnaire, [ca. August/September 1966], AV Papers, box 31 (second quote). Owing to an agreement with the Berea College Archives, I am unable to reveal the name of this Volunteer.

24. "[Report:] Linda and I went back to Fonde . . ." [The Fonde Volunteer to Dan Fox], [ca. fall 1966], AV Papers, box 31. All surnames have been omitted from this statement.

25. [Interview with Residents of Weeksbury, KY], [ca. 1965], AV Papers, box 33.

26. Ellen Weisman to [Dan] Fox, [ca. October 1965], AV Papers, box 35.

27. Ibid. (first quote); Ellen Weisman to Dan Fox, February 26, 1966 (second quote), AV Papers, box 35. On the phenomenon of quiescence, see Gaventa, *Power and Powerlessness*.

28. AV Background Information, [Chapter] VII Case Study—Report on Verda, [ca. 1966] (Daugherty's statements), AV Papers, box 8; Oral History Interviews with George Brosi, November 3, 1990, Berea, KY, and Flem Messer, October 26, 1990, Danville, KY, WOP Oral History Project.

29. The new Appalachian Volunteer outlook can be found in AV Background Information, [ca. 1966], AV Papers, box 8, and Notes on the Appalachian Volunteers, [ca. 1967], AV Papers, box 13.

30. Memorandum, P. F. Ayer to All Staff Members, November 1, 1965, AV Papers, box 34; Memorandum, Eastern Kentucky Report, Frank Prial to Bill Haddad, OEO, June 7, 1965 (last quote), AV Papers, box 27. See also Jack Ciaccio to Sidney Woolner, June 21, 1965, OEO Papers/AV Papers, box 27.

31. AV Background Information, [Chapter] VII Case Study—Report on Verda, [ca. 1966] (quote), AV Papers, box 8.

32. Donald R. Fessler, President, CSM Board of Directors, to Members of the C.S.M. Board of Directors, April 18, 1966, AV Papers, box 5. On the drawbacks to the move to Bristol, see Disadvantages—Tri-Cities, [ca. 1966], AV Papers, box 4.

33. Donald R. Fessler to Members of the C.S.M. Board of Directors, April 18, 1966 (Fessler quote), AV Papers, box 5; Advantages—Tri-Cities, [ca. 1966], AV Papers, box 4 (other quotes).

34. Horton, "The Appalachian Volunteers," 51 (committee quote); [Draft of Form Letter to Presidents of Eastern Kentucky Colleges from Perley Ayer], [ca. 1964] (other quotes), CSM Papers, box 104. This document states: "It is the hope that in the end Appalachian Volunteers may became an independent permanent organization." See also Loyal Jones to Thomas Anderson, Editor in Chief, State Farm Publication, May 26, 1964, CSM Papers, box 100; and Loyal Jones to Brady Black, Editor of the *Cincinnati Enquirer*, April 22, 1964, CSM Papers, box 103. The Kentucky Development Committee was a state-sponsored agency that attempted to coordinate economic development strategies in Kentucky.

35. Tentative Letter, Perley Ayer to Donald Fessler (Perley Ayer Writes Don Fessler, CSM President), [ca. April 20, 1966], AV Papers, box 5.

36. Ibid.

37. Donald R. Fessler to Members of the C.S.M. Board of Directors, April 18, 1966, AV Papers, box 5.

38. Memorandum, P. F. Ayer to Milton Ogle, March 19, 1964, CSM Papers, box 114.

39. Memorandum, Perley Ayer to Phil Conn, March 31, 1964, CSM Papers, box 103. Ayer sent a similar memorandum to Flem Messer that same day. See Perley Ayer to Flem Messer, March 3, 1964, AV Papers, box 4. On November 17, 1965, the CSM held another staff meeting that only one AV attended, and then only for a "few minutes." Ayer questioned whether this nonparticipation was

"an indication of AV attitude." See Memorandum, Perley Ayer to Milton Ogle, November 20, 1965, AV Papers, box 4. On Wells and Blair, see Memorandum, P. F. Ayer to Milton Ogle, January 27, 1966, AV Papers, box 5.

40. Memorandum, P. F. Ayer to Milton Ogle, June 25, 1965, AV Papers, box 5. In another communiqué to Ogle, Ayer again reprimanded the AV director for the "evidence that our Appalachian volunteer staff considers itself an independent agency, somewhat disinclined to operate as team members of the Council staff." See Memorandum, P. F. Ayer to Milton Ogle, March 5, 1965, AV Papers, box 27. See also Memorandum, P. F. Ayer to Mace Crandall, December 30, 1964, CSM Papers, box 103, in which Ayer criticized Crandall for a press release "because of its failure to make any direct implication of the Council as the sponsoring agency [of the AVs]."

41. You Are Responsible: Some Thoughts on the Appalachian Volunteer Summer Project, [ca. spring 1966], AV Papers, box 5.

42. Ibid.

43. Memorandum, P. F. Ayer to Dan Fox, April 9, 1966, AV Papers, box 5.

44. Ibid.

45. Memorandum, Daniel Fox to P. F. Ayer, March 7, 1966, AV Papers, box 5.

46. Ayer to Fox, April 9, 1966, AV Papers, box 5.

47. Comments on the AV-VISTA Program, [ca. 1966], AV Papers, box 5. Unfortunately, the document does not reveal who the Volunteers "of unquestioned integrity and personal dedication" were.

48. Ibid.

49. Ibid. All the Appalachian Volunteers interviewed denied these charges.

50. Ibid.

51. On Ayer's attempt to stop the AV move, see Tentative Letter, Perley Ayer to Donald Fessler, [ca. April 1966], AV Papers, box 5. On the "secret meeting," see Oral History Interview with Loyal Jones, November 19, 1990 (first quote), Berea, KY, WOP Oral History Project. P. F. Ayer to Milton Ogle, May 4, 1966 (second quote), AV Papers, box 5; P. F. Ayer to Milton Ogle, May 2, 1966 (third quote), AV Papers, box 5; P. F. Ayer to Daniel Fox, May 2, 1966 (last quote), AV Papers, box 5.

52. Letter of Resignation Submitted by Thirteen Members of the AV Staff to Dr. Fessler and Members of the Board, May 3, 1966, AV Papers, box 5; Statement of Don Fox and Milton Ogle to Jim Hampton of the *Louisville Courier-Journal*, May 5, 1966 (Mimeo), AV Papers, box 4.

53. Memorandum, Perley Ayer to [CSM] Board of Directors, June 3, 1966, AV Papers, box 5.

54. Oral History Interview with Loyal Jones, November 19, 1990, Berea, KY, WOP Oral History Project.

55. Joe Barker to Loyal Jones, May 24, 1966, AV Papers, box 5.

56. Southern Conference Educational Fund, the Southern Mountain Proj-

ect, a Statement of Purpose and Program, September 1, 1967, AV Papers, box 10. On the increasing radicalization of protest in the United States at this time, see esp. Matusow, *The Unraveling of America;* and Anderson, *The Movement and the Sixties.*

6. Operation Rolling Thunder

1. Oral History Interview with Joe Mulloy, November 11, 1990, Huntington, WV, WOP Oral History Project.

2. Ibid. For additional comments concerning how the CSM sought to give its early AVs "meaningful experiences," see Oral History Interview with Roslea Johnson, June 24, 1991, Des Moines, IA, WOP Oral History Project.

3. Oral History Interview with Joe Mulloy, November 11, 1990, Huntington, WV, WOP Oral History Project.

4. First General Membership Meeting of Appalachian Volunteers, Southeastern Christian College, May 15, 1966, AV Papers, box 7.

5. Perley Ayer to Theodore Berry, OEO, May 12, 1966, AV Papers, box 5; Perley Ayer to Sidney Woolner, OEO, May 12, 1966, AV Papers, box 5; Perley Ayer to Milton Ogle, June 8, 1966, AV Papers, box 4; Memorandum, P. F. Ayer to CSM Board of Directors, June 3, 1966, AV Papers, box 5. The final figures for AV funding in June 1966 are contained in Milton Ogle to Dunn & Bradstreet, Inc., June 21, 1966, AV Papers, box 22.

6. Harry M. Caudill to Milton Ogle, May 4, 1966, AV Papers, box 21.

7. On the demographics of the summer project, see Memorandum, Milton Ogle to George Peck, September 20, 1967, AV Papers, box 27; and Daniel Fox to John G. Collins III, July 20, 1966, AV Papers, box 33. On the community intern program, see Whisnant, *Modernizing the Mountaineer,* 192; and Horton, "The Appalachian Volunteers," 72.

8. Memorandum, Milton Ogle to Sanford Kravitz and Padraic Kennedy, December 17, 1965 (second and third quotes), AV Papers, box 26; and Memorandum, Sanford Kravitz and Padraic Kennedy to Dan Fox and Milt Ogle, December 2, 1965 (first and last quotes), AV Papers, box 26.

9. Michael Kline to Manuel Strong, Assistant Director, Middle Kentucky Area Community Action Program, June 17, 1966 (quote), AV Papers, box 31; [Report of the AV Summer 1966 Project], [1966], AV Papers, box 8. The schools listed on this report were Elkhorn, Buffalo, Barewallow, Evarts, Kidlow, Jones Creek, Verda, Black Starr, Persimmon Fork, Baker's Fork, Bear Creek, and Goose Creek. See also Cases of Group Action, Place: Whitley County, Kentucky, October 1966, AV Papers, box 21. This report also highlighted activity in Wolfe and Breathitt counties.

10. Ayer, "College Volunteers to Serve Appalachia"; Whisnant, *Modernizing the Mountaineer,* 193.

11. Community Action Program Application—Component 2: Appalachian Volunteer Community Interns [attached to A Proposal to the OEO . . . Demonstration Grant for AV Program, 1965], AV Papers, box 3.

12. Ibid. (quote); Guidelines for Community Councils, [1966], AV Papers, box 8.

13. Community Action Program Application—Component 3: Appalachian Volunteers Summer Project 1966 [attached to A Proposal to the OEO . . . Demonstration Grant for AV Program, 1965], AV Papers, box 3.

14. Whisnant, *Modernizing the Mountaineer,* 191. Unfortunately, Whisnant does not reveal who these fieldmen were. Robert Coles, Brief and Over-All Evaluation of the Appalachian Volunteers during the Summer of 1966, AV Papers, box 12.

15. Flem Messer to Bankers Trust Co., New York, September 12, 1966, AV Papers, box 27; Robert Coles to Dan Fox, July 25, 1966, AV Papers, box 12; James E. Clay to John Gaines, August 30, 1966, and Bristol Office to John Gaines, December 30, 1966, AV Papers, box 23.

16. Bruce Boyens's, Jerry Knoll's, and Gail Hadley's Responses to Question 3 in a [Survey on a Possible] AV-VISTA Meeting, December 1966, AV Papers, box 7.

17. David Thoenen, Cathy Lochner, Carol Wolfenden, and Candy Colin surveys, AV Papers, box 7.

18. [Conference Questionnaires], David Altschul, Robin Buckner, and Carol Wolfenden, December 1966, AV Papers, box 7. On the anti-strip-mining movement in Kentucky and the rest of Appalachia, see Montrie, *To Save the Land and People.*

19. [Conference Questionnaires], Sandra R. Hall, Jerry Knoll, Karyn Palmer, and Patricia Ann Dicky, AV Papers, box 7. See also [Conference Questionnaires], James Larry Myers, Penny Caldwell, and A. Marks, AV Papers, box 7.

20. [Conference Questionnaires], Judith Jacobs, Ed Turner, Anne L. Chambers, John Zysman, and Karen Spitulnik, AV Papers, box 7.

21. [Conference Questionnaires], Sheila Musselman, Rita O'Donnell, and John Campbell, AV Papers, box 7.

22. "Vista Denied More Schools," *Louisville Courier-Journal,* June 27, 1966; Neureul Miracle to Council of the Southern Mountains, May 30, 1966, AV Papers, box 5.

23. Jestyn Portugill to Aaron Paul, July 6, 1966, and Aaron Paul to Jestyn Portugill, July 8, 1966, AV Papers, box 28. See also Dan Fox to Mitchell Ginsberg, Welfare Commissioner, City of New York, July 5, 1966, AV Papers, box 23.

24. Appalachian Volunteer—VISTA Associate End-of-Service Questionnaire, August/September, 1966 (first quote), AV Papers, box 31; [Report] by Judy Stewart to Dan [Fox], [ca. September 1966] (second quote), AV Papers,

box 12. On the issue of quiescence, about which Stewart essentially spoke, see Gaventa, *Power and Powerlessness.*

25. Notes on the Appalachian Volunteers, [ca. 1967], AV Papers, box 13. See also The Appalachian Volunteers: A Force for Change in Appalachia, [ca. 1968], AV Papers, box 3.

26. Notes on the Appalachian Volunteers, n.d., AV Papers, box 13.

27. Ibid.

28. Community Action Program Application—Component 4: Outpost Education [attached to A Proposal to the OEO . . . Demonstration Grant for AV Program], 1965, AV Papers, box 3.

29. Jack Rivel to Mrs. Charles D. Gloster, September 21, 1966 (first quote), AV Papers, box 23; Notes on the Appalachian Volunteers, n.d. (other quotes), AV Papers, box 13.

30. Notes on the Appalachian Volunteers, n.d., AV Papers, box 13.

31. Ibid. See also Whisnant, *Modernizing the Mountaineer,* 190.

32. Minutes of the Ad-Hoc Executive Board of the Appalachian Volunteers Meeting, July 27, 1966, Barbourville, KY, AV Papers, box 7.

33. Cases of Group Action, Place: Whitley County, Kentucky, Date: October 1966 (token response), AV Papers, box 21; [Report], Whitley County, [ca. October 1966] (all other quotes), AV Papers, box 8. See also Milton Ogle to Sanford Kravitz, OEO, April 26, 1966, AV Papers, box 27.

34. Bill Wells, N. E. Area Prospectus, [ca. autumn 1966], AV Papers, box 8.

35. The Problem of Participation in Community Action Programs: Impressions and Suggestions, Appalachian Community Meeting, August 21–22, 1966, Washington, DC, AV Papers, box 8.

36. Ibid.

37. Bill Wells to "Hoot," November 29, 1966, AV Papers, box 20.

38. AV Background Information, Section II: Appalachia—the Welfare States, n.d., AV Papers, box 8.

39. Ibid.

40. Ibid.

41. Ibid.

42. Notes on the Appalachian Volunteers, n.d., AV Papers, box 13.

43. AV Background Information, Section IV: An Indictment of the Coal Industry, n.d., AV Papers, box 8.

44. Ibid.

45. Ibid. See also Montrie, *To Save the Land and People.*

46. Appalachia Speaks II, Appalachian Volunteers Winter Meeting, Marshall University, Huntington, WV, January 28, 1967, AV Papers, box 7.

47. AV Background Information, Section IV: An Indictment of the Coal Industry, n.d., AV Papers, box 8.

48. Ibid.

49. Thoughts on Being a VISTA Volunteer in Perry County, Kentucky [attached to By Way of Introduction (a booklet by a VISTA volunteer who had recently returned to the Berkeley campus of the University of California)], n.d., AV Papers, box 3.

50. Jamie Huff to [Jack] Rivel, October 6, 1966 (first quote), and David Harris to [Jack] Rivel, [October 1966] (second quote), AV Papers, box 30. For the letters about the accidents, see Emily Creech to Ann Pollards, October 24, 1966, James Miniard to Ann Pollards, [October 6, 1966], and Mr. and Mrs. David Turner to Ann Pollards, October 24, 1966, AV Papers, box 30. The teacher and the county superintendent had the same surname.

51. To Whom It May Concern from We—the People of Buffalo, n.d., AV Papers, box 30.

52. Tom Rhodenbaugh to Julia McKeon, October 25, 1966 (first quote), AV Papers, box 26; Stephen Daugherty to Joseph Nolan, Regional Director, U.S. Postal Service, November 18, 1966 (second quote), AV Papers, box 29; The A.V. Experience Summary Statement, [ca. 1966] (last quote), AV Papers, box 31.

53. [Draft Letter], Milton Ogle to Robert Kennedy, November 1, 1966, AV Papers, box 25.

54. Joe's Prospectus, [ca. 1967], AV Papers, box 8. On the Freedom Schools conducted by civil rights workers in Mississippi in 1964, see Carson, *In Struggle;* McAdam, *Freedom Summer;* and Sitkoff, *The Struggle for Black Equality.* On Highlander, see Glen, *Highlander.*

55. Memorandum, Thomas Rhodenbaugh to Jack Ciaccio, October 27, 1966, and Appalachian Volunteers in Wise County, Virginia, by James Sommerville, AV Papers, box 8.

56. Appalachian Volunteers in Wise County, Virginia, by James Sommerville, AV Papers, box 8.

57. Memorandum, Thomas Rhodenbaugh to Jack Ciaccio, October 27, 1966, AV Papers, box 8. See also Raleigh County, West Virginia, [1966], AV Papers, box 8. On the events in Mingo County, see Perry, *"They'll Cut off Your Project."* See also Whisnant, *Modernizing the Mountaineer,* 191–92.

58. This Is Not a Memorandum to Mike, Gibbs, Steve, et al. from Milton Ogle, October 19, 1966, AV Papers, box 21.

59. Milton Ogle to Fr. Austin J. Staley, St. Vincent College, Latrobe, PA, March 28, 1967, AV Papers, box 31.

60. Highlights of Community Action in the Middle Kentucky River Area, January 1966–November 1966 (other quotes), AV Papers, box 8; Tom Rhodenbaugh to Rick Bank, April 3, 1967 (last quote), AV Papers, box 20.

61. Tom Rhodenbaugh to Rick Bank, April 3, 1967, AV Papers, box 20.; Memorandum, Thomas Rhodenbaugh to Jack Ciaccio, October 27, 1966, AV Papers, box 8; Appendix II: Details of the Kentucky AV Program as Excerpted from the Quarterly Report to the Board of Directors (Draft), [1967], AV Papers,

box 7; Whisnant, *Modernizing the Mountaineer,* 200, 210. See also Caudill, *My Land Is Dying.*

62. Appendix II: Details of the Kentucky AV Program as Excerpted from the Quarterly Report to the Board of Directors (Draft), [1967] (on the Evarts outpost), AV Papers, box 7; A.V.s in Harlan County, [1967] (on HELL), AV Papers, box 8.

63. A.V.s in Harlan County, [1967], AV Papers, box 8.

64. On the AV activities in Floyd County, see Appendix II: Details of the Kentucky AV Program as Excerpted from the Quarterly Report to the Board of Directors (Draft), [1967], AV Papers, box 7; Floyd County, [1967], AV Papers, box 8; Washington White Paper: Floyd County Report, [1966], AV Papers, box 8; Future Appalachian Volunteer Operations in Floyd County, Kentucky, 1966, AV Papers, box 8; Report on Community Action Efforts of Appalachian Volunteers from Prestonsburg Office by Flem Messer, [1966], AV Papers, box 8; Meeting at Frankfort, [1967], AV Papers, box 30; and The People of Little Mud Creek, [1967], AV Papers, box 30.

65. Appendix II: Details of the Kentucky AV Program as Excerpted from the Quarterly Report to the Board of Directors (Draft), [1967] (quote), AV Papers, box 7; Appalachian Volunteers in Letcher County, Ky., Summer 1967, AV Papers, box 8.

66. Appendix II: Details of the Kentucky AV Program as Excerpted from the Quarterly Report to the Board of Directors (Draft), [1967], AV Papers, box 7; White Paper Report: Wise, Scott, Letcher and Pike Counties, [1966] (quotes), AV Papers, box 8.

67. The October 7th Meeting at Frankfort, October 18, 1966, AV Papers, box 30.

68. Minutes of the Appalachian [Volunteer] Board Meeting, June 10, 1967, Beckley, WV, AV Papers, box 7.

69. Appalachia Speaks II, Appalachian Volunteers—Winter Meeting, Marshall University, Huntington, WV, January 28, 1967 (first quote), and Minutes of the Appalachian [Volunteer] Board Meeting, June 10, 1967, Beckley, WV (other quotes), AV Papers, box 7.

70. Minutes of the Appalachian [Volunteer] Board Meeting, June 10, 1967, Beckley, WV, AV Papers, box 7 (other quotes); Minutes of May 6, 1967, Appalachian Volunteers Board Meeting (last quote), AV Papers, box 7.

7. Peace without Victory

1. Harrison and Klotter, *A New History of Kentucky,* 413 (*Hazard Herald* quote); Sexton, ed., *The Public Papers of Governor Louis B. Nunn,* 186 (Nunn quote re "decent, law-abiding, constructive citizens"). On Nunn's conservative ideology and silent majority, see esp. Ernst and Baldwin, "The Not So Silent

Minority"; and Oral History Interview with Louie Nunn, July 6, 1993 (other Nunn quotes), Horse Cave, KY, WOP Oral History Project.

2. Oral History Interview with Louie Nunn, July 6, 1993, Horse Cave, KY, WOP Oral History Project.

3. Ibid.

4. Minutes of the Appalachian [Volunteer] Board Meeting, June 10, 1967, Beckley, WV, and Minutes of [Appalachian Volunteer Board Meeting], July 22, [1967], AV Papers, box 7.

5. Dennis Forbes to Tom Rhodenbaugh, April 17, 1967, AV Papers, box 23; Minutes of the Appalachian [Volunteer] Board Meeting, June 10, 1967, Beckley, WV (comments about 1966 Summer Project), AV Papers, box 7.

6. Minutes of May 6, 1967, Appalachian Volunteers Board Meeting, AV Papers, box 7.

7. Chapter 2: The AV Stand or Which Side Are You On, n.d., AV Papers, box 8.

8. Ibid.

9. Ibid.

10. On the meeting, see Milton Ogle to AV Board Member[s], April 20, 1967, AV Papers, box 7. Jack Rivel to Mrs. Pinson, Pinson Hotel, Pikeville, May 1, 1967, AV Papers, box 27; Pikeville and a Central AV Office, [1967] (quote), AV Papers, box 8; Minutes of the AV Staff Meeting, March 6–8, 1967, AV Papers, box 7.

11. Joel Hasslen to Milton Ogle, April 26, 1967, AV Papers, box 24.

12. Oral History Interview with Flem Messer, October 26, 1990, Danville, KY, WOP Oral History Project (quotes); Flem Messer to John M. Yost, Vice President, Citizens Bank of Pikeville, October 26, 1965, AV Papers, box 26.

13. Flem Messer to John Yort, Vice President, Citizens Bank of Pikeville, October 26, 1965, and Flem Messer to Perley Ayer, November 1, 1965 (quotes), AV Papers, box 26.

14. For an account of the accomplishments of the AVs in the Persimmon Fork community and in Knott and Perry counties, see Appalachian Volunteers Third Progress Report, May 1964, and [Appalachian Volunteers] Fourth Progress Report, June 1964, on the Contract between Area Redevelopment Administration of the U.S. Department of Commerce and the Council of the Southern Mountains, AV Papers, box 3. The defensive posture of the county elite is highlighted in Oral History Interview with Flem Messer, October 26, 1990, Danville, KY, WOP Oral History Project. On the roving pickets, see Whisnant, *Modernizing the Mountaineer*, 188–89; and Tharpe, "Appalachian Committee for Full Employment." Evidence to the effect that, apart from his association with the bank, Yost was well connected among the county elite is contained in a letter from Messer to Ayer in which Messer relates that the president of Pikeville College cautioned Messer about Yost, telling him "not to underestimate Mr. Yost's

power and influence." See Flem Messer to Perley Ayer, November 1, 1965, AV Papers, box 26.

15. Flem Messer to Dr. B. H. Jarman, President, Pikeville College, April 2, 1965, AV Papers, box 26.

16. Alan McSurely, A New Political Union, January 17, 1967, AV Papers, box 9; *Modernizing the Mountaineer,* 197 (Whisnant quote).

17. Alan McSurely, A New Political Union, January 17, 1967, AV Papers, box 9.

18. Milton Ogle to Dr. Robert Coles and Dr. Joseph Brenner, April 29, 1967, AV Papers, box 12.

19. Whisnant (*Modernizing the Mountaineer,* 198) claimed that some on the Volunteer staff felt that McSurely's "ideas deserved discussion" and that "he should be given a chance to prove himself." On the broad form deed, see Eller, *Miners, Millhands, and Mountaineers,* 55–56. On the AV anti-strip-mining activities, see esp. Appalachia Speaks II, Appalachian Volunteers Winter Meeting, Marshall University, Huntington, WV, January 28, 1967, and Milton Ogle to Howard Carson, President of the West Virginia Senate, February 3, 1967, AV Papers, box 7; and Thomas Rhodenbaugh to Alan M. Lerner, New York City Law Students' Civil Rights Research Council, January 24, 1967, AV Papers, box 26.

20. For more on AGSLP, see chapter 6 above. For the Volunteers' anti-strip-mining efforts in West Virginia, again see chapter 6. On Daugherty in Harlan County, see AV Background Information, [Chapter] VII Case Study—Report on Verda, AV Papers, box 8. For Letcher County, see Millstone, "Strip-Mining Feud in Kentucky." See also Whisnant, *Modernizing the Mountaineer,* 200. On the anti-strip-mining movement and AGSLP, see Montrie, *To Save the Land and People.*

21. Peterson, *Coaltown Revisited,* 137. For the number of lawyers, see Jackson, "In the Valley of the Shadows." See also Mason, "The 'Subversive' Poor." On Easterling, see Whisnant, *Modernizing the Mountaineer,* 200.

22. While Mulloy himself denies that he ever met McSurely prior to August 1967, Whisnant (*Modernizing the Mountaineer,* 200) claims that the two were, in fact, in contact beginning in March 1967 and that McSurely indeed affected Mulloy's attitudes and ideas about politics. Mulloy's denial is in Oral History Interview with Joe Mulloy, November 10, 1990, Huntington, WV, WOP Oral History Project.

23. Joe Mulloy, Report on Intern Activities of Edith Easterling, January 4, 1967, AV Papers, box 25; Whisnant, *Modernizing the Mountaineer,* 200.

24. Whether by design or just the result of bad timing, the meeting at Highlander could not have been more ill advised. At that time, the Highlander Center still was reeling from an attack in May 1967 by local and Tennessee state officials who sought to expose Highlander's "subversive" activities and wanted "to use all legal means to cut this cancerous growth from our state." On the

Highlander Center, see Glen, *Highlander*, 214; and Minutes of Highlander Workshop Meeting, June 3–4, [1967], AV Papers, box 9.

25. Minutes of Highlander Workshop Meeting, June 3–4, [1967] (first quote), AV Papers, box 9; Oral History Interviews with Joe Mulloy, November 11, 1990 (Mulloy quotes), Huntington, WV, Loyal Jones, November 19, 1990, Berea, KY, and George Brosi, November 3, 1990, Berea, KY, WOP Oral History Project; Whisnant, *Modernizing the Mountaineer*, 200–201; Horton, "The Appalachian Volunteers," 85. See also Carawan and Carawan, *Voices from the Mountains*, 48, 88–94. According to an AV report: "Strip-mining operators saw the decision [to suspend mining on Jink Ray's land] as a potential body blow to the industry. 'Hell' one of them later told an AV staff member, 'if it can happen on Island Creek it can happen anywhere.'" A Special Report to Governor Edward T. Breathitt, AV Papers, box 8.

26. Oral History Interviews with Joe Mulloy, November 19, 1990, Huntington, WV (quote), Milton Ogle, April 5, 1991, Charleston, WV, and Loyal Jones, November 19, 1990, Berea, KY, WOP Oral History Project; Horton, "The Appalachian Volunteers," 86; Whisnant, *Modernizing the Mountaineer*, 201.

27. Report of the September 1967 Pike County Grand Jury, September 11, 1967 (Mimeo) (quotes), AV Papers, box 10. For the opinion in the federal court case, see *Alan McSurely et al. v. Thomas B. Ratliff et al.*, 282 F. Supp. 848 (1967). Whisnant, *Modernizing the Mountaineer*, 201–4; Horton, "The Appalachian Volunteers," 86–87. The Bradens were then living in Louisville. They turned themselves in to the Pike County authorities the day after the indictment.

28. See *Braden v. Commonwealth of Kentucky*, 291 S.W.2d 843, 844 (1956). For the Pennsylvania case, see *Commonwealth v. Nelson*, 377 Pa. 58, 104 A.2d 133. See also *Commonwealth of Pennsylvania v. Nelson*, 350 U.S. 497, 76 S. Ct. 481 (1956). These federal statutes include the Smith Act of 1940 and subsequent amendments. See 18 U.S.C. sec. 2385 (1940). In the earlier case, Braden was charged with sedition against the state of Kentucky. In 1967, he, along with the others, was charged with sedition against Pike County. Some argue that this was the crucial difference, but it was not. The significance lies in the fact that the Kentucky court's decision was binding for the Louisville district only. Because they were in a different judicial district, the courts in Pike County were not bound by the earlier judgment.

29. Report of the September 1967 Pike County Grand Jury, September 11, 1967 (Mimeo), AV Papers, box 10.

30. The Appalachian Volunteers: A Report to the Public, August 17, 1967, AV Papers, box 10. On the decision to cut funding, see Statement on Appalachian Volunteers Situation in Kentucky by Albert Whitehouse, Director of Kentucky Office of Economic Opportunity, September 11, 1967, AV Papers, box 11.

31. Gillis Brassfield to Governor Edward T. Breathitt, August 20, 1967, AV Papers, box 9; "Do We Really Need These 'Helpers'?"; Statement on Appala-

chian Volunteers, September 8, 1967 (Whitehouse comments; emphasis added), AV Papers, box 11; Appalachian Volunteers, Minutes of Board Meeting, Mingo County, West Virginia, August 26, 1967 (Ogle remarks), AV Papers, box 7. For Breathitt's tentative decision to refuse AV funding, see Ramsey, "13 Poverty Program Heads Protest Appalachian Volunteers' Fund Loss"; and Boyd, "Cut Off Is Illegal, AV Boss Claims." For a collection of letters for and against the Appalachian Volunteers, see the Edward T. Breathitt Papers, Kentucky Department of Libraries and Archives, Frankfort.

32. Horton, "The Appalachian Volunteers," 100 (quote); and Whisnant, *Modernizing the Mountaineer,* 206.

33. On the draft deferments, see George A. Woodring to Miss Marty Dixon, American Friends Service Committee, May 18, 1967, AV Papers, box 30; Bill Wells to Perley Ayer, March 9, 1965, AV Papers, box 30; Joel Hasslen to [Selective Service] Local Board No. 96, St. Paul, MN, May 7, 1967, AV Papers, box 24; Dan Fox to [Selective Service] Local Board No. 8, Camden, N.J., April 12, 1966, AV Papers, box 35 (for Rivel); Thomas Rhodenbaugh to Selective Service Local 113, Akron, Ohio, March 24, 1966, AV Papers, box 35; Dan Fox to [Selective Service] Local Board No. 14, New York City, April 20, 1966 (for Kramer); Douglas Yarrow to [CSM], March 30, 1965, AV Papers, box 28; Jack Rivel to Breck Fugate, October 14, 1966, AV Papers, box 23; and Walter Hays to [AVs], September 10, 1966, AV Papers, box 28. Cooper's wishes are in Linda Cooper, [Conference Questionnaire], December 1966, AV Papers, box 7. On Mulloy, see Oral History Interview with Joe Mulloy, November 11, 1990, Huntington, WV, WOP Oral History Project.

34. Appalachian Volunteers Fire Joe Mulloy, [Press Release], [December 1967], and Statement by Joe Mulloy, December 2, 1967, AV Papers, box 11.

35. Walls quotes concerning Easterling are in Memorandum, David Walls to AV Staff, November 6, 1967, AV Papers, box 11. Whisnant, *Modernizing the Mountaineer,* 204.

36. Appalachian Volunteers Fire Joe Mulloy, [Press Release], [December 1967] (first quote), AV Papers, box 11. On the question of procedural impropriety, see Tom Bethell to Milton Ogle, December 6, 1967, AV Papers, box 11; W. M. Peck to Milton Ogle, December 6, 1967 (third quote), AV Papers, box 11; and Whisnant, *Modernizing the Mountaineer,* 205. Ogle's quotes in Milton Ogle to Richard Cartwright Austin, December 11, 1967, AV Papers, box 11. David Walls to AV Staff, November 6, 1967 (last quote), AV Papers, box 11.

37. On the resignations, see AV Papers, box 11. Michael Clark to Milton Ogle, December 4, 1967 (first two quotes), Steve Daugherty to Milton Ogle, December 4, 1967, and Tom Bethell to Milton Ogle, December 5, 1967, AV Papers, box 11.

38. W. Va. AV's to Bristol Office, December 4, 1967, Memorandum, Eric Metzner, West Virginia Volunteers, to West Virginia Appalachian Volunteers

Staff, December 7, 1967, Steve Daugherty to Milton Ogle, December 4, 1967 ("moral force"), and Memorandum, Tom Bethell to Edith Easterling, David Walls, AV Staff, December 10, 1967 (last quote), AV Papers, box 11.

39. Memorandum, Edith Easterling to Steve Daugherty, Michael Clark, et al., December 6, 1967, AV Papers, box 11.

40. Ibid. (emphasis added).

41. *Acts of the General Assembly, 1968,* chap. 237 (HR 84), p. 903 (quote); Conspiracy Exposed: City, KUAC Work Together to Cover-Up Injustices, AV Papers, Part II, box 5.

42. "KUAC Investigating in the Mountains." According to the AVs, the request for the hearings originated with Tom Ratliff, the commonwealth's attorney in Pike County who prosecuted the sedition case of 1967. See Horton, "The Appalachian Volunteers," 108; The Joint Legislative Committee on Un-American Activities, Hearings Held at Pikeville, Kentucky, October 15 and 16, 1968, AV Papers, Part II, box 5.

43. Statement by David Walls, AV Acting Director, October 7, 1968 (quote), AV Papers, Part II, box 5. Not surprisingly, the argument that Communists will deny they are Communists was used in Carl Braden's first sedition conviction in 1954. See Ross, "The Domestic Anti-Communist Movement and Carl Braden." For an example of how this clever political trick worked in Louisiana politics in the 1950s, see Whitfield, *The Culture of the Cold War,* 30.

In a January 24, 2008, e-mail to the author, David Walls explained the AVs' position vis-à-vis KUAC: "As I remember the times, the thought that we would voluntarily appear [before the committee] was entirely out of the question. It would have betrayed our own, and our liberal allies' (including foundation, etc.), notions of the necessary civil libertarian response to an Un-American Activities committee. We were stretching our principles to talk with them informally in our Prestonsburg office. We had hoped that we'd be subpoenaed, and could challenge KUAC's authority and constitutionality in court. They were smart not to get to that point."

44. Horton, "The Appalachian Volunteers," 109 (quotes). Though KUAC used its subpoena power, the vast majority of witnesses required to testify were hostile to the AV position. These included the director and associate director of the Big Sandy Community Action Program, an organization that had been hostile toward the AVs for many years, an employee of that organization, a Pike County deputy sheriff, a prominent Pikeville lawyer who represented the water district the Volunteers were battling, the director of that water district, the county magistrate of the Marrowbone District, and the jailor for Pike County. Only one member of the Pike County Citizens Association, an organization sympathetic to the AVs, was subpoenaed, and even he disassociated his organization from the Volunteers. Remember, no AVs were subpoenaed. They were merely "invited" to attend. Surely, given their protests and avowals not to co-

operate, those conducting the hearings knew that the Appalachian Volunteers would refuse to appear before KUAC. This essentially gave the committee a free hand in condemning the organization. See Walls's explanation in previous note.

45. The Joint Legislative Committee on Un-American Activities, Hearings Held at Pikeville, Kentucky, October 15 and 16, 1968, pp. 6, 141, 71, 95, 92, AV Papers, Part II, box 5. The transcript is replete with attacks on the AVs.

46. Ibid., 175, 95, 245, 95, 246.

47. Not only did witnesses claim that the AVs threatened to destroy the chances for the establishment of the much-needed water system if their plan was not followed, but one witness, the county magistrate, claimed that his job was threatened, an AV telling him: "You have been very popular in this vicinity but when we get through, you ain't gonna be." See The Joint Legislative Committee On Un-American Activities, Hearings Held at Pikeville, Kentucky, October 15 and 16, 1968, p. 42, AV Papers, Part II, box 5.

48. Ibid., 86–87.

49. Ibid., 89. For an excellent discussion of the history of the Highlander Folk School, see Glen, *Highlander*.

50. The Joint Legislative Committee on Un-American Activities, Hearings Held at Pikeville, Kentucky, October 15 and 16, 1968, pp. 168, 173, 171, 172, 28, 227, 228, AV Papers, Part II, box 5. In another statement, a certain witness believed "that these programs can only be conducted by the State organization, set up by the State, by local people and local administration, whereby the County Judge or his subordinates can see that the people working in the program are legitimate." See ibid., 27.

51. Ibid., 187, 149, 28.

52. Kentucky Un-American Activities Committee Interim Report quoted in Horton, "The Appalachian Volunteers," 110. The report is also reprinted in *Appalachian Lookout* 1 (January–February 1969): 11–13. Given that KUAC began its hearings with no preconceptions and that the hearings were one-sided for only two days, this was a very interesting conclusion.

53. Hulett C. Smith's letter is reprinted in full in "Speech by Senator Robert Byrd (W.VA)," 27620.

While I concentrate primarily on the AV experience in eastern Kentucky, the organization did make a notable presence in the Mountain State. It attained, in the short term, a degree of success organizing poor rural West Virginians, especially in Raleigh County. Nevertheless, the Raleigh County Community Action Program, which the AVs managed to control in the summer of 1966, remained small and minimally funded. Moreover, by August 1967, as Governor Smith's statements illustrate, the AVs' days in West Virginia were numbered. On the funding in West Virginia and the Volunteers, see Whisnant, *Modernizing the Mountaineer*, 193–94, 200, 206. For an examination of the War on Poverty in West Virginia's Mingo County, see Perry, *"They'll Cut off Your Project"*; and Barnes, "A Case Study of the Mingo County Economic Opportunity Commission." For Byrd's remarks, see "Speech by Senator Robert Byrd (W.VA)," 27621.

54. On the move to Prestonsburg, see Horton, "The Appalachian Volunteers," 100; and Suggested Agenda, AV Board of Directors Meeting, February 8, 1969, AV Papers, box 7. Evaluation Report of the Appalachian Volunteers, June 24 to July 3, 1968, Mid Atlantic Region (II), OEO, August 1, 1968, AV Papers, box 13; Economic Opportunity Act of 1964, Title V (quote).

55. Cloward, "The War on Poverty," 55; AV Background Information, Section I: Men and Jobs, n.d. (second quote), AV Papers, box 8.

56. Ibid.; AV Background Information, Section I: Men and Jobs, n.d. (first quote), AV Papers, box 8; Horton, "The Appalachian Volunteers," 101 (last quote). On the Floyd County AGSLP chapter, see Suggested Agenda, AV Board of Directors Meeting, February 8, 1969, AV Papers, box 7.

57. West Virginia Report, David Biesmeyer, February 5, 1968, and [Attachment] Quarterly Report, October 31, 1968, AV Papers, box 9.

58. Bertrand Harding, Acting Director, OEO, to David Biesmeyer, President, Designs for Rural Action, May 21, 1969 (first quote), and Neal Kingsolving to Richard Nixon, June 16, 1969 (second quote), OEO Papers, NN 3-381-92-19, box 20.

59. Suggested Agenda, AV Board of Directors Meeting, February 8, 1969, [Section] V (first quote), and Suggested Agenda, AV Board of Directors Meeting, February 8, 1969, [Section] III: Goals, Priorities and Problems (second quote), AV Papers, box 7.

60. The Program of the Appalachian Volunteers, Inc., April, 1969, AV Papers, box 9.

61. Howard Thorkelson to Robert Coles, September 30, 1968, AV Papers, box 21; Whisnant, *Modernizing the Mountaineer,* 208. On the PCCA, see Contract between the Appalachian Volunteers and the Pike County Citizens Association, [1969], AV Papers, box 7.

62. 4 Months Report on Roy J. Cantrell, May 14, 1968, Three Months Report, Truman Jent, November 15, 1968 (quote), Economic Consultation, August 22–23, 1968, Summary Statement, Bennett Poage, Three Month Report, February 15, 1969, Clifford Atchley [Logan County], and Report for Last Three Months, Josephine Combs, February 13, 1969, AV Papers, box 9.

63. Memorandum, Douglas G. Robinson to Appalachian Volunteers Files, January 7, 1970 (quotes), AV Papers, box 11; The Program of the Appalachian Volunteers, Inc., April, 1969, AV Papers, box 9.

64. Prior to 1968, OEO grants to the AVs exceeded $500,000 per year. See Memorandum, Douglas G. Robinson to Appalachian Volunteers Files, January 7, 1970 (quotes), and Complaint, In the United States District Court for the District of Columbia, February 28, 1970, AV Papers, box 11.

65. Memorandum, Douglas G. Robinson to Appalachian Volunteers Files, January 1, 1970, AV Papers, box 11; Memorandum, David Walls to AV Board and Staff, June 3, 1969, AV Papers, box 7.

66. Appalachian Volunteers Board Meeting Minutes, June 6, 1970, and Complaint, In the United States District Court for the District of Columbia, February 28, 1970, AV Papers, box 11; Whisnant, *Modernizing the Mountaineer,* 208.

67. "Council of the Southern Mountains Seek New Paths"; Business Meeting [Minutes] 57th Annual Conference, Council of the Southern Mountains, Fontana Village, NC, April 10, 1969, CSM Papers, box 173; Glen, "The War on Poverty in Appalachia," 53–54.

68. The Council of the Southern Mountains in Transition, July 1970, and Business Meeting [Minutes] 58th Annual Conference, Council of the Southern Mountains, Lake Junaluska, NC, April 25–26, 1970, CSM Papers, box 173; Loyal Jones to Council Members and Friends, September 24, 1969, CSM Papers, box 159; Glen, "The War on Poverty in Appalachia," 54–55.

69. "Council of the Southern Mountains Seek New Paths"; Glen, "The War on Poverty in Appalachia," 53–57.

Conclusion

1. Ross, "A Kentucky Mine Town Speaks Its Mind" (quote). See also Ross, *Machine Age in the Hills.* On Reconstruction, see Foner, *Reconstruction.* Waller's *Feud* illustrates how "modernizers" from outside the region used a negative image of Appalachians to justify their exploitation of the region. Two additional important works that investigate the creation of an Appalachian "otherness" are Shapiro's *Appalachia on Our Mind* and Batteau's *The Invention of Appalachia.*

2. In *Poverty Knowledge,* O'Connor argues that this version of liberalism still dominates American ideology today.

3. Glen ("The War on Poverty in Appalachia," esp. 56) suggested this fault in the OEO strategy in the mountains. For an in-depth discussion of the history of community action, see Matusow, *The Unraveling of America,* 122–26, 243–71; and Kravitz, "The Community Action Program." Economic Opportunity Act of 1964, Public Law 88–46, Title II, Sec. 2 (quote).

Most former AVs interviewed claimed that the "maximum feasible participation" clause was paramount in their strategizing. See Oral History Interviews with Flem Messer, February 26, 1990, Danville, KY, Joe Mulloy, November 10, 1990, Huntington, WV, Milton Ogle, April 5, 1991, Charlestown, WV, and Jack Rivel, February 12, 1991, Berea, KY, WOP Oral History Project. For an excellent discussion of the roles that political resources play in a pluralist democracy, see Dahl, *Dilemmas of Pluralist Democracy.* On the fact that, in eastern Kentucky, the coal companies controlled both politics and economics, including welfare systems, see Whisnant, *Modernizing the Mountaineer,* 105 and chap. 9; and Caudill, "Corporate Fiefdom," and "The Permanent Poor."

4. Harold Kwalwasser to Tom, March 14, 1967, AV Papers, box 25 (emphasis added). The recipient was either Tom Bethell or Tom Rhodenbaugh.

5. Memorandum, David Walls to AV Staff, November 6, 1967, AV Papers, box 11. See chapter 7 above. See also Dittmer, *Local People.*

6. "A Tax Paying Citizen" to Blanche Dreyfuss, January 10, 1967, AV Papers, box 22. In a report to the AV staff, the same Volunteer who established the Blue Springs PTA commented: "The main work I have done in Rockcastle County it seems, for the past 6 months is convincing people I am not a communist." See Rockcastle County [Report], n.d., AV Papers, box 9.

7. Moynihan, *Maximum Feasible Misunderstanding,* 134 (first quote), 135–36 (second quote).

8. Statement on Appalachian Volunteers, September 8, 1967, AV Papers, box 11 (first two quotes); Statement on Appalachian Volunteers Situation in Kentucky, September 11, 1967, AV Papers, box 13 (last two quotes). In a letter to the OEO director, Sargent Shriver, that same month, Governor Breathitt himself expressed "concern over 'mounting damage to the entire anti-poverty program stemming from the actions of . . . the Volunteers stationed in Kentucky.'" See A Special Report to Governor Edward T. Breathitt, [1967], AV Papers, box 8.

9. Gaventa, *Power and Powerlessness,* 110. For an examination of how civil rights activists experienced similar attacks, see esp. Carson, *In Struggle.*

10. The Joint Legislative Committee on Un-American Activities, Hearings Held at Pikeville, Kentucky, October 15 and 16, 1968, pp. 71–72, AV Papers, Part II, box 5, discusses the possibility that the AVs and McSurely hoped to distribute Communist literature in the county.

11. Ibid., 84–85.

12. See Gaventa, *Power and Powerlessness,* 254 (quote); and Dahl, *Dilemmas of Pluralist Democracy,* 43–45.

13. "Speech by Senator Robert Byrd (W.VA)," 27621 (Byrd's remarks); Matusow, *Unraveling of America,* 395 (last quote).

14. Introduction: History and Description of CSM and Mountain Life and Work, [ca. 1983] (first quote), Council of the Southern Mountains Papers, 1970–1989, and [Notes], [ca. 1980] (second and third quotes), box 1, Special Collections, Hutchins Library, Berea College, Berea, KY. In early 2007, Berea College opened to researchers the "Second Part" of the Council of the Southern Mountains Papers. Covering the years 1970–1989, this collection contains the various commission records and, of course, documents the activities of the CSM after the reorganization of 1969–1970.

Bibliography

Archival Sources

Appalachian Volunteers Papers, Hutchins Library, Berea College, Berea, KY.

Appalachian Volunteers Papers, Part II, Hutchins Library, Berea College, Berea, KY.

Council of the Southern Mountains Papers, 1913–1970, Hutchins Library, Berea College, Berea, KY.

Council of the Southern Mountains Papers, 1970–1989, Hutchins Library, Berea College, Berea, KY.

Edward T. Breathitt Papers, Kentucky Department of Libraries and Archives, Frankfort, KY.

Ford Foundation Grants Files, Ford Foundation Archives, Ford Foundation, New York.

John D. Whisman Papers, Margaret I. King Library, University of Kentucky, Lexington.

Office of Economic Opportunity Papers, National Archives II, College Park, MD.

War on Poverty in Appalachian Kentucky Oral History Project, Margaret I. King Library, University of Kentucky, Lexington.

Primary Sources

Acts of the General Assembly of the Commonwealth of Kentucky, 1968. Frankfort, KY, 1969.

Ayer, Jack. "College Volunteers to Serve Appalachia." *Louisville Courier-Journal,* June 14, 1966.

"Berea Sociologist Raps Welfare 'for Free' as Creating Dependency." *Jackson County Sun* (McKee, KY), June 8, 1961, 1.

Bigart, Homer. "Kentucky Miners: A Grim Winter." *New York Times,* October 20, 1963, 1, 79.

Boyd, Richard. "Appy Volunteers Are Accustomed to Controversy." *Bristol, TN-VA, Herald Courier,* August 27, 1967.

———. "Cut Off Is Illegal, AV Boss Claims." *Bristol, TN-VA, Herald Courier,* August 25, 1967.

Cloward, Richard. "The War on Poverty: Are the Poor Left Out?" *Nation* 204 (August 2, 1965): 55–60.

"Council of the Southern Mountains Seek New Paths." *Berea College Pinnacle,* May 2, 1970.

"Do We Really Need These 'Helpers'?" *Jackson, KY, Times,* August 24, 1967.

Hoskins, Kenneth. "Appalachian Volunteers Evaluate Project." *Kentucky Kernel* 56 (March 30, 1965): 1, 8.

"KUAC Investigating in the Mountains." *Whitesburg, KY, Mountain Eagle*, December 5, 1968, 1.

MacDonald, Dwight. "Our Invisible Poor." *New Yorker*, January 19, 1963, 82–132.

Mason, Gene L. "The 'Subversive' Poor." *Nation* 207 (December 30, 1968): 721–24.

Merrill, P. D. "Strategy in the War on Poverty." *Leslie County News* (Hyden, KY), December 9, 1965, 2, 4.

Mobley, Joe. "A Hard Look at Tomorrow." *Mountain Life and Work* 35 (Summer 1960): 5–10.

The Public Papers of the Presidents of the United States: Lyndon Baines Johnson, 1963–64. 2 vols. Washington, DC: U.S. Government Printing Office, 1965.

The Public Papers of the Presidents of the United States: Lyndon Baines Johnson, 1966. 2 vols. Washington, DC: U.S. Government Printing Office, 1967.

Ramsey, Sy. "13 Poverty Program Heads Protest Appalachian Volunteers' Fund Loss." *Louisville Courier-Journal*, August 24, 1967.

Ross, Malcolm. "A Kentucky Mine Town Speaks Its Mind." *New York Times*, May 1, 1932, sec. 9.

Rural Poverty: Hearings before the National Advisory Commission on Rural Poverty: Tucson, Memphis, Washington, DC. Washington, DC: U.S. Government Printing Office, 1967.

"Speech by Senator Robert Byrd (W.VA)." *Congressional Record* 113, pt. 20 (October 3, 1967): 27, 618–624.

The Speeches of Senator John F. Kennedy: Presidential Campaign of 1960. Washington, DC: U.S. Government Printing Office, 1961.

Tharpe, Everette. "Appalachian Committee for Full Employment: Background and Purpose." *Appalachian South* 1 (Summer 1965): 44–46.

Weller, Jack E. *Yesterday's People: Life in Contemporary Appalachia.* Lexington: University of Kentucky Press, 1965.

Zeh, John. "University Students Protest—against Poverty, Indifference." *Kentucky Kernel* (University of Kentucky), February 9, 1965.

Secondary Sources

Alinsky, Saul. *Reveille for Radicals.* Chicago: University of Chicago Press, 1946.

Anderson, Terry. *The Movement and the Sixties: Protest in America from Greensboro to Wounded Knee.* Oxford: Oxford University Press, 1995.

Aspen Institute. *Measuring Community Capacity Building: A Workbook-in-Progress for Rural Communities.* Washington, DC: Aspen Institute—Rural Economic Policy Program, 1996.

Bailey, Robert, Jr. *Radicals in Urban Politics: The Alinsky Approach.* Chicago: University of Chicago Press, 1972.

Banner, Lois. *Elizabeth Cady Stanton: A Radical for Women's Rights.* New York: Little, Brown, 1980.

Barnes, John. "A Case Study of the Mingo County Economic Opportunity Commission." Ph.D. diss., University of Pennsylvania, 1970.

Batteau, Allen. *The Invention of Appalachia.* Tucson: University of Arizona Press, 1990.

Beik, Mildred Allen. *The Miners of Windber: The Struggles of New Immigrants for Unionization, 1890s–1930s.* University Park: Pennsylvania State University Press, 1996.

Berry, Chad. *Southern Migrants, Northern Exiles.* Urbana: University of Illinois Press, 2000.

Billings, Dwight, Gurney Norman, and Katherine Ledford, eds. *Confronting Appalachian Stereotypes: Back Talk from an American Region.* Lexington: University Press of Kentucky, 1999.

Bingham, Mary Beth. "Stopping the Bulldozers: What Difference Did It Make?" In *Fighting Back in Appalachia: Traditions of Resistance and Change,* ed. Stephen L. Fisher, 17–30. Philadelphia: Temple University Press, 1993.

Birdwhistell, Terry L., and Susan Emily Allen. "The Appalachian Image Reexamined: An Oral History View of Eastern Kentucky." *Register of the Kentucky Historical Society* 81 (Summer 1983): 287–302.

Blumenthal, Sidney. "The Years of Robert Caro." *New Republic* 202 (June 1990): 29–36.

Bowles, Samuel, Herbert Gintis, and Melissa Osborne Groves, eds. *Unequal Chances: Family Background and Economic Success.* Princeton, NJ: Princeton University Press, 2005.

Boyer, Paul S. *Promises to Keep: The United States Since World War II.* New York: Houghton Mifflin, 1999.

Brauer, Carl M. *John F. Kennedy and the Second Reconstruction.* New York: Columbia University Press, 1977.

———. *Presidential Transitions: Eisenhower through Reagan.* Oxford: Oxford University Press, 1986.

Brown, James S., and George Hillery Jr. "The Great Migration." In *The Southern Appalachian Region: A Survey,* ed. Thomas R. Ford, 54–78. Lexington: University of Kentucky Press, 1962.

Brundage, W. Fitzhugh. *The Southern Past: A Clash of Race and Memory.* Cambridge, MA: Belknap/Harvard University Press, 2005.

Burnham, Robert A. "The Mayor's Friendly Relations Committee: Cultural Pluralism and the Struggle for Black Advancement." In *Race and the City: Work, Community, and Protest in Cincinnati, 1820–1970,* ed. Henry L. Taylor Jr., 258–79. Urbana: University of Illinois Press, 1993.

Burns, James MacGregor, ed. *To Heal and to Build: The Programs of Lyndon B. Johnson.* New York: McGraw-Hill, 1968.

Cable, Sherry. "From Fussin' to Organizing: Individual and Collective Resistance at Yellow Creek." In *Fighting Back in Appalachia: Traditions of Resistance and Change,* ed. Stephen L. Fisher, 69–84. Philadelphia: Temple University Press, 1993.

Cameron, Ardis. *Radicals of the Worst Sort: Laboring Women in Lawrence, Massachusetts, 1860–1912.* Urbana: University of Illinois Press, 1995.

Campbell, John C. *The Southern Highlander and His Homeland.* New York: Sage, 1921.

Carawan, Guy, and Candie Carawan. *Voices from the Mountains.* Urbana: University of Illinois Press, 1982.

Caro, Robert. *The Years of Lyndon Johnson: The Path to Power.* New York: Knopf, 1982.

———. *The Years of Lyndon Johnson: Means of Ascent.* New York: Knopf, 1990.

Carson, Clayborne. *In Struggle: SNCC and the Black Awakening of the 1960s.* Cambridge, MA: Harvard University Press, 1981.

Caudill, Harry M. *Night Comes to the Cumberlands: A Biography of a Depressed Area.* Boston: Little, Brown, 1963.

———. "The Permanent Poor: Lessons of Eastern Kentucky." *Atlantic Monthly* 213 (June 1964): 49–53.

———. "Corporate Fiefdom: Poverty and the Dole in Appalachia." *Commonweal* 89 (January 24, 1969): 523–25.

———. *My Land Is Dying.* New York: Dutton, 1971.

———. *A Darkness at Dawn: Appalachian Kentucky and the Future.* Lexington: University Press of Kentucky, 1976.

———. *The Watches of the Night.* Boston: Little, Brown, 1976.

Ceaser, James. *Liberal Democracy and Political Science.* Baltimore: Johns Hopkins University Press, 1990.

Cobb, James. *The Selling of the South: The Southern Crusade for Industrial Development.* Urbana: University of Illinois Press, 1982.

Coles, Robert. *Children of Crisis: A Study of Courage and Fear.* New York, Dell, 1964.

Conkin, Paul. *The Southern Agrarians.* Knoxville: University of Tennessee Press, 1988.

Conti, Eugene. *Mountain Metamorphoses: Culture and Development in East Kentucky.* Ann Arbor, MI: University Microfilm International, 1980.

Corbin, David Alan. *Life, Work, and Rebellion in the Coal Fields: The Southern West Virginia Miners, 1880–1922.* Urbana: University of Illinois Press, 1981.

Crook, William H., and Ross Thomas. *Warriors for the Poor: The Story of VISTA, Volunteers in Service to America.* New York: Morrow, 1969.

Dahl, Robert A. *A Preface to Democratic Theory.* Chicago: University of Chicago Press, 1956.

———. *Polyarchy: Participation and Opposition.* New Haven, CT: Yale University Press, 1971.

———. *Dilemmas of Pluralist Democracy: Autonomy vs. Control.* New Haven, CT: Yale University Press, 1982.

Dallek, Robert. *Lone Star Rising: Lyndon Johnson and His Times, 1908–1960.* New York: Oxford University Press, 1991.

Davies, Gareth. "War on Dependency: Liberal Individualism and the Economic Opportunity Act of 1964." *Journal of American Studies* 26, no. 2 (August 1992): 205–31.

Davis, Allen. *Spearheads for Reform: The Social Settlements and the Progressive Movement, 1890–1914.* New Brunswick, NJ: Rutgers University Press, 1984.

Degler, Carl N. *Place over Time: The Continuity of Southern Distinctiveness.* Baton Rouge: Louisiana State University Press, 1977.

Devine, Donald. *The Political Culture of the United States: The Influence of Member Values on Regime Maintenance.* Boston: Little, Brown, 1972.

Dittmer, John. *Local People: The Struggle for Civil Rights in Mississippi.* Urbana: University of Illinois Press, 1994.

Donovan, John C. *The Politics of Poverty.* New York: Pegasus, 1967.

Drake, Richard. *A History of Appalachia.* Lexington: University Press of Kentucky, 2001.

Duke, David C. *Writers and Miners: Activism and Imagery in America.* Lexington: University Press of Kentucky, 2002.

Dunaway, Wilma. *The First American Frontier: Transition to Capitalism in Southern Appalachia, 1700–1860.* Chapel Hill: University of North Carolina Press, 1996.

Dunn, Durwood. *Cades Cove: The Life and Death of a Southern Appalachian Community.* Knoxville: University of Tennessee Press, 1988.

Ehrenreich, Barbara. *Fear of Falling: The Inner Life of the Middle Class.* New York: Pantheon, 1989.

Eller, Ronald D. *Miners, Millhands, and Mountaineers: Industrialization of the Appalachian South, 1880–1930.* Knoxville: University of Tennessee Press, 1982.

Ergood, Bruce, and Bruce Kuhre. *Appalachia: Social Context, Past and Present.* Dubuque, IA: Kendall, Hunt, 1976.

Ernst, John, and Yvonne Baldwin. "The Not So Silent Minority: Louisville's Antiwar Movement, 1966–1975." *Journal of Southern History* 73 (February 2007): 105–42.

Evans, Rowland, and Robert Novak. *Lyndon B. Johnson: The Exercise of Power.* New York: New American Library, 1966.

Fairclough, Adam. "Historians and the Civil Rights Movement." *Journal of American Studies* 24 (1990): 387–98.

Fetterman, John. "Volunteers Are a Bargain in Dollars or People." *Louisville Courier-Journal*, March 19, 1964, 12.

———. "Young Samaritans in Appalachia." *Louisville Courier-Journal*, March 15, 1964, sec. 4, pp. 3–4.

———. *Stinking Creek*. New York: Dutton, 1970.

Fink, Leon. *Workingman's Democracy: The Knights of Labor and American Politics*. Urbana: University of Illinois Press, 1983.

Finks, P. David. *The Radical Vision of Saul Alinsky*. New York: Paulist, 1984.

Fishback, Price. *Soft Coal, Hard Choices: The Economic Welfare of Bituminous Coal Miners, 1890–1930*. Oxford: Oxford University Press, 1992.

Fisher, Stephen L., ed. *Fighting Back in Appalachia: Traditions of Resistance and Change*. Philadelphia: Temple University Press, 1993.

Fleming, Daniel B. *Kennedy vs. Humphrey, West Virginia, 1960: The Pivotal Battle for the Democratic Presidential Nomination*. Jefferson, NC: McFarland, 1992.

Foner, Eric. *Tom Paine and Revolutionary America*. New York: Oxford University Press, 1976.

———. *Reconstruction: America's Unfinished Revolution, 1863–1877*. New York: Harper & Row, 1988.

Ford, Thomas R., ed. *The Southern Appalachian Region: A Survey*. Lexington: University of Kentucky Press, 1962.

Forderhase, Nancy. "Eve Returns to the Garden: Women Reformers in Appalachian Kentucky in the Early Twentieth Century." *Register of the Kentucky Historical Society* 85 (Summer 1987): 237–61.

Foster, Stephen William. "Politics, Expressive Form, and Historical Knowledge in a Blue Ridge Resistance Movement." In *Fighting Back in Appalachia: Traditions of Resistance and Change*, ed. Stephen L. Fisher, 303–15. Philadelphia: Temple University Press, 1993.

Fox, John, Jr. "The Southern Mountaineer." *Scribner's* 29 (April 1901): 387–99; 29 (May 1901): 556–70.

———. *The Little Shepherd of Kingdom Come*. New York: Scribner's, 1903.

———. *Trail of the Lonesome Pine*. New York: Scribner's, 1908.

Fraser, Steve, and Gary Gerstle, eds. *The Rise and Fall of the New Deal Order, 1930–1980*. Princeton, NJ: Princeton University Press, 1989.

Fried, Richard. *Nightmare in Red: The McCarthy Era in Perspective*. New York: Oxford University Press, 1990.

Frost, William Goodell. "Our Contemporary Ancestors in the Southern Mountains." *Atlantic Monthly* 83 (March 1899): 311–19.

Fukuyama, Francis. *The Social Virtues and the Creation of Prosperity*. New York: Free Press, 1995.

Gaddis, John. *Strategies of Containment: A Critical Appraisal of Postwar American National Security Policy.* New York: Oxford University Press, 1982.

Galbraith, John Kenneth. *The Affluent Society.* Boston: Houghton Mifflin, 1958.

Garrow, David J. *Bearing the Cross: Martin Luther King, Jr. and the Southern Christian Leadership Conference.* New York: Morrow, 1986.

Gaventa, John. *Power and Powerlessness: Quiescence and Rebellion in an Appalachian Valley.* Urbana: University of Illinois Press, 1980.

————. "The Poverty of Abundance Revisited." *Appalachian Journal* 15 (Fall 1987): 24–33.

Gitlin, Todd. *The Sixties: Years of Hope, Days of Rage.* New York: Bantam, 1993.

Gitlin, Todd, and Nanci Hollander. *Uptown: Poor Whites in Chicago.* New York: Harper & Row, 1970.

Glen, John M. *Highlander: No Ordinary School, 1932–1962.* Lexington: University Press of Kentucky, 1988.

————. "The War on Poverty in Appalachia—a Preliminary Report." *Register of the Kentucky Historical Society* 87 (Winter 1989): 40–57.

————. "The War on Poverty in Appalachia: Oral History from the 'Top Down' and the 'Bottom Up.'" *Oral History Review* 22 (Summer 1995): 67–93.

Goodwyn, Lawrence. *Democratic Promise: The Populist Movement in America.* New York: Oxford University Press, 1975.

Grantham, Dewey. *The Life and Death of the Solid South: A Political History.* Lexington: University Press of Kentucky, 1988.

Greenstein, Robert. "Losing Faith in Losing Ground." *New Republic,* March 25, 1985, 12–17.

Grisham, Judy. "A Hollow Place: Hillfolk Live in a World of Their Own Where Poverty Is a Password and Home Is Home." *Kentucky Kernel* 67 (April 20, 1966): 5.

Hamby, Alonzo. *Liberalism and Its Challengers: FDR to Reagan.* New York: Oxford University Press, 1985.

Hampton, Jim. "Volunteers Pioneer Classes at Mill Creek." *Louisville Courier-Journal,* August 9, 1964, sec. 4, p. 4.

Harney, Will W. "A Strange Land and Peculiar People." *Lippincott's* 12 (October 1873): 429–38.

Harrington, Michael. *The Other America: Poverty in the United States.* New York: Macmillan, 1963.

Harrison, Lowell, and James Klotter. *A New History of Kentucky.* Lexington: University Press of Kentucky, 1997.

Haveman, Robert H., ed. *A Decade of Federal Anti-Poverty Programs: Achievements, Failures, and Lessons.* New York: Academic, 1977.

————. *Poverty Policy and Poverty Research: The Great Society and the Social Sciences.* Madison: University of Wisconsin Press, 1987.

Heale, M. J. *American Anticommunism: Combating the Enemy Within, 1830–1970.* Baltimore: Johns Hopkins University Press, 1990.

Heath, Jim F. *Decade of Disillusionment: The Kennedy-Johnson Years.* Bloomington: Indiana University Press, 1975.

Hennen, John C. *The Americanization of West Virginia: Creating a Modern Industrial State, 1916–1925.* Lexington: University Press of Kentucky, 1996.

Hevener, John. *Which Side Are You On? The Harlan County Coal Miners, 1931–1939.* Urbana: University of Illinois Press, 1978.

Hirschman, Albert O. "Social Conflicts as Pillars of Democratic Market Society." *Political Theory* 22 (May 1994): 203–18.

Hodgson, Godfrey. *America in Our Time: From World War II to Nixon—What Happened and Why.* New York: Doubleday, 1976.

Horton, Billy D. "The Appalachian Volunteers: A Case Study of Community Organization and Conflict." M.A. thesis, University of Kentucky, 1971.

Isserman, Andrew. "Appalachia Then and Now: An Update of 'The Realities of Deprivation' Report to the President in 1964." *Journal of Appalachian Studies* 3 (Spring 1997): 43–69.

Jackson, Bruce. "In the Valley of the Shadows: Kentucky." *Transaction* 8 (June 1971): 28–38.

Jencks, Christopher. "How Poor Are the Poor?" *New York Review of Books,* May 9, 1985, 41–49.

Johnson, Lyndon B. *A Time for Action: A Selection from the Speeches and Writings of Lyndon B. Johnson, 1954–63.* New York: Atheneum, 1964.

———. *The Vantage Point: Perspectives of the Presidency, 1963–69.* New York: Holt, Rinehart & Winston, 1971.

Jones, Loyal, Thomas Parrish, and A. H. Perrin. "Problems in Revisionism: More Controversy in God's Grand Division." *Appalachian Journal* 2 (1975): 171–91.

Judkins, Bennett M. "The People's Respirator: Coalition Building and the Black Lung Association." In *Fighting Back in Appalachia: Traditions of Resistance and Change,* ed. Stephen L. Fisher, 225–41. Philadelphia: Temple University Press, 1993.

Katz, Michael. *The Undeserving Poor: From the War on Poverty to the War on Welfare.* New York: Pantheon, 1989.

———. *Improving Poor People: The Welfare State, "the Underclass," and Urban Schools as History.* Princeton, NJ: Princeton University Press, 1995.

———. *In the Shadow of the Poorhouse: A Social History of Welfare in America.* New York: Basic, 1996.

Kavanaugh, Dennis. *Political Culture.* London: Macmillan, 1972.

Kelman, Steven. *Push Comes to Shove: The Escalation of Student Protest.* Boston: Houghton Mifflin, 1970.

Kiffmeyer, Thomas. "From Self-Help to Sedition: The Appalachian Volunteers in Eastern Kentucky, 1964–1970." *Journal of Southern History* 64 (February 1998): 65–94.

Kravitz, Sanford. "The Community Action Program—Past, Present, and Its Future?" In *On Fighting Poverty: Perspectives from Experience*, ed. James L. Sundquist, 52–69. New York: Basic, 1969.

Lancourt, Joan E. *Confront or Concede: The Alinsky Citizen-Action Organizations*. Lexington, MA: Heath, 1979.

Lasch, Christopher. *The New American Radicalism, 1889–1963: The Intellectual as a Social Type*. New York: Vintage, 1967.

Levitan, Sar. *Federal Aid to Depressed Areas: An Evaluation of the Area Redevelopment Administration*. Baltimore: Johns Hopkins University Press, 1964.

Lewis, Helen. "Fatalism or the Coal Industry? Contrasting Views of Appalachian Problems." *Mountain Life and Work* 46 (December 1970): 4–15.

Lewis, Helen, Linda Johnson, and Donald Askins, eds. *Colonialism in Modern America: The Appalachian Case*. Boone, NC: Appalachian Consortium Press, 1978.

Lewis, Ronald. *Transforming the Appalachian Countryside: Railroads, Deforestation, and Social Change in West Virginia, 1880–1920*. Chapel Hill: University of North Carolina Press, 1998.

Lewis, Ronald, and Dwight Billings. "Appalachian Culture and Economic Development: A Retrospective View on the Theory and Literature." *Journal of Appalachian Studies* 3 (Spring 1997): 3–42.

Lilienthal, David E. *TVA: Democracy on the March*. New York: Harper, 1953.

Matusow, Allen J. *The Unraveling of America: A History of Liberalism in the 1960s*. New York: Harper Torchbooks, 1984.

McAdam, Doug. *Freedom Summer*. New York: Oxford University Press, 1988.

McNeil, W. K. *Appalachian Images in Folk and Popular Culture*. Ann Arbor, MI: UMI Research, 1989.

Michel, Gregg L. *Struggle for a Better South: The Southern Student Organizing Committee, 1964–1969*. New York: Palgrave Macmillan, 2004.

Milkis, Sidney, and Jerome Mileur, eds. *The Great Society and the High Tide of Liberalism*. Amherst: University of Massachusetts Press, 2005.

Miller, Jim. *Democracy Is in the Streets: From Port Huron to the Siege of Chicago*. New York: Simon & Schuster, 1987.

Millstone, James C. "Strip-Mining Feud in Kentucky." *Congressional Record* 113 (August 17, 1967): 29114.

Montgomery, David. *Beyond Equality: Labor and the Radical Republicans, 1862–1872*. New York: Knopf, 1967.

———. *The Fall of the House of Labor: The Workplace, the State, and American Labor Activism*. Cambridge: Cambridge University Press, 1987.

Montrie, Chad. *To Save the Land and People: A History of Opposition to Sur-*

face Mining in Appalachia. Chapel Hill: University of North Carolina Press, 2003.

Moynihan, Daniel P. *Maximum Feasible Misunderstanding: Community Action in the War on Poverty.* New York: Free Press, 1969.

Murray, Charles. *Losing Ground: American Social Policy, 1950–1980.* New York: Basic, 1984.

Newman, Paul. *Fries's Rebellion: The Enduring Struggle for the American Revolution.* Philadelphia: University of Pennsylvania Press, 2004.

O'Connor, Alice. "Community Action, Urban Reform, and the Fight against Poverty: The Ford Foundation's Gray Areas Program." *Journal of Urban History* 22 (July 1996): 586–625.

———. *Poverty Knowledge: Social Science, Social Policy, and the Poor in Twentieth-Century U.S. History.* Princeton, NJ: Princeton University Press, 2001.

O'Neill, William. *Coming Apart: An Informal History of America in the 1960s.* New York: Quadrangle, 1971.

Paludan, Phillip Shaw. *Victims: A True Story of the Civil War.* Knoxville: University of Tennessee Press, 1981.

Parmet, Herbert. *JFK: The Presidency of John F. Kennedy.* New York: Dial, 1983.

Parrish, Thomas. *To Make a Difference: The Story of the Appalachian Fund, 1950–1990.* Berea, KY: Berea College Press, 1990.

Patterson, James T. *America's Struggle against Poverty, 1900–1985.* Cambridge, MA: Harvard University Press, 1986.

———. *Grand Expectations: The United States, 1945–1974.* New York: Oxford University Press, 1996.

Perry, Huey. *"They'll Cut off Your Project": A Mingo County Chronicle.* New York: Praeger, 1972.

Peterson, Bill. *Coaltown Revisited.* Chicago: Regnery, 1972.

Photiadis, John D. *The Changing Rural Appalachian Community and Low Income Family: Implication for Community Development.* Morgantown: West Virginia University, Office of Research and Development, 1980.

———. *Community and Family Change in Rural Appalachia.* Morgantown: West Virginia University Press, 1985.

Photiadis, John D., and Harry K. Schwarzweller. *Change in Rural Appalachia: Implication for Action Programs.* Philadelphia: University of Pennsylvania Press, 1970.

Pope, Daniel. "Introduction: The Nature and Significance of Radicalism in American History." In *American Radicalism,* ed. Daniel Pope, 1–14. Oxford: Blackwell, 2001.

Powaski, Ronald E. *The Cold War: The United States and the Soviet Union, 1917–1991.* New York: Oxford University Press, 1998.

Pudup, Mary Beth, Dwight Billings, and Altina Waller, eds. *Appalachia in the*

Making: The Mountain South in the Nineteenth Century. Chapel Hill: University of North Carolina Press, 1995.

Putman, Robert. *Making Democracy Work: Civic Traditions in Modern Italy.* Princeton, NJ: Princeton University Press, 1993.

Reed, B. F. *My Life in Coal.* Lexington, KY: America's Publishing and Printing Co., 1985.

Reeves, Thomas C. *The Life and Times of Joe McCarthy.* New York: Stein & Day, 1982.

Rogin, Michael Paul. *The Intellectuals and McCarthy: The Radical Specter.* Cambridge, MA: MIT Press, 1967.

Ross, Malcolm. *Machine Age in the Hills.* New York: Macmillan, 1932.

Ross, Steve. "The Domestic Anti-Communist Movement and Carl Braden: Guilty of Sedition." Paper presented at the Ohio Valley History Conference, Western Kentucky University, Bowling Green, KY, October 1990.

Rossinow, Doug. *The Politics of Authenticity: Liberalism, Christianity, and the New Left in America.* New York: Columbia University Press, 1998.

Roszak, Theodore. *The Making of a Counter Culture: Reflections on the Technocratic Society and Its Youthful Opposition.* Garden City, NY: Doubleday, 1969.

Sale, Kirkpatric. *SDS.* New York: Random House, 1973.

Salstrom, Paul. *Appalachia's Path to Dependency: Rethinking a Region's Economic History, 1730–1940.* Lexington: University Press of Kentucky, 1994.

Sanders, Marion. *The Professional Radical: Conversations with Saul Alinsky.* New York: Harper & Row, 1965.

Scharz, Jordan A. *The New Dealers: Power Politics in the Age of Roosevelt.* New York: Knopf, 1993.

Schram, Sanford. *Words of Welfare: The Poverty of Social Science and the Social Science of Poverty.* Minneapolis: University of Minnesota Press, 1995.

Schrecker, Ellen. *No Ivory Tower: McCarthyism and the Universities.* New York: Oxford University Press, 1986.

Sellers, Charles. *The Market Revolution: Jacksonian America, 1815–1846.* New York: Oxford University Press, 1991.

Semple, Ellen Church. "The Anglo-Saxons of the Kentucky Mountains: A Study in Anthrogeography." *Bulletin of the American Geographic Society* 42 (August 1910): 561–94.

Sexton, Robert F., ed. *The Public Papers of Governor Louis B. Nunn, 1967–1971.* Lexington: University Press of Kentucky, 1975.

Shapiro, Henry D. *Appalachia on Our Mind: The Southern Mountains and Mountaineers in the American Consciousness, 1870–1920.* Chapel Hill: University of North Carolina Press, 1978.

Shifflett, Crandall. *Coal Towns: Life, Work, and Culture in Company Towns of Southern Appalachia, 1880–1960.* Knoxville: University of Tennessee Press, 1991.

Sitkoff, Harvard. *The Struggle for Black Equality, 1954–1980.* New York: Hill & Wang, 1981.

Stock, Catherine McNicol, and Robert D. Johnston, eds. *The Countryside in the Age of the Modern State: Political Histories of Rural America.* Ithaca, NY: Cornell University Press, 2001.

Sundquist, James L., ed. *On Fighting Poverty: Perspectives from Experience.* New York: Basic, 1969.

———. "Origins of the War on Poverty." In *On Fighting Poverty: Perspectives from Experience,* ed. James L. Sundquist, 6–33. New York: Basic, 1969.

———. *Politics and Policy: The Eisenhower, Kennedy, and Johnson Years.* Washington, DC: Brookings, 1986.

Taylor, Henry L., Jr., ed. *Race and the City: Work, Community, and Protest in Cincinnati, 1820–1970.* Urbana: University of Illinois Press, 1993.

Thelen, David. *Paths of Resistance: Tradition and Dignity in Industrializing Missouri.* New York: Oxford University Press, 1986.

Thomas, Jerry Bruce. *An Appalachian New Deal: West Virginia in the Great Depression.* Lexington: University Press of Kentucky, 1998.

Tucker, Bruce. "Imagining Appalachians: The Berea Workshop on the Urban Adjustment of Southern Appalachian Migrants." In *Appalachian Odyssey: Historical Perspectives on the Great Migration,* ed. Phillip Obermiller, Thomas Wagner, and Bruce Tucker, 97–120. Westport, CT: Praeger, 2000.

Vance, Rupert B. "The Region: A New Survey." In *The Southern Appalachian Region: A Survey,* ed. Thomas R. Ford, 1–8. Lexington: University of Kentucky Press, 1962.

Walkowitz, Daniel J. *Worker City, Company Town: Iron and Cotton-Worker Protest in Troy and Cohoes, New York, 1855–1884.* Urbana: University of Illinois Press, 1978.

Waller, Altina L. *Feud: Hatfields, McCoys, and Social Change in Appalachia, 1860–1900.* Chapel Hill: University of North Carolina Press, 1988.

Walls, David S., and John B. Stephenson, eds. *Appalachia in the Sixties: Decade of Reawakening.* Lexington: University Press of Kentucky, 1972.

Waxman, Chaim, ed. *Poverty: Power and Politics.* New York: Grosset & Dunlap, 1968.

Weise, Robert. "Remaking Red Bird: Isolation and the War on Poverty in a Rural Appalachian Locality." In *The Countryside in the Age of the Modern State: Political Histories of Rural America,* ed. Catherine McNicol Stock and Robert D. Johnston, 258–78. Ithaca, NY: Cornell University Press, 2001.

Wells, John Calhoun. "Poverty amidst Riches: Why People Are Poor in Appalachia." Ph.D. diss., Rutgers University 1977.

Whisnant, David E. "Workers in God's Grand Division: The Council of the Southern Mountains." *Appalachian Journal* 2 (Autumn 1974): 7–45.

———. *Modernizing the Mountaineer: People, Power, and Planning in Appalachia.* Boone, NC: Appalachian Consortium Press, 1980.

———. "Second Level Appalachian History: Another Look at Some Fotched-on Women." *Appalachian Journal* (Winter–Spring 1982): 115–23.

———. *All That Is Native and Fine: The Politics of Culture in an American Region.* Chapel Hill: University of North Carolina Press, 1983.

White, Theodore H. *The Making of the President, 1960.* New York: Atheneum, 1961.

Whitfield, Stephen J. *The Culture of the Cold War.* Baltimore: Johns Hopkins University Press, 1991.

Williams, John Alexander. *Appalachia: A History.* Chapel Hill: University of North Carolina Press, 2002.

Wilson, Charles M. "Elizabethan America." *Atlantic Monthly* 144 (August 1929): 238–44.

Windmiller, Marshall. *The Peace Corps and Pax Americana.* Washington, DC: Public Affairs, 1970.

Wofford, John G. "The Politics of Local Responsibility: Administration of the Community Action Program—1964–1966." In *On Fighting Poverty: Perspectives from Experience,* ed. James L. Sundquist, 70–102. New York: Basic, 1969.

Wood, Gordon. *The Radicalism of the American Revolution.* New York: Knopf, 1992.

Woodward, C. Vann. *Tom Watson: Agrarian Rebel.* New York: Rinehart, 1938.

———. *Origins of the New South, 1877–1913.* Baton Rouge: Louisiana State University Press, 1951.

———. *The Strange Career of Jim Crow.* 3rd ed. New York: Oxford University Press, 1974.

Yarmolinsky, Adam. "The Beginnings of OEO." In *On Fighting Poverty: Perspectives from Experience,* ed. James L. Sundquist, 34–51. New York: Basic, 1969.

Young, Alfred. *The American Revolution: Explorations in the History of American Radicalism.* De Kalb: University of Northern Illinois Press, 1976.

Zieger, Robert. *For Jobs and Freedom: Race and Labor in America since 1865.* Lexington: University Press of Kentucky, 2007.

Zinn, Howard. *SNCC: The New Abolitionists.* Boston: Beacon, 1965.

Index